". . . Little sensible advice has been offered parents on how they can go about it in a practical way, or at least how to get beyond the Richard Scarry-Bernstein-Bear syndrome. Jim Trelease has filled this vacuum with a book that is a wonder of success in its completeness of down-to-earth, yet intelligent, approaches to reading aloud."

—*Family Journal*

"At our house we have been making a concerted effort to read more to our children. This book has helped me zero in on good choices, almost all of which have been hits."

—*Parents' Press*

"Certain books are naturals—*Winnie-the-Pooh* for five-year-olds, or 'A Visit From St. Nicholas' for the whole family—but where do you go from there? *The Read-Aloud Handbook* includes a guide to more than 300 books, from picture books for infants through novels and anthologies for eigth graders."

—*McCall's*

"Trelease's book is a treasury of titles he recommends for their read-aloud values, and is well worth a place on any parent's, teacher's or school volunteer's shelf for that reason alone."

—*National School Volunteer Program*

PENGUIN HANDBOOKS
THE READ-ALOUD HANDBOOK

Jim Trelease is a frequent lecturer to parents, teachers, and professional groups on children, literature, and television. A graduate of the University of Massachusetts, he was for twenty years an award-winning artist and writer for *The Springfield* (Mass.) *Daily News*. His work also has appeared in the Sunday book review sections of *The Washington Post* and *The New York Times*.

The first edition of *The Read-Aloud Handbook* spent four months on *The New York Times* bestseller list and sold a quarter of a million copies in its first year. With the British edition, published in 1984, it is now available in more than thirty countries.

Despite a speaking schedule that carries him to every part of the United States, Mr. Trelease is still a regular visitor to classrooms near his home in the Connecticut River Valley, sharing with children his career as a writer and his love of children's books. He lives in Springfield, Massachusetts, with his wife, Susan, and their two children.

Jim Trelease's lectures are available on 16 mm. film and on ninety-minute audio cassette. For information, write Reading Tree Productions, 51 Arvesta Street, Springfield, MA 01118.

"What you learn in childhood is carved on stone. What you learn in old age is carved on ice."

—David Kherdian,
The Road from Home: The Story of an Armenian Girl.

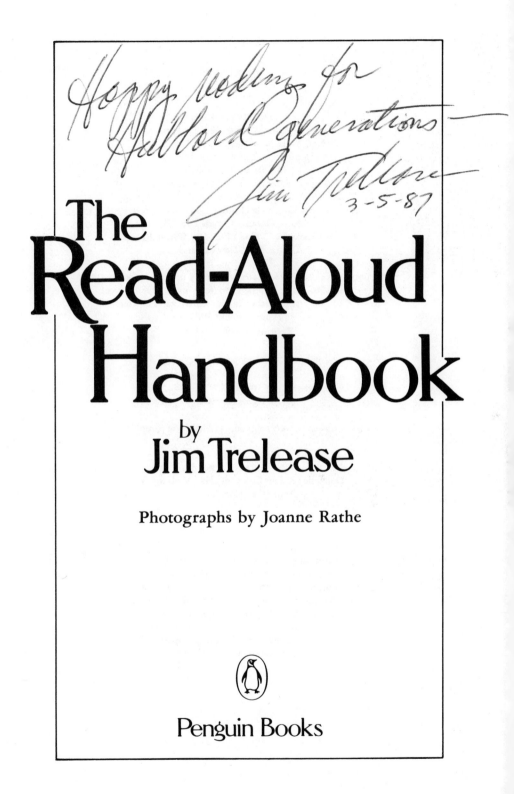

Happy reading for
Halford generations —
Jim Trelease
3-5-87

The
Read-Aloud
Handbook

by
Jim Trelease

Photographs by Joanne Rathe

Penguin Books

PENGUIN BOOKS
Viking Penguin Inc., 40 West 23rd Street,
New York, New York 10010, U.S.A.
Penguin Books Ltd, Harmondsworth,
Middlesex, England
Penguin Books Australia Ltd, Ringwood,
Victoria, Australia
Penguin Books Canada Limited, 2801 John Street,
Markham, Ontario, Canada L3R 1B4
Penguin Books (N.Z.) Ltd, 182–190 Wairau Road,
Auckland 10, New Zealand

First published in the United States of America in Penguin Books 1982
Reprinted 1982 (three times), 1983 (four times), 1984 (twice)
Revised edition first published in the United States of America
in Penguin Books 1985
Reprinted 1985, 1986

Published simultaneously in Canada

Portions of this work were originally published in pamphlet form.

Printed in the United States of America by
R. R. Donnelley & Sons Company, Harrisonburg, Virginia
Set in Garamond No. 3

To Elizabeth and Jamie—
the best audience a reader-aloud could hope to find.

And to Alvin R. Schmidt,
a ninth-grade English teacher who found the time
twenty-seven years ago
to write to the parents of one of his students to tell
them that they had a talented child. The vote
of confidence has never been forgotten.

Contents

Acknowledgments

This book could not have been written without the support and co-operation of many friends, associates, neighbors, children, teachers and editors. I especially wish to acknowledge my everlasting gratitude to Mary A. Dryden, principal of New North Community School in Springfield, Massachusetts, for beginning it all by persuading me to visit her class fifteen years ago when she was teaching fifth grade.

I am deeply indebted to the editors of *The Springfield Daily News* for their long-standing support of staff involvement with the community's school children. It was this policy which provided the initial impetus for my experiences in the classroom. At the same time, I am particularly grateful to Associate Editor Jane Maroney of *The Springfield Morning Union,* whose guiding hand helped shape the initial concept of this book, Ruth Danckert, children's book editor of *The Springfield Sunday Republican,* and George R. Delisle of *The Springfield Daily News.*

For their assistance in preparing the photographs used in the book I am grateful to the following: Margo and Leigh Anderson; Dolores, Nathan, Shameka, and Nina Brice; Catherine Bryson; Hanh Bui; Karen Chartier and the children of Elias Brookings School; Ellie, Jonathan, Amy and Melissa Fernands; Jennifer Haley; Kristen Hallahan; Jack,

Pat, John, Brian, Catie and Colleen Hoar; Nancy, Julie, Mark, Mary and Sheila Holland; Patricia Kelleher; Kathy, Ryan, Paul, Moira and Patrick Kelly; Mark Mamuszka; Linda and Meaghan McCormick; Debbie and Owen McLaughlin and the children of Holyoke Montessori Internationale; Mary, Danny, Darby and Jessica McLaughlin; Michael Nozzolillo; Scott Rogan; Christopher Rooney; Andy and Jennifer Rostek; Todd Stewart; Jeff Sullivan and the children of New North Community School; Brian, Denis, Janet and Jeanne Trelease; and Susie, Christopher and Jennifer Wing.

In addition, I would like to thank my neighbor Shirley Uman, whose enthusiasm for my idea spilled over at a family reunion within hearing distance of a literary agent, Raphael Sagalyn, who carried it home for me to Penguin Books; Bernice E. Cullinan of New York University for her candid and painstaking advice; and my editor at Penguin, Kathryn Court, for her encouragement, thoroughness, understanding, and good humor.

Introduction to the Second Edition

If we would get our parents to read to their preschool children 15 minutes a day, we could revolutionize the schools.
—Ruth Love,
Superintendent of Chicago Public Schools (1981)

Karen Chartier is a sixth-grade teacher in Springfield, Massachusetts, who begins school every year by reading aloud to her class. This particular year she began with a novel. Her wide-eyed new students listened attentively on that first day as she finished the first page and turned to the second.

At that moment, a student in the front row raised his hand. "Mrs. Chartier, you forgot to show us the picture on that first page," he said.

"Oh, I didn't forget," she explained. "It's just that this book doesn't have any pictures."

The student frowned for a second and then asked, "Then how are we supposed to know what the people look like in the story?"

That student has a problem, and so do millions of his peers in this nation of 44 million children where two out of every three children can't read, won't read, or hate to read. What that teacher was trying to do for that child and that class is what this book is all about: reading aloud to children to awaken their sleeping imaginations and improve their deteriorating language skills. Where this is done in school, it improves the atmosphere of the classroom. When it is done at home, it improves the quality of family life. But wherever it is done, the overwhelming result is that it improves children's attitudes toward books and reading.

These are facts that have been proven in hundreds of studies (many are referred to throughout this book) by educators and psychologists in thousands of classrooms and homes. The results are so decisive they are beyond debate. This handbook is an outgrowth of those findings, as well as a response to the only major decline in literacy skills since the founding of this nation. I have tried to bring to the writing a personal point of view—that of a parent, journalist, and frequent classroom instructor. In addition to my firsthand experiences with my own children and many schoolchildren, I have included those of other parents and teachers.

I had been reading aloud to my daughter Elizabeth for several years when I was invited to speak to a sixth-grade class about my career as an artist with *The Springfield Daily News.* (I had been doing these talks on a weekly basis in the Connecticut River Valley for several years.)

After spending an hour with the class, talking about newspapers, illustrations, and cartoons, I gathered my materials and prepared to leave, when I noticed a book on the shelf near the door. It was *The Bears' House* by Marilyn Sachs, and it caught my eye immediately because I'd just finished reading it to my daughter.

"Who's reading *The Bears' House?*" I asked the class. Several girls' hands went up.

"I just finished reading it," I said. Their eyes lit up. They couldn't believe it. This man, who had just told them stories about how he got started in newspapers, this man, whose drawings and stories they had been clipping out of the paper for the last month—this man was reading one of *their* books?

So I explained about my children, Elizabeth and Jamie, and how I read to each of them every night. I told them how, when my children were little, they were most interested in the pictures. That was fine with me because I was an artist and I was interested in the pictures, too. I told them how much I'd loved Maurice Sendak's *Where the Wild Things Are* because of how he drew the monsters. I loved to scan the Little Tim books to see how Edward Ardizzone drew the ocean and *Make Way for Ducklings* to see how Robert McCloskey drew the ducks.

"And did you know," I said, when I saw them perk up at the mention of the *Ducklings* classic, "that Mr. McCloskey had a dreadful time trying to draw those ducks? He finally brought six ducklings up to his apartment in order to get a closer look. In the end, because they kept moving around so much, do you know what he did? You may find this hard to believe, but I promise you it's true: In order to get them to hold still, he put them to sleep by getting them drunk on champagne!"

The class clapped and cheered their approval of McCloskey's unorthodox approach.

I went on to explain that as my children grew older, our read-aloud stories became longer and I began to realize that not only were the pictures beautiful in children's books but the stories were, too. "Now those books have become my hobby. We hated so much to return our favorites to the library, we decided to buy copies for ourselves. Today we have hundreds and hundreds." Again the eyes widened in wonder.

Then we talked about *The Bears' House:* what it was about (for those in the room who had not read it); what the students liked about it; and what else they had read by the same author. I asked the rest of the class what they had read lately. There was an avalanche of hands and a chorus of books. It was forty-five minutes before I could say good-bye. I stepped out into the corridor, where the teacher thanked me for coming. "But most of all," she said, "thank you for what you said about the books. You have no idea what it means for them to hear it from someone outside the classroom."

In the days following the visit I pondered what had happened in that classroom. The teacher subsequently wrote to say that the children had begged and begged to go to the library that afternoon in order to get some of the books I'd talked about. I wondered what it was that I had said that was so different. I had only talked about my family's favorite books.

All I was doing was giving book reports. As soon as I called it that I realized what was so special about it. It probably was the first time any of those children had ever heard an adult give not only a book report but an unsolicited book report—and that's the best kind.

How many of them had ever heard a teacher say, "You'll have to bear with me today, class, I'm a little fuzzy-headed this morning. I stayed up until three o'clock this morning reading the most wonderful book. I just couldn't put it down. Would you like to hear what the book was about?" Of course they would!

I had talked animatedly about the characters, dramatically about the plots, warmly about the authors. I'd teased the children's interest by giving them a book report. But an even better description of it would be "a commercial." I'd started by selling them on newspapers and a career. And I'd concluded by selling them on books and reading.

From that day to this, I've never visited a class without asking before I left: "What have you read lately?" Speaking at nearly thirty schools a year over the last dozen years, I've exchanged book reports with thousands of children. Out of those numbers and years certain patterns emerged that spurred me to write this book:

- Since the late 1960s there had been a dramatic decline in the number of books read by the children whose classrooms I'd visited.
- The decline was so sharp that by 1979 when I asked, "What have you read lately?" the children were naming their classroom textbooks. That happened not once but numerous times.
- Lack of interest in reading was apparent in both public and private schools, in suburban as well as urban locales. In one private school, the entire sixth grade couldn't name more than five books they had read in the last three months. Either ignoring or ignorant of the reading problem at her school, the principal confided to me later that the school had begun to turn the corner—there was now a waiting list for enrollment. I shuddered and wondered if prospective students really knew what they were waiting for.
- While the decline was general, it was not all-inclusive. Some classes overwhelmed me with their responses; they loved books and read voraciously. In each case that contagious enthusiasm was a direct result of a teacher's attitude. He or she loved books and shared that affection by reading aloud and talking to the class about books.
- In many cases, when teachers and parents witnessed the children's responses to my "commercials," they asked for a list of

"good read-alouds." Some had tried reading aloud previously and had been stung by a dull book: the children were bored, the reader was bored, and the book was put away along with the whole idea of reading aloud.

When I realized there was no available read-aloud book list other than brief ones included in children's literature textbooks, I decided to compile my own. Because I worked for a newspaper at the time and had access to modern typesetting facilities, the task seemed a simple one: I would write a short how-to booklet for parents, teachers, and librarians on reading aloud to children, with a list of recommended titles. To be candid, I never imagined the events that were to follow. Initially it was a modest self-publishing venture (it cost me $650—the family vacation money—for the first printing), with local bookstores taking copies on consignment. Within three years, the booklet sold more than 20,000 copies in thirty states and Canada. By that time (1982), Penguin Books had seen a copy and asked me to expand it into the first edition of the book you are reading now.

Six months later, a new mother in Arlington, Virginia, read a letter to "Dear Abby" decrying the decline in reading among children. The Virginia woman had just finished *The Read-Aloud Handbook* and immediately wrote to call "Abby's" attention to it. Within ten days of the publication of her letter and "Abby's" response, Penguin Books had orders for 120,000 copies of the book.

I share that background with you not in a self-congratulatory way but rather as evidence in support of a proposition. I propose that you— one parent, one grandparent, or one teacher—can make a lasting difference if you are willing to stand up for what you believe and value. Those who value the printed word cannot afford to wait for someone else to endorse or advertise it. The budget on my little thirty-page booklet was so small, there was no money for radio, television, magazine, or newspaper advertising. Its success rested upon one ad only— word-of-mouth. And it is that same word-of-mouth approach that best sells the love of reading to children.

Very little of what is in this book is original. There are thousands of psychologists, librarians, and educators who know how remarkably effective reading aloud to children can be. What I have done is to collect evidence in support of its resurrection, to describe the various aids and techniques for reading aloud most effectively, and to provide an introductory booklist. I hope to persuade parents, teachers, and librarians to return to, or continue, an old practice and to help them make that practice a habit. This is not a book on teaching your child *how* to read. Instead, it is a book on teaching your child to *want* to read. All too often we mistakenly try to interest the child in reading *after* we've tried teaching him to read.

The length of this book is deceiving. One does not need to read a two-hundred-page book in order to read aloud to children. It is not that complicated. The first half of the book deals with the need to read aloud to children: when to do it and how to do it, supported by personal experiences. I also discuss television, the largest stumbling block to reading enjoyment and achievement in this country, and how families can begin to cope with its pervasive influence. Because they both foster and are nurtured by reading, public and home libraries are the subject of one chapter. There is also a cautionary note for computer-age parents and educators bent on using reading to build "superbabies."

The second half of the book is the Treasury of Read-Alouds, a listing of recommended titles, ranging from picture books to novels. The listing is based on first-hand experience and is intended for the busy parent and teacher who doesn't have time to take a course in children's literature. The list is meant to take the guesswork out of reading aloud. These are stories with strong narratives that have excited children's interests and reading appetites. Needless to say, the whole Treasury need not be read at once. If your child is 3 years old, the picture book section is all you need for now.

This second edition of *The Read-Aloud Handbook* differs from the first in several respects. Though none of the fundamentals has changed, the statistics that indicate a need for reading aloud have been updated—including those that ring hopeful notes. Evidence of recent education reform and new parenting patterns have also been noted. My travels throughout the United States over the last four years have exposed me to some inspiring teachers and parents; I have tried to share my visits with as many of these as space allows. Finally, 8,000 new children's books have been published since the first edition, and I've culled from these what I hope are some of the best read-alouds and included them with many of the recommendations from the first edition.

One of the keys to success in reading aloud to children is matching the right books to the right child and coupling both with the right attitude by the reader. Taken as a whole, the Treasury of Read-Alouds should go a long way toward achieving that goal. For example, your 10-year-old may not want to hear the story of a Little League pitcher dying of leukemia (*Hang Tough, Paul Mather* by Alfred Slote). If your child is a nature lover, he might initially prefer to hear about the city boy, Sam Gribley, who ran away to the mountains, determined to live through the winter in communion with nature (*My Side of the Mountain* by Jean George).

Whenever I think of *My Side of the Mountain,* I am reminded of a Massachusetts family's experience with it, as well as the old adage: "Anyone can count the seeds in a single apple but only God can count the apples in a single seed." A mother wrote to tell me of the unexpected fruit born from her family's reading: "About a year ago my husband began reading *My Side of the Mountain* to our two sons, ages 10 and 8. He read each evening at six p.m. The boys are friendly with an older boy in the neighborhood, Scott, age 12, who happened by on the first evening of the book. He wanted them to come over to his house to play with his new Atari cartridges, but when he saw my husband reading aloud he was disgusted and said he'd wait outside or at home. He actually looked embarrassed, witnessing his friends sitting on their father's lap being read to!

"He was really into stoicism and independence at that time; nevertheless, with a brownie in hand I was able to persuade him to wait for the boys inside our house, in the same room where the disgraceful 'babying' was taking place. I could never do justice with words to the change in his facial expression while waiting. It went from disgust, to puzzlement, to interest, to total involvement. From then on, each evening at six p.m., Scott would 'happen' to stop by for the boys, and each night with less and less effort he was coaxed into waiting while Sam Gribley's story unfolded.

"I had never seen Scott with library books before, but the following week I saw him by chance at the bus stop—with a copy of *My Side of the Mountain.* Since then his mother tells me he's read it five times."

Reading aloud is such a multifaceted experience that adults often benefit from it as much as the children—especially today when many new parents were themselves raised on television. Their bedtime stories were viewed, not heard; *The Three Bears* was replaced by "My Three Sons," while *Aladdin and the Wonderful Lamp* gave way to "I Dream of Jeannie." I can't begin to estimate the number of parents and teachers who have confessed to me that reading aloud to their children has introduced them not only to scores of books they never read as children, but also to the joy of reading that had never been a part of their own childhood.

I remember the father who stopped me in a bookstore one day to tell me how much the experience had meant to him. He said, "I heard you speak several years ago, before your book came out, and since then I have not missed a night reading to my son. My son is 4 years old now and we're into novels as well as picture books and poetry. But as much as he loves those stories, they could not possibly mean as much to him as they have to me. You see, my mother and father were Hispanic, and they didn't speak or read English; therefore, they never read to me. And when I began to read in school, the teacher directed me to nonfiction in the library. I read and I read," the father explained. Pausing for a second, he added, "But until now—reading side by side with my son—I never knew there were books that can make you laugh and make you cry, that could touch your heart."

I was touched by his candidness and asked where he had heard me speak. He smiled and said, "I was one of the twenty pediatricians you addressed at Bay State Medical Center."

I can promise—as will anyone who reads aloud—once you begin the daily experience of reading aloud to children, it will become one of the best parts of your day and the children's day. Those minutes and hours will be cherished for years to come.

My children and I have sat in a one-room schoolhouse with Carol Ryrie Brink's *Caddie Woodlawn,* chased monsters with Maurice Sendak and Mercer Mayer, captured owls with Farley Mowat in *Owls in the Family,* and sweated it out in Mr. McGregor's garden with Peter Rabbit.

We have mourned the death of a father in *A Day No Pigs Would Die,* roamed the backwoods of the Ozarks with Wilson Rawls in *Where the Red Fern Grows,* groped down the dark subway passages of New York City with Felice Holman in *Slake's Limbo,* and swallowed magic potions with Judy Blume in *Freckle Juice.*

With *James and the Giant Peach* by Roald Dahl, we crossed the shark-infested waters of the North Atlantic; we battled a Caribbean hurricane in Theodore Taylor's *The Cay.* We have searched for wayward brothers and sisters, evaded wolves, lost friends, and learned how to make new ones. We have laughed, cried, shaken with fright, and shivered with delight. And, best of all, we did it together.

Along the way we discovered something about the universality of human experience—that we, too, have many of the hopes and fears of the people we read about.

The cost of such a wondrous experience is well within your means as a parent or teacher. It does not require purchasing an expensive teaching machine for the home or passing new education taxes to increase the size of the faculty; you don't need a college or high school diploma. Nor is the cost of books an issue. The free public library will supply all the books you could read in a lifetime. The cost is your time and interest. If you are willing to invest both, you can pick up a book, turn to a child, and begin today. I promise, you will never want the experience to end.

The fact of the matter is, because it is done with children, there probably is no end to the experience; it goes on touching generation after generation. I read to my children not because of early childhood classes in college (I took none) or because our pediatrician told us to (he did not), but because my father had read to me. Therefore, when it was my turn, I knew there was a torch that was supposed to be passed from one generation to the next. More than half a century ago there was a poor Quaker woman who took in a foundling child and began reading Dickens to him every night. Surely she could not have dreamed the words and stories would have such an enormous impact; the boy, James Michener, would write his first book at age 39 and his thirty-second at age 78. In between there would be bestsellers translated into fifty-two languages, selling more than 60 million copies, and enjoyed by countless millions of readers.

A NOTE ON PRONOUNS

In the interests of smooth reading, I have generally avoided using "he or she" and instead I usually refer to the child as "he" and to the teacher as "she." This does reflect the numbers: a greater percentage of boys than girls have reading problems, and by far the larger proportion of elementary-school teachers is female. But of course this book is aimed at *all* adults—parents, teachers, loving neighbors—for the benefit of *all* children.

You may have tangible wealth untold:
Caskets of jewels and coffers of gold.
Richer than I you can never be—
I had a Mother who read to me.

> —"The Reading Mother" by Strickland Gillilan,
> from *Best Loved Poems of the American People*

The
Read-Aloud
Handbook

1
Why Read Aloud?

Perhaps it is only in childhood that books have any deep influence on our lives . . . in childhood all books are books of divination, telling us about the future, and like the fortune-teller who sees a long journey in the cards or death by water, they influence the future. I suppose that is why books excited us so much. What do we ever get nowadays from reading to equal the excitement and the revelation of those first fourteen years?

—Graham Greene, from
The Lost Childhood and Other Essays

In an era when electronic information is at one's fingertips, when satellites bring the world's wonders and excitement into our living rooms, why read aloud to children?

Answered simply, the initial reasons are the same reasons you talk to a child: to reassure, to entertain, to inform or explain, to arouse curiosity, and to inspire—and to do it all personally, not impersonally with a machine. All those experiences create or strengthen a positive attitude about reading, and attitude is the foundation stone upon which you build appetites. A secondary reason, and of great importance in an age of rising illiteracy, is the established fact that regular

1

reading aloud strengthens children's reading, writing, and speaking skills—and thus the entire civilizing process.

One of the primary learning methods for children is imitation.[1] They imitate what they hear and what they see. It is this ability to imitate that allows the 15-month-old child to say his first words. By age 2, the average child expands his vocabulary to include nearly three hundred words. That figure is tripled in the next year, and between ages 3 and 5 he learns about fifty new words a month—not one of which is on a flash card. Considering that the average adult uses only 1800 different words in his daily vocabulary, the child's language development can only be considered monumental in scope.

Many parents are unaware of their role as a prime model in their child's language development. Much more obvious to them is the child's quickness to imitate television—especially the commercials. No matter how often children see a particular commercial, the same look of fascination returns to their eyes each time they watch it.

How great an effect does the commercial have on a child? At this imitative stage, the influence can be enormous. And, as I will point out in Chapter 7, it can be devastating in its long-range effects. I suspect that a few years ago you could find more 5-year-olds who could say McDonald's commercial for "two all-beef patties, special sauce, lettuce, cheese, pickles, onions, on a sesame-seed bun" than children who could recite their own telephone numbers and addresses.

This kind of commercial success does not happen by chance. It is carefully calculated by the agencies on Madison Avenue that are spending upwards of $50,000 a minute to ensure that your child is enraptured by the commercial.

That rapture is built upon a formula—admittedly an unofficial formula, but most certainly one that guides the advertising agencies. It was devised in the 1950s when they realized what a powerful tool they held in television.

When you break down the formula, you discover the following guildelines for selling to children:

1. Send your message to the child when he or she is still at a receptive age. Don't wait until he's 17 to try to sell him chocolate breakfast cereal. Get him when he's 5 or 6 years old.

2. Make sure the message has enough action and sparkle in it to catch and hold the child's attention. Avoid dull moments.

3. Make the message brief enough to whet the child's appetite, to make him want to see and hear it again and again. It should be finished before the child becomes bored.

We, as parents and teachers, would do well to learn something from Madison Avenue. We should take that three-part sales formula and use it to sell our product. And we most certainly have a product to sell. When the U.S. Department of Education is telling us that one out of every five American adults is functionally illiterate (which means that 20 percent of the adults in this country cannot read the directions on a can of soup), and that another 34 percent is only marginally literate (barely able to address an envelope), it is time for every educated adult to sell one product before all others in our homes and in our classrooms, and that product is READING.[2]

Despite some recent literacy gains among children, thanks to state policies of accountability along with Title I and Chapter I, and Project Head Start (which frequently incorporate read-aloud practices within the daily curriculum), these remain difficult times in which to sell reading in America. Consider these statistics:

- Ninety-eight percent of the homes in America have a television set and nearly one out of every two families has more than one set.
- The average set is on for seven hours a day (up from five hours in 1960).[3]
- The nation's 3-year-olds are now watching as much TV as the 10-year-olds—an average of thirty hours a week. As a result, the average kindergarten graduate has already seen more than 5,000 hours of television in his young lifetime. That is more time than it takes to obtain a bachelor's degree.[4]
- Teenagers account for 84 percent of the nation's movie admissions.[5]

Competing with that kind of monopoly is no small sales task. But it can be done. You, all by yourself, can instill a desire for books and reading in an entire family or class. If a plastic box in your living room can turn on your child to chocolate breakfast cereal, then you should be able to do ten times as much—because you are a sensitive, loving, and caring human being. (They have yet to invent the television set that can hug a child.) Using the television formula, here's the way to do it:

1. You read to children while they are still young enough to want to imitate what they are seeing and hearing.
2. You make sure the readings are interesting and exciting enough to hold their interest while you are building up their imaginations.
3. You keep the initial readings short enough to fit their attention spans and gradually lengthen both.

Few tasks present man with as monumental a challenge and few tasks are as far-reaching in their consequences as the challenge of learning to read. In describing his own childhood agonies with the printed word, Nobel Prize winner John Steinbeck once wrote, "Some people there are who, being grown, forget the horrible task of learning to read. It is perhaps the greatest single effort that the human undertakes, and he must do it as a child. An adult is rarely successful in the undertaking. . . . For a thousand thousand years these humans have existed and they have only learned this trick—this magic—in the final ten thousand of the thousand thousand."[6] In pursuit of that magic and in an effort to ease the agony for young minds, the Federal government alone spends nearly $20 billion a year on teaching people how to read.

Nevertheless, for all the buying power and brain power expended in this war on ignorance, we as a nation have sustained some heavy losses in the last two and a half decades. During the last three years, American education has received the most exhaustive examination and analysis in its history. And having scrutinized classroom, teacher, and pupil, the experts generally agree that as a nation we are not doing as good a job as we used to do or can do.

The experts' nearly unanimous call for change obviously rang true with educators. Since the appearance of the first report in 1983 ("A Nation at Risk"), local and national reforms have resulted in higher reading scores in previously troubled urban centers such as New York, Chicago, New Orleans, Houston, and Atlanta. Longer school days are now in effect in at least sixteen states; eighteen states now demand more advanced teacher qualifications; and high school graduation requirements are higher in thirty-five states. Thirty percent of the nation's kindergartens are now all-day, and the learning gap between white and black students, as well as urban and suburban youths, has narrowed. The International Reading Association indicates that we have a higher percentage of children reading on grade level than at any time in history, and the book industry supports this with steady gains in sales over the last four years.

Those are all positive signs and hopefully that will not wilt beside the academic road, as American math and science programs did between 1960 and 1980. But the good news is overshadowed by the gloomy academic and cultural reports of the last decade. Consider these statistics:

- The school dropout rate has climbed to 27 percent, (Japan's is 5 percent, the Soviet Union's 2 percent), and one out of every twelve students is absent each school day (one out of six in city schools).[7]
- Eighty-one percent of U.S. colleges and universities (including the Ivy League) have to provide remedial reading and composition courses for incoming freshmen. In 1980, the University of California employed 280 full-time remedial instructors—teaching what amounts to high school material to college students.[8]
- Between 1970 and 1980, the number of college preparatory high school students enrolled in remedial reading classes increased by 900 percent.[9]
- In a survey conducted by the National Assessment of Educational Progress, it was found that 53 percent of 17-year-olds could not write a letter correcting a billing error and 85 percent could not write a persuasive statement.[10]

Pinpointing the origin of such failure is as frustrating as the "chicken or the egg" argument. The politicians talk about the rising tide of mediocrity in the classroom, but educators are quick to point out the rising tide of mediocrity outside the classroom—in the home and community. It started out there, say the teachers, and spilled into the schools. Origin notwithstanding, our entire culture is showing strains of the infection:

- In 1982, 30 percent of Army recruits read at levels between fourth and eighth grades and only 2.8 percent of the 674,700 enlisted men and women were able to read on the level of high school seniors.[11]
- Newspaper readership is down to only 55 percent of adults, leaving almost half the people to receive all their information from television. An average of twelve newspapers a year either fold or merge.[12]

- In the book industry, 80 percent of the books published are financial failures.[13] The United States is one of the largest, wealthiest, and most educated nations in the world, but we rank only twenty-fourth in per capita book buying.[14]
- Forty-four percent of our adults never read a book in the course of a year.[15]
- Ten percent of the U.S. public is reading 80 percent of the books.[16]
- In the nation's prisons, 60 percent of the inmates are illiterate and 85 percent of juvenile offenders have reading problems.[17]
- The U.S. illiteracy rate is four times higher than the Soviet Union's and five times higher than Cuba's.[18]

Defenders of the status quo will point to the high influx of illiterate immigrants over the last twenty years as a cause of the illiteracy rates—an increase in the number of adults who never had the benefit of our educational system. That argument loses much of its strength when you consider the reading appetites of those who can read and are graduates of our system: the bestselling weekly magazine on U.S. newsstands is *TV Guide;* in second place is the periodical that declared in 1983 that John Kennedy, Marilyn Monroe and Grace Kelly were still alive—*The National Enquirer. TV Guide* and *The National Enquirer* are read not by illiterate immigrants but by graduates of our homes and classrooms.

Obviously, if we are spending immense amounts of time and money in successfully teaching children to read but they in turn are choosing *not* to read, we can only conclude that something is wrong. In concentrating exclusively on teaching the child *how* to read, we have forgotten to teach him to *want* to read. There is the key: desire. It is the prime mover, the magic ingredient. There is no success story written today—whether in the arts, business, education, athletics— in which desire does not play the leading role. Somehow we lost sight of the teaching precept: What you make a child love and desire is more important than what you make him learn.

Contrary to popular opinion, desire is not something we are born with or that must come first from within. Winners aren't born, they're made; hundreds of coaches have taken teams with losing reputations, instilled desire in them, and inspired them to championships. Readers aren't born, they're made; thousands of teachers instill desire each year in children who have been branded by parents and previous teachers as "losers," and by the end of the school year their desire to excel is a mainstay in their lives. Desire is planted—planted by parents and teachers who work at it.

How does one begin to instill in children the desire to read? That is something I believe we can learn from the man who has broken all records in the desire league, "Ronald McDonald." How did McDonald's instill that desire for their product and convince the American people that they "deserve a break today"? They did it by advertising over and over again, week after week, singing new praises, extolling new tastes, announcing new products.

Most parents do much the same thing with their children prior to their beginning school. They praise the virtues of school, the kindness of the teacher, the excitement of making new friends. In essence, they give the child a commercial for school. Unfortunately, it is only after the child has started school that most parents begin to think about motivating the child to be interested in books. The truth is that they should have begun motivating him years before. They should have started giving him book commercials in the first year of his life. They should have been reading to him and selling him early on the joys and discoveries waiting inside the covers of books.

Assuming this was not done, it is in school that the child begins to make his first noble efforts at reading—sound by sound, syllable by syllable, word by word. It is at this point that many parents and teachers make a mistake. They misread the child's early reading efforts as a sign that he loves to read and therefore doesn't need to be sold on it, or that continued reading by the adult to the child will rob the child of his initiative to read on his own. An indication of how widespread such reasoning is can be found in a national survey of teachers' read-aloud practices.[19] It was found that more than 60 percent of the third- and fourth-grade teachers did not read aloud regularly to their classes. By sixth grade, that percentage climbed to 74 percent. Interestingly, the grades that show the largest declines in read-aloud practices are the same grades that show the first signs of a national decline in grade-level reading performances by children—third and fourth grades.

At home, television combines with the parents' general disinterest in books to smother the beginning reader's desire to read the book he brought home from school or from the library. A Gallup Poll taken during the 1970s showed that 82 percent of the elementary-grade children polled had not read a book in the preceding month, although they each averaged more than one hundred hours of television during the same period. With increased television viewing and the introduction of video games, it's highly unlikely those statistics have improved.

In the classroom, too many of our children too quickly come to associate books and reading with ditto sheets, workbooks, tests, and homework. "Reading? That's work, not fun," they will tell you. Nearly 70 percent of the 233,000 sixth-graders polled by the California Department of Education in 1980 reported that they rarely read for pleasure. (In the same poll, an identical percentage of the students admitted to being heavy television watchers—four or more hours a day.)[20]

The "reading is work" mentality that children associate with books is supported in the findings of Richard Allington of the State University of New York.[21] Allington observed that remedial-reading classes spent a remarkably small amount of time reading in context without interruption. In fact, the average student read only forty-three consecutive words before being interrupted for questions or corrections. The poorest readers received the heaviest doses of skills instruction and consequently spent the least amount of time on the very objective—READING.

I am not suggesting that we abandon the teaching of reading skills. They are, I am afraid, a necessary evil and most of today's children would never learn to read without them. However, I am suggesting that we balance the scales in our children's minds. It is imperative that we let our children know there is something more to reading than the practicing, the blendings, the vowel sounds, something more to it than the questions at the end of the chapter. And we must let them know this early, before they have permanently closed the door on reading for the rest of their lives.

The way to achieve this is to read to them every day, allowing them to finally sample the excitement and pleasures they've been practicing for but aren't quite ready or willing to accomplish on their own.

It can be done. Whether you are a teacher or a parent, don't tell me there isn't enough time—we find time for what we value. As a parent, I know first-hand how much time is wasted in a typical family day. And I know teachers who daily find the time to teach the skills *and* the love of reading—by reading to the class. If you care enough, you'll find the time.

Before a child can have an interest in reading, he must first have an awareness of it. The child who is unaware of the riches of literature certainly can have no desire for them.

Mrs. Ann Hallahan of Springfield, Massachusetts, offers an example of that axiom. Assigned at mid-year to teach a sixth-grade class of remedial students, Mrs. Hallahan shocked her new students by reading to them on her first day in class. The book was *Where the Red Fern Grows.*

A hardened, street-wise, proud group (mostly boys), they were insulted when she began reading to them. "How come you're reading to us? You think we're babies or something?" they wanted to know. After explaining that she didn't think anything of the kind but only wanted to share a favorite story with them, she continued reading *Where the Red Fern Grows.* Each day she opened the class with the next portion of the story and each day she was greeted with groans. "Not again today! How come nobody else ever made us listen like this?"

Mrs. Hallahan admitted to me later, "I almost lost heart." But she persevered, and after a few weeks (the book contained 212 pages), the tone of the class's morning remarks began to change. "You're going to read to us today, aren't you?" Or, "Don't forget the book, Mrs. Hallahan."

"I knew I had a winner," she confesses, "when on Friday, just when we were nearing the end of the book, one of the slowest boys in the class went home after school, got a library card, took out *Where the Red Fern Grows,* finished it himself, and came to school on Monday and told everyone how it ended.

"I didn't care about that. All I cared about was that I'd found the right key to open the lock on that boy's mind."

If the boy's parents had taken the time to introduce him to the book, the same task would have been accomplished. And if they had done it early enough, it's very probable he wouldn't have been in a remedial-reading class in the first place.

Amidst all the workbook pages and academic jargon, we daily overlook the very purpose of literature: to provide meaning in our lives. That, of course, is the purpose of all education. Child psychologist Bruno Bettelheim says that the finding of this meaning is the greatest need and most difficult achievement for any human being at any age. Who am I? Why am I here? What can I be? [22]

In his widely acclaimed work *The Uses of Enchantment,* Bettelheim writes that the two factors most responsible for giving the child this belief that he can make a significant contribution to life are: parents/teachers and literature.

Literature is considered such an important medium because—more than television, more than film, more than art or opaque projectors—literature brings us closest to the human heart. And of the two forms of literature (fiction and nonfiction), the one that brings us closest and presents the meaning of life most clearly to the child is fiction. That is the reason nearly all the recommendations for read-alouds at the back of this book are fiction.

What is it about fiction that brings it so close to the human heart? Three-time Pulitzer Prize–winning novelist and poet Robert Penn Warren declares that we read fiction because:

• We like it.
• There is conflict in it—and conflict is at the center of life.
• Its conflict wakes us up from the tedium of everyday life.
• It allows us to vent our emotions with tears, laughter, love, and hate.
• We hope its story will give us a clue to our own life story.
• It releases us from life's pressures by allowing us to escape into other people's lives.[23]

The child who has become accustomed to the tedium of the classroom cannot help but be awakened by the conflict in stories like *James and the Giant Peach* by Roald Dahl or *Mrs. Frisby and the Rats of NIMH* by Robert C. O'Brien. The awkward, freckle-faced 8-year-old discovers a ray of hope when she hears Hans Christian Andersen's *The Ugly Duckling*. It is through fiction's escapism—putting ourselves in the place of Snow White or Casey at the Bat or Mike Mulligan—that we stimulate the soul of creativity: the imagination. And it is this role-playing that leads us to an awareness of others and, most importantly, of ourselves.

Can we really believe that a child is going to develop a sense of "self" doing reading skills for forty minutes a day, five days a week, thirty weeks a year? Does an uninterrupted diet of skill and drill make a child want to escape *into* the world of books or *away* from it? It stands to reason that, given a yearly dropout rate of 27 percent and daily absenteeism running to 4 million students, the status quo is not adequate. Would you be satisfied with a surgeon who lost 27 percent of his patients? How long would an airline stay solvent if 27 percent of its passengers said, "I'll never fly again!"

We must remember a key ingredient in reading a book—the pleasure it brings into our lives, something a growing number of parents and teachers boil down to a dirty word: fun. Like the supervisor who walks by and sees the teacher reading to the class: "There's got to be something wrong here," he reasons. "The teacher's enjoying it, the class is enjoying it. How much learning can be taking place if they're all having a good time?" Noticeably absent from Robert Penn Warren's list of reasons for reading were book reports, vocabulary tests, and right or wrong answers. Books are meant to be savored and enjoyed, and those who use them exclusively to cross-examine children, to the certain destruction of their enjoyment, should, in the words of Alfred North Whitehead, "be prosecuted for soul-murder." In compiling the eight-year report that experts described as "probably the most comprehensive study ever made of American schools" (A Place Called School), John Goodlad found laughter and overt displays of feeling to be rarities. Our classrooms, said Goodlad, are "emotionally flat." [24]

Fun and successful learning should go hand in hand. No one knows that better than Katherine Randolph, a fifth-grade teacher in the Boston public schools. Randolph's racially balanced, self-contained classes at Higginson Elementary score nearly twice as high as other Boston reading classes, and better than 88 percent of the nation's fifth grades. "I always find the time to read for ten or fifteen minutes a day," she explains. "Excitement is a very contagious thing in a classroom, and children are immediately infected by it. My enthusiasm shows the children that classwork is not just something the *kids* should like—the *teacher* likes it, too!" [25] Similar success stories with reading aloud can be found in Chapter 5.

Reading aloud to children stimulates their interest, their emotional development, and their imagination. There is also a fourth area which is stimulated by reading aloud and it is a particularly vital area in today's world. It is the child's language. We have seen children's spongelike reaction to television commercials. They continue this imitative behavior with words until their language development peaks around age 13. They will speak the language primarily as they have heard it spoken.

Now, if the child hears the English language only as it is spoken by Archie Bunker, Laverne and Shirley, or Fonzie, then he has no alternative but to model his own speech on theirs. The danger with such modeling is that it is very different from the English language a student is asked to read, write, and speak in school or in the business world. A large portion of television's language is "street talk"—jargon and slang. It is poorly constructed and imprecise. It is hardly what a child needs as a model.

Children raised on a heavy diet of television and rock music are most readily recognized by a speech pattern that is punctuated every half-dozen words by "You know?" and "I mean, like . . ." The primal grunts and groans of a rock album may or may not have their merits as entertainment, but most decidedly they have neither the meaning nor the sensitivity children need to express their feelings clearly.

Literature's words, as opposed to those of the electronic media, offer a wealth of language for children to use. Because good literature is precise, intelligent, colorful, sensitive, and rich in meaning, it offers the child his best hope of expressing what he feels.

Hundreds of tests have been conducted to measure the effects of reading aloud upon language skills, and the results have been significantly positive.

In one study, twenty classes of Harlem 7-year-olds were read to for twenty minutes a day for one school year.[26] At the end of that time, the children were tested and compared with a control group that had not been read to. The experimental group showed significantly higher gains in vocabulary and reading comprehension.

In light of such statistics from one-year programs, imagine the results of a read-aloud program spread over several years. Imagine its effects upon both language and imagination.

For teachers and parents to ignore the warnings of widespread disinterest and illiteracy is to invite disaster for our children and our culture. Our goal is that all able-minded children read, write, and speak to their fullest capacities, and the road to it is clearly marked and defined. The first step in that direction is to pick up our books and begin reading to our children. By making books a priority in our lives, a nation in which 90 percent of the children can read and choose to read, instead of the present 50 percent, is not inconceivable. Invariably, children buy what the culture sells. For example, no nation in the world values the printed word as much as Japan. The vast majority of Japanese parents read aloud to their children. One-half the magazines published for Japanese children are geared for preschoolers and the early primary grades. The result of such priorities, despite children having to master 1,900 alphabet characters compared to our twenty-six, is one of the highest literacy rates in the world—99 percent.

On the other hand, the United States prizes entertainment, and our children reflect this value. Curious about our cultural heroes, editors at the *World Almanac and Book of Facts* polled 4000 American eighth-grade students in 1981: Whom do you most admire or whom would you most want to be like when you grow up? There were no politicians, lawyers, scientists, writers, or business leaders in the top thirty choices. There were, however, three athletes—and the rest were entertainers (and only five of those were women). Top vote getter? Burt Reynolds.

Such results should come as no surprise if you recall that teenagers account for 84 percent of all movie admissions. But imagine what could be accomplished if we as a nation used just half the enthusiasm in selling the three R's that we save for selling the three B's (ball-games, Burt Reynolds, and Brooke Shields)? What if we sold ideas, words, and books with the same creativity we use to sell designer jeans and shampoo? Why—we might end up with people whose attention span for the printed word is longer than the time it takes to read T-shirts or record jackets.

2
When to Begin Read-Aloud

Children who are not spoken to by live and responsive adults will not learn to speak properly. Children who are not answered will stop asking questions. They will become incurious. And children who are not told stories and who are not read to will have few reasons for wanting to learn to read.

—Gail E. Haley,
1971 Caldecott Medal acceptance speech

"How old must the child be before you start reading to him?" That is the question I am most often asked by parents. The next most often asked question is: "When is the child too old to be read to?"

In answer to the first question, let me share an anecdote involving a junior high school English teacher who happened to be a proud new father and was assuring me that as soon as his daughter was a year old, he and his wife would start reading to her every day. "That's wonderful, Bill," I said. "But why not read to her now?"

"What?" he asked incredulously. "At six months she won't understand the words I'm reading to her." Conceding there was some

14

truth in that, I asked him if he *talked* to his daughter. Taken aback momentarily, he said proudly, "Of course, we *talk* to her."

"Why are you talking to her?" I asked. "At six months she doesn't understand the words you're saying." He sheepishly conceded the irony in the situation: if the child is old enough to talk to, she is old enough to read to; after all, it's the same English language. Obviously, from infancy until six months of age we are concerned less with "understanding" than with "conditioning" the child to your voice and to the sight of books.

Dr. T. Berry Brazelton, chief of the child development unit of Boston Children's Hospital Medical Center, says that new parents' most critical task during these early stages is learning how to calm the child, how to bring it under control, so he or she can begin to look around and listen when you pass on information.[1] Much the same task confronts the classroom teacher as she faces a new class each September.

The human voice is one of the most powerful tools a parent has for calming the child. At the earliest stages—there is even some evidence to suggest as early as the sixth or seventh month in the womb—a child is capable of discerning tone of voice: positive or negative, soothing or disturbing. A child's sense of hearing is so acute that when a male and female speak simultaneously to an infant only a few hours old, he will always turn toward the woman's voice. The evidence seems to point to his months of listening to the female voice while *in utero*. Thus it is easy for him to start associating certain tones of voice with comfort and security. The baby is being conditioned—his first class in learning.[2]

In exactly the same way that the child is conditioned by a soothing tone of voice to expect calmness and security, so, too, can the child be conditioned to the sound of the reading voice. Over a period of months the child will recognize it as an unthreatening sound, one that is associated with warmth, attention, and pretty pictures, and he will gravitate naturally to that sound.

Dorothy Butler demonstrates this thesis in *Cushla and Her Books,* where the parents began reading aloud to Cushla Yeoman at 4 months of age.[3] By 9 months the child was able to respond to the sight of certain books and convey to her parents that these were her favorites. By age 5 she had taught herself to read.

What makes Cushla's story so dramatic is the fact that she was born with chromosome damage which caused deformities of the spleen, kidney, and mouth cavity. It also produced muscle spasms—which prevented her from sleeping for more than two hours a night or holding anything in her hand until she was 3 years old—and hazy vision beyond her fingertips.

Until she was 3, the doctors diagnosed Cushla as "mentally and physically retarded" and recommended that she be institutionalized. Her parents, after seeing her early responses to books, refused; instead, they put her on a dose of fourteen read-aloud books a day. By age 5 the psychologists found her to be well above average in intelligence and a socially well-adjusted child.

If such attention and reading aloud could accomplish so much with Cushla, think how much can be achieved with children who have none or few of Cushla's handicaps.

Historical research offers the evidence of Puritan New England, where in 1765 John Adams noted that "a native American who cannot read or write is as rare an appearance as . . . a comet or an earthquake." Such verbal competence in our forefathers is attributed to the fact that the colonial child was exposed from infancy to the family's daily oral reading of the Bible.[4]

The crucial timing of such exposure has been discovered only in recent years, most powerfully by Professor Benjamin Bloom's famous study of 1,000 children's development profiles.[5] His findings demonstrated that 50 percent of the intelligence a child will have at maturity is already formed by age 4—at least a year before the child enters kindergarten.

The key is to *gently* match the skill with the developing interest. It is commonplace for the children of diplomats to learn easily both their parents' language and that of the country in which they are stationed—providing both tongues are introduced while the child has this voracious appetite for words. Back in the 1930s, Myrtle Mc-Graw, a psychologist doing a study of twins, routinely taught an 11-month-old boy to roller skate as he was also learning to walk. His twin, who did not receive skates until almost a year later, experienced considerably more difficulty in learning to skate.[6] The same concept can be applied to an early introduction of rich vocabulary and the concept of books.

Much of a child's intense mental growth during these early years can be attributed to the fact that he is at the height of his imitative powers during this period. Not only will they imitate the sounds of their home and family (and television set), but they will imitate also the actions of their parents, grandparents, and siblings. They are their first role models, their "superheroes." If the child sees these heroes reading and involved with books, experience shows us that it is very likely that he will wish to do the same.

Martin Deutsch's study "The Disadvantaged Child and the Learning Process" demonstrates what happens when the role models do not stimulate the child.[7] In homes where conversation, questions, and reading are not encouraged, the child eventually enters school markedly short of the basic tools he will need to accomplish his tasks. He will ask fewer questions, use shorter sentences, and have both a smaller vocabulary and a shorter attention span than his more advantaged classmates.

In studying methods to reverse such verbal shortcomings among children, Harvard psychologist Jerome Kagan found intensified one-to-one attention to be especially effective.[8] His studies indicated the advantages of reading to children and of listening attentively to their responses to the reading, but they also point to the desirability of reading to your children separately, if possible. I recognize this approach poses a problem for working mothers and fathers with more than one child. But somewhere in that seven-day week there must be time for your child to discover the specialness of you, one-on-one— even if it is only once or twice a week.

This is a good time to ask ourselves exactly why we are reading to children. Living as we do in a society that is so success-oriented, it is a common mistake for parents to associate books only with skills. "If I read to my child," reasons the parent, "he will be that much smarter and he'll eventually be way ahead of the others in school." On and on drones the achievement syndrome. The objective in reading to children is not to build "superbabies" or children who are hurried into adulthood. But just as a child's body is fed, so, too, should be his mind. When the child can name the people and things in his environment, he can begin to ask questions and express his needs and fears. The sooner the child can put his feelings into words, the more human and civilized he becomes.

There is, however, a difference between feeding the mind and pushing the mind. The achievement syndrome is discussed at length in Chapter 5, but for the moment let me state that early interest in a child's intellectual growth is important and admirable. But you can expect negative consequences if this interest takes the form of an obsession with teaching your child to read, says Dr. Brazelton, who, along with his hospital work, research, and writing, has been a practicing pediatrician in Cambridge, Massachusetts, for twenty-six years.

"I've had children in my practice," Brazelton explained to National Public Radio's John Merrow, "who were reading from a dictionary at the age of 3½ or 4, and had learned to read and type successfully by the age of 4. But those kids went through a very tough time later on. They went through first grade successfully, but second grade they really bombed out on. And I have a feeling that they'd been pushed so hard from outside to learn to read early, that the cost of it didn't show up until later."[9]

Testimony to the importance of an *unforced* learning schedule in these formative years comes from all corners of the fields of psychology and education—including one that dates back nearly three thousand years: "Avoid compulsion and let early education be a manner of amusement. Young children learn by games; compulsory education cannot remain in the soul," was the advice offered by Plato to parents.

None of these experts is saying that "early reading" is intrinsically bad; rather, they feel the early reader should arrive at that station naturally, on his own, without a structured time each day when the mother or father sits down with him and teaches him letters, sounds and syllables. That is the way Scout learned in Harper Lee's *To Kill a Mockingbird*—by sitting on the lap of a parent and listening, listening as the parent's finger moves over the pages, until gradually, in the child's own good time, a connection is made between the sound of a certain word and the appearance of certain letters on the page.

Prior to speaking to a group of children at a local library one day, I was stopped in the hallway by a grandmother. "Want to see something amazing?" she asked. When I expressed an interest, she sat on the floor, put her grandson on her lap, and handed him a book. The child, 3½ years old, began at once to read—easily, without stumbling, using marvelous expression and pointing to each word as he read. Anticipating my question, the grandmother whispered, "I began reading to him eight months ago. I'd put him on my lap and point to the words as I read. And then a month ago, it all fell into place for him."

"How does he like it?" I asked.

"He doesn't like it—he *loves* it," she said.

Much of that woman's achievement was accomplished by gradually conditioning her grandchild to look and listen when a book was being read. His senses of sight and hearing were pleased each time, along with the emotional pleasure of having Grandma's attention. By repeating this situation over and over again with a variety of books, the child developed a concept: Books are objects to be enjoyed; they bring pleasure.

By building this concept in the child's mind, the grandparent laid the foundation for the next accomplishment: the boy's attention span. Without a concept of what is happening and why, a child cannot and will not attend to something for any appreciable amount of time.

Here, for example, are two concepts entirely within the grasp of a 3-year-old: the telephone can be used to receive calls as well as make calls; books contain stories that give me pleasure if I listen and watch.

A nursery-school teacher told me recently of her experiences on the first day of school with these two concepts. All morning the 3-year-olds in her new class used the toy telephone to make pretend calls to their mothers for reassurances that they would be picked up and brought home. They dialed make-believe numbers, often talked for extended periods of time, and used telephone etiquette.

Understanding the concept of the telephone, these children were able to use and enjoy it for a considerable length of time. Their telephone attention span was excellent.

Let's compare that with story time in the same class. Thirty seconds after the story began, several of the children stood up and moved away from the circle, obviously bored. More children quickly joined them. Within two minutes, half the children had abandoned the story.

The difference between the attention spans for each of these two activities is based on the *concept* that each child brought to the activity. Where a child had little or no experience with books, it was impossible for him to have a concept of them and the pleasure they afford. No experience means no concept; no concept means no attention span.[10]

Parents and teachers are always fascinated with children who apparently "teach themselves" to read. However, as we have seen with Cushla and the grandchild at the local library, these children *do* have teachers—their role models. The majority of children who arrive in kindergarten already knowing how to read have never been formally taught to read, but they didn't pick it up out of thin air, either.

Over the past twenty-five years, studies done on "early readers," as well as those done on children who respond to initial classroom instruction without difficulty, indicate four factors which are present in the home environment of nearly every early reader.[11]

1. The child is read to on a regular basis. This is the most often cited factor among early readers. In Dolores Durkin's comprehensive

1966 study of early readers, every one of the seventy-nine children had been read to regularly. Additionally, the parents were avid readers and led by example. The reading aloud included not only books but package labels, street and truck signs, billboards, et cetera.

2. A wide variety of printed material—books, magazines, newspapers, comics—is available in the home.

3. Paper and pencil are readily available for the child. Durkin explained, "Almost without exception, the starting point of curiosity about written language was an interest in scribbling and drawing. From this developed an interest in copying objects and letters of the alphabet."

4. The people in the child's home stimulate the child's interest in reading and writing by answering endless questions, praising the child's efforts at reading and writing, taking the child to the library frequently, buying books, writing stories that the child dictates, and displaying his paperwork in a prominent place in the home.

I want to emphasize that these four factors were present in the home of *every* child who was an early reader. None of these factors requires much more than interest on the part of the parent. There are no elaborate sound systems or learning machines involved, no bachelor or master's degrees; just a free public library card, some pencils and crayons, and cheap paper. (A small blackboard is another excellent aid if you want to go one step further.)

Beyond the materials, the program requires time: time to read to the child, time to post his drawings on the refrigerator door, time to answer questions, time to point out signs along the highway.

Time, declares the typical parent after a parent-teacher association meeting, is a rare commodity in her home. She works, her husband works, they don't have a lot of time to spare. I can identify with her plight and sympathize—having been there myself when for fourteen years I worked two jobs and my wife worked one. But in fairness, I must point out the things for which we *do* find the time—how many trips a week to the mall? how many times out for cigarettes? how many hours of television each night?

"Just when you think there isn't enough time for the night's reading," I tell the parent, "remind yourself how short is your daughter's childhood. I promise you that twenty years from now your television set will still be there—some of tonight's shows may even be in reruns—but I can also guarantee that twenty years from now your daughter will no longer be your little girl, she probably won't even be living in the same state, let alone your home. Given those guarantees, which is more precious: that time together with *The Secret Garden* or tonight's episode of 'Dallas'? Which can you least afford to miss?"

I often wonder afterwards if such parents really understand, if they understand about the language bridges a parent builds with a child during those few minutes a day, bridges to adventure and imagination and, just as importantly, the emotional bridges between parent and child.

I recall the teacher in New Hampshire who told me the story of Beth, and I wonder if those busy parents would have understood about Beth. "I've been a first-grade teacher for seventeen years," the teacher said, "and I have never had a child who didn't *want* to learn to read. That is, until this year.

"This year I had Beth as a student. The more I worked with her the more convinced I became that Beth didn't *want* to learn to read. Then I began to suspect that she already knew how to read but wouldn't admit it for some reason."

When the teacher talked to Beth's mother, she found the mother had similar suspicions. The following day the teacher took her student aside and said, "Beth, I think you've been fooling us. Do you know that? I think you already know how to read but for some reason you don't *want* to read. Is that true, Beth?"

Beth nodded.

"Will you tell me why?" asked the teacher.

"No," Beth replied.

At this point, the teacher asked a question that allowed Beth an escape route. "Do you think you could *ever* tell me why?"

The child thought for a moment and said, "Tomorrow."

The next morning Beth looked up at her teacher and whispered, "After lunch."

Sequestered in a room by themselves after lunch, Beth confided to the teacher that she was the oldest of four children. "The only time all day when I have my mother all to myself is when she reads to me at bedtime," she explained. She was afraid that if she admitted to being able to read by herself, then that was what she would be doing each night: reading alone. Beth felt her mother would go off to read to her sisters and brother and leave her without that intimate sharing time each night. As soon as the parent and teacher were able to convince Beth that her mother would continue their bedtime reading ritual, Beth became one of the best readers in the class.

"When do you start reading aloud to classroom children?" asks the teacher. On the very first day of school—whether you are teaching nursery school or kindergarten or seventh grade. And the way you hold that book, the warmth you extract from it, the laughter, the interest, and the emotion—all will tell your class something about you and how you feel about books, and the special place books and reading are going to hold in your class this year. The fifth-grade student who until now has associated books only with remedial classes or workbooks is going to experience a special treat on that first day. He's going to be introduced to a whole new concept of books and reading. He's going to be conditioned to the idea that books mean pleasure as well as work. You're going to show him the other side of the coin.

A fellow teacher suggested to Deborah Murphy that "when introducing a book to your class, you caress and hold it in your hands as you would a well-loved and precious treasure. While holding the book in this way, tell the children how you feel about the story, any personal experiences you might have had with it." But Murphy, a third- and fourth-grade teacher in a Connecticut inner-city magnet school, is a self-described "no-time-to-waste" teacher, and she doubted the effectiveness of such an approach.

But she gave it a try. She had a favorite book—*Tal, His Marvelous Adventures with Noom-zor-noom*—long out of print and now treasured by her. "With great skepticism," Murphy says, "I introduced *Tal* in this way—speaking about it and touching it as I would a well-respected old friend. And as the weeks passed I saw the children begin to reflect this feeling in the way they would carry the book to me at reading time and in the way they would turn the pages."

And then one day there was a fire drill, and as Deborah Murphy herded the class out the door, reminding them not to think of it as a drill but as a real fire and that nothing mattered except getting out of the school quickly, she saw a boy detour past her desk to save the copy of *Tal*. "I realized then," she concedes, "my friend *Tal* was treasured not only by me."

It's important for the teacher, just as it is for the parent, to establish early in her own mind exactly why she is reading to the class. This should ease any concern about reading aloud being a "time waster."

The best answer is found in the definition of a teacher outlined by Nathan Pusey while president of Harvard.[12] "The close observer soon discovers that the teacher's task is not to implant facts but to place the subject to be learned in front of the learner and, through sympathy, emotion, imagination, and patience, to awaken in the learner the restless drive for answers and insights which enlarge the personal life and give it meaning." He could not have described the functions of reading aloud more accurately if he had been trying to. Children's literature arouses their imaginations, emotions, and sympathies. It awakens their desire to read, enlarges their lives, and provides a sense of purpose and identity for children.

Yes, you have to teach reading skills and math skills. They are necessary. But don't make the mistake of thinking they are the purpose of teaching or even the heart of the curriculum. Reading skills are facts; they have no life unto themselves and cannot motivate. I've yet to find the child who fell in love with vowels, consonants, or the questions at the end of the chapter.

On the other hand, *Charlotte's Web* by E. B. White can be loved by and will motivate a class. Most children and young adults have a strong need for books that curl up inside their lives, that take up residence in their dreams and ambitions.

Charlotte and her friends fill that need in young children; they reach out and beckon to their emotions and hopes and fears. There is no more important social experience in a child's life than friendship. And friendship is what *Charlotte's Web* is all about. It is the rare child who meets *Lassie Come Home* by Eric Knight or Jack London's *The Call of the Wild* and does not carry its story, its emotions, and its courage into the rest of his life.

I was unpacking a case of books before addressing a preschool parents group when a woman standing nearby gushed with pleasure when I put *Lassie Come Home* on the table.

"That book," she said, picking it up and caressing it, "and the teacher who read it to my sixth-grade class moved me more than any book or teacher I ever had in school. I can hardly wait for my daughter to be old enough for me to share this with her."

When you take time to read to your class you are not neglecting the curriculum. Reading *is* the curriculum. The principal ingredient of all learning and teaching is language. Not only is it the tool with which we communicate the lesson, it is also the product the student hands back to us—whether it is the language of math or science or history.

In that light, the classroom teacher who reads aloud helps the class to become better listeners and develop greater verbal skills. The more they hear other people's words, the greater becomes their desire to share their own through conversation and writing. The principal in Connecticut who interrupted a fourth-grade teacher's daily read-aloud ("You're wasting time. Get busy," he said) obviously didn't recognize a language arts class when he saw one. There are four language arts: they begin with the art of listening and proceed to the art of speaking, the art of writing, and the art of reading. The teacher, incidentally, told me it was futile to argue the point but she did have her day in the sun two weeks later when the principal had to be out of town all day for a convention. "Do you know what we did all day?" she asked me. "We read *Stone Fox* [by John Reynolds Gardiner]. We cried about it, we talked about it, then we wrote and drew about it. And it was the best day we had all year."

A common mistake is to relegate reading aloud to just the reading or language arts classes. When children love books, it ripples through every part of the curriculum—an aspect not always understood by those who have never taught reading. I am frequently called upon to address a school system's entire faculty—including math, science, art, music, and physical education teachers. My first task is to convince those teachers outside the reading faculty that reading *is* the curriculum and therefore *every* teacher's business. (At this point, the reading teachers nod agreement but the rest of the faculty is unconvinced.)

Take, for example, vocabulary, spelling, and writing skills—three areas in which English and reading teachers come under constant attack. "Sure," says the history teacher, "I'd love to give more essay questions on exams. But those damn English teachers haven't taught these kids how to write." And the science teacher adds, "Their spelling is even worse, and most have the vocabulary of a squirrel." (Everyone is now agreeing—even the English teachers acknowledge that such disparagement takes place.)

How do we improve vocabulary, spelling, and writing? By reading, reading, reading. Vocabulary and spelling words are not learned best by looking them up in the dictionary. You learn the meanings and spellings in the same way teachers learn the names of new students each September: by meeting them again and again, making the connection between the face and the name. The more often you encounter a student, the quicker and better you learn his name. Nearly everyone spells by memory, not by rules. When in doubt, you write the word out several different ways and choose the one that looks correct. The more a child meets words and sees how they are used in sentences and paragraphs, the better he will know, understand, and spell words. Conversely, the less you read, the fewer words you meet and the less certain you are of meaning.[13]

Anyone who knows anything about writing will tell you that nothing improves writing like writing. By the same token, I don't know a single writer who isn't also a reader. It's the same with baseball players—the good ones sit and watch an incredible number of innings, observing how others play the game. Among other things, reading is sometimes a spectator sport: you're watching how the all-stars play the game of writing, how they aim words to catch meaning.

If parents and schools want better readers—and consequently better writers, speakers, and spellers—it will happen naturally if children are interested in reading. Unfortunately, children are not born interested in anything. Not one player in the history of the NFL was born wanting to play football, but somewhere along the way—at home or school—seeds of football interest were sown and nurtured. Reading interest grows wherever people take the time to plant *and* nurture the seed. In the educator's mind, is reading there to support the curriculum, or is the curriculum there to support reading? Do your students (and children) ever see you with something other than a textbook or gradebook in your hand? Do they see and hear you reading for the fun of it? Have you shared with your class a book you stayed awake reading until two in the morning? Have you read a magazine piece to your students about something that really interested you? Have you let your guard down and shown your enthusiasm lately? And, I might add, if you are not enthusiastic about reading you are in the wrong profession.

If you want your science class, history class, or civics class to be alive, then wrap the facts and figures, the dates and battles, in flesh and blood. Open your history class with five minutes from *My Brother Sam Is Dead* by James and Christopher Collier. Read *My Side of the Mountain* by Jean George to your science class each day. Or, in *any* class, read *North to Freedom* by Anne Holm or *American Beat* by Bob Greene because they deal with the human condition—the things that set us above and apart from computers.

"But," says a teacher, "these are just stories. I've got a curriculum to cover. I don't have time for *stories!*" Far from suggesting the curriculum be abandoned, I say it should be enriched and bought to life by story. It should be reassuring to know that many of the best teachers—Aesop, Socrates, Confucius, Jesus—used stories to teach their lessons. The Bible has survived the centuries as much for the stories as for its curriculum.

Whether you are acting as a parent or as a teacher, when you read aloud to children you are fulfilling one of the noblest duties of cultured man. It is this sharing and enrichment that allows a culture to grow among people. Artists, writers, and musicians alone cannot keep a culture alive. They must be backed by the enthusiasm of a multitude of parents and teachers—people who treasure their heritage and will devote their energies to keeping its flame aglow. The mother who sits through music and dance recitals, the father who puts down the evening paper to help his son with a drawing of a tree, the teacher who reads to her class every day—they are the lifeblood of a culture. To them, more than to the artists, must fall the responsibility to "pass it on."

Almost like clockwork, after every speech I give on reading aloud, a worried parent approaches me and asks, "When is it too late? Is there a time when children are too old to be read to?" It is never too late, they are never too old—but it is never going to be as beneficial or as easy as it is when they are 2 years old or 6 years old.

Novelist and teacher Paula Fox, winner of the 1974 Newberry Medal for *The Slave Dancer,* read to her students at a branch of New York State University just as she had to her fifth-grade students years before. She found the older students loved the readings just as much as the younger ones had. "There was no tension of accomplishment or grades connected with the readings. It simply *was,* as literature should be," Fox explained.[14]

Because she has a captive audience, the classroom teacher holds a distinct advantage over the parent who suddenly wants to begin reading to a 13-year-old. Regardless of how well intentioned the parent may be, reading aloud to an adolescent at home can be difficult. During this period of social and emotional development, teenagers' out-of-school time is largely spent coping with body changes, sex drives, vocational anxieties, and the need to form an identity apart from that of their families. These kinds of concerns and their attendant schedules don't leave much time for Mom's and Dad's reading aloud.

But the situation is not hopeless. When the child is in early adolescence, from 12 to 14, try sharing a small part of a book, a page or two, when you see he is at loose ends. This only has to be several times a week. Mention that you want to share something with him that you've read; downplay any motivational or educational aspects connected with the reading.

The older the child, the more difficult he is to corral. Here, as in early adolescence, you must pick your spots for reading aloud. Don't suggest that your daughter listen to a story when she's sitting down to watch her favorite television show or waiting for her boyfriend to call. Along with timing, consider the length of what you read. Keep it short—unless you see an interest for more.

Dorothy Mulligan, former director of editorial services for the National School Volunteer Program in Alexandria, Virginia, confirms that there is no age limit to reading aloud. This is how she picked her spots for read-aloud:

"One summer our 22-year-old son had his four wisdom teeth pulled. A week later, after the stitches came out, one socket began to bleed. Late that night, the oral surgeon had to put in more stitches. Despite painkillers, Greg was miserable during the night. Nothing would calm him. And then I recalled what I had done for the kids whenever they were sick at night.

"First, I tried some of Greg's favorite authors—Mark Twain, Ray Bradbury, et cetera—but I couldn't find a section with enough action to still his moans. I lightbulb appeared in a balloon above my head; I reached for a *Reader's Digest*.

"Greg immediately quieted to listen to an article about how the music was selected to go into the space capsules. He is a violinist and one of the selections for the capsule was his favorite string quartet. Then I read about the kidnapping of a young girl, and then two more articles. By now he was lying quietly and told me he wanted to go to sleep."

Mrs. Mulligan says that her 17-year-old son, Mark, came down with a viral infection a few weeks later. The illness bothered him most at night.

"Several nights in a row he would vomit and complain of abdominal discomfort. This time I didn't wonder what to do—I got a *Reader's Digest*.

"I read about a 9-year-old who desperately needed to catch a fish for his family's dinner. Mark loves animals and never wants any living thing to be hurt, but he listened intently—until he fell asleep before the article ended."

Frequently, if the parent picks the right time and place, he or she can kill two birds with one stone—or story. Mrs. Mulligan recalls the week she and her family vacationed in a rustic cabin in Pennsylvania, minus television.

"That week I was reading *The Wheel on the School* [by Meindert DeJong], about children in a small Dutch school who put a wheel on the rooftop for a stork to use as a nest. I assumed that I was reading only for the younger three children, but learned differently when Greg, then 14, and my husband asked me not to read until they returned from playing tennis."

I found a similar situation when one of Elizabeth's girlfriends listened one evening to the chapter I was reading to Elizabeth from *Good Old Boy* by Willie Morris. She went home and insisted that her father get the book and read it to the entire family. The oldest son later used the book in a comparison study he did for eighth-grade English in which he compared *Good Old Boy* with *Tom Sawyer*.

The desire to read is not born in a child. It is planted—by parents and teachers.

Novelist and short-story writer Roald Dahl offers an example of this in an essay, "Lucky Break," from his book *The Wonderful Story of Henry Sugar*.

Tucked away in English boarding schools from age 8 to 18, Dahl's academic childhood was a disaster. "Those were days of horror," he writes, "of fierce discipline, of no talking in the dormitories, no running in the corridors, no untidiness of any sort, no this or that or the other, just rules, rules and still more rules that had to be obeyed. And the fear of the dreaded cane hung over us like the fear of death all the time." His teachers described him on his report cards as "incapable" and "of limited ideas." He hated school and school obviously hated him.

At last there came a ray of hope. One Saturday morning the boys were marched to the assembly hall. The masters departed for the local pubs and in walked Mrs. O'Connor, a neighborhood woman hired to "babysit" the boys for two and a half hours. Instead of babysitting, Mrs. O'Connor chose to read, talk about, and bring to life the whole of English literature. Her enthusiasm and love of books were so contagious and spellbinding that she became the highlight of the school week for Roald Dahl. As the weeks slipped by, she kindled his imagination and inspired a deep love of books. Within a year he'd become an insatiable reader, and Dahl credits Mrs. O'Connor with turning him into a reader, and thus a writer. Today, more than fifty years later, I know of no author who so captivates children, who so excites their imaginations, as Roald Dahl. His *James and the Giant Peach* is the finest read-aloud I have ever known.

How many minds and imaginations have remained unstirred because there was no Mrs. O'Connor? That child in your home or classroom—the one who never seems to be listening, who never completes his work on time, who appears to be forever looking out the window as though waiting for someone—is waiting for someone like Mrs. O'Connor. How long are you going to keep him waiting?

3
The Stages
of Read-Aloud

Few children learn to love books by themselves. Someone has to lure them into the wonderful world of the written word; someone has to show them the way.
—Orville Prescott, from
A Father Reads to His Children

Staring at the thousands of books in the children's section of the local library, a parent is filled with the same panic that faces the beginning artist with an empty canvas: Where to begin?

I suggest that you first consider the child's age and maturity; then make your selections accordingly. Let's start with the infant level and work our way upward.

Until a child is six months old, I don't think it matters a great deal what you read, as long as you are reading. What is important up to this stage is that the child becomes accustomed to the rhythmic sound of your reading voice and associates it with a peaceful, secure time of day. Mother Goose, of course, is always appropriate, but my neighbor read aloud Kipling when she was nursing her daughter, who is now at Princeton.

The major stumbling block in all this for many parents is the awkwardness. "I feel silly," said one woman. "It's like reading to the wall." Research in the last three years has clearly shown the fallacies in this image of the infant as deaf, dumb, and vegetable-like. The parent who needs convincing need only consider these recent discoveries in infant learning:

- One-day-old babies can be calmed with tape recordings of their own cries and within days are able to distinguish their own cries from those of peers and older babies. [1]
- Twelve-day-old babies can imitate an adult sticking out a tongue. [2]
- Ten-week-olds, with strings attached to slide projectors that change with movement of the wrist, will watch the changing slides attentively for an average of 14 minutes. [3]
- Ten-week-old babies recognize their mother's voice from all others. [4]
- Three-month-olds consistently showed distress when the sound-track was placed out of synchronization with the video portion of a film showing a woman reciting nursery rhymes. [5]
- Nine-month-olds recognize themselves in the mirror. [6]
- Thirteen-month-olds can tell the difference between boy and girl babies—even when clothes are swapped. [7]
- Girls often talk before boys, studies show, because mothers talk to daughters more than to sons. [8]

Most of these abilities are preprogramed at birth into the child's life. But like flowers out of water, they will wilt and be lost if they are not cared for over the next two years. Study after study shows us that when curiosity is not fostered between 6 and 24 months, it will not be there at age 10.

Between 6 and 10 months of age, the child's sight and hearing are attuned enough for him to recognize familiar faces, objects, and voices. Therefore your book selections for the next year should be ones that stimulate those two senses—colorful pictures and exciting sounds upon which the child can focus easily. One of the reasons old Mother Goose has lasted so long is that she fills so well this rhythmic requirement.

Hickory, dickory, dock,
The Mouse ran up the clock!

"But," you ask, "where's the plot? The meaning?" At this stage, Mother Goose isn't there for the plot. She's there to take all those sounds and syllables, those endings and blendings, to mix them in with the rhythm and rhyme of language, to be fed to a child who already takes delight in rocking back and forth in his crib repeating a single syllable over and over: "Ba, ba, ba, ba, ba . . ."

Since Mother Goose so wisely populated her rhymes with people as well as animals, the child's visual world is also expanded—particularly with many of the exciting recent editions. My favorite Mother Goose is the one edited by Watty Piper and illustrated by the Hildebrandt brothers. The pictures, large and brightly painted, are perfect for young children. Grade-school children also can enjoy Mother Goose, especially in Wallace Tripp's collection, *Granfa' Grig Had a Pig,* which contains hundreds of minutely detailed drawings that add not only a sense of humor to the rhymes but an element of sense as well. Tomie dePaola also has an excellent *Mother Goose* edition. Each year sees another artist's version of Mother Goose in print and I hope the list grows longer and longer.

Have you ever noticed how many of the Mother Goose rhymes can be applied to a child's everyday activities? "Hush-a-Bye Baby" (sleeping and waking); "Deedle, Deedle, Dumpling" (going to bed); "One, Two, Buckle My Shoe" (getting dressed); "Pat-a-Cake" (eating); "Little Jack Horner" (eating); "London Bridge" (falling down); "Jack and Jill" (falling down); "Little Bo Peep" (losing toys); "Humpty Dumpty" (falling down); "What Can the Matter Be?" (crying); "Rub-a-Dub-Dub" (bathing).

Many parents find that singing or reciting these rhymes during the appropriate activity further reinforces both rhyme and activity in the child's mind. Long-playing records of these rhymes are available at your library and local record store.

Mother Goose is your child's first language lesson. Author and editor Clifton Fadiman, writing in *Empty Pages* as the chairman of the Council for Basic Education's Commission on Writing, notes: "If you read the most famous of all rhymes, 'Jack and Jill,' your child will, after listening to the third line, have learned the excellent word *fetch.* This word has a useful, precise meaning, a little different from *get.* It should not be allowed to disappear. Mother Goose will see to that."[9]

Recent research has proven that speech and music are stored in separate parts of the brain.[10] Therefore, when you sing a nursery rhyme to your child you are expanding even wider your child's early learning. Later, when your child becomes interested in the alphabet, pick up Joan Walsh Anglund's *In a Pumpkin Shell,* a Mother Goose alphabet book.

One factor that is often overlooked by parents is the inability of children under 18 months of age to easily understand complicated illustrations that adults recognize instantly. Book illustrations consisting of many little figures running here and there may be charming to adults but they are incomprehensible to young children. An adult can recognize instantly a three-dimensional rabbit when it is reduced to one dimension on a page, but a 14-month-old child is just beginning this complicated process. To help the child in this task, the picture books you choose now should be uncomplicated—a single image to a page and preferably in color. Black-and-white drawings don't seem to make sense until after age 2. Plot, if there is any, is secondary to the image. Among the very best for this purpose are those by Dutch author-artist Dick Bruna.

Internationally recognized, the Bruna books are masterpieces of simplicity: simple black outlines, solid colors of red, yellow, blue, and green against plain backgrounds. His subjects are simple enough to border on caricature. Bruna packs language, story, emotion, and color into 12 pages. After *Mother Goose,* among your first books should be one of the more than fifty little Dick Bruna books (see Index to Treasury).

During the toddler stage, an important parental role is serving as a kind of welcoming committee for the child, welcoming him to your world. Just think of yourself as the host of a huge party. Your child is the guest of honor. Naturally, you want to introduce him to all the invited guests in order to make him feel at home.

You do this by helping him learn the names of all the objects that surround him, the things that move, things that make noises, the things that shine. Picture books are perfect teaching vehicles at this stage. Point to the various items illustrated in the book, call them by name, ask the child to say the name with you, praise him enthusiastically for his efforts. Picture books like *The First Words Picture Book* and *The Early Words Picture Book* by Bill Gillham are excellent teaching vehicles at this stage.

Dr. Fitzhugh Dodson, psychologist and author of *How to Parent* and *How to Father,* recommends that you include your department store mail-order catalogues in this "label-the-environment" activity. With your help and reinforcement, your 11-month-old can be pointing correctly to household items as you say them.

The very best picture book at this stage may be the one you cannot buy in a store or borrow from the library. It is one you make with photographs taken in your home and of your family. Making sure the images are not smaller than 4 inches, label each with easy-to-read letters, place the picture on cardboard, and cover it entirely with a piece of self-sealing clear plastic. Metal rings through punch holes will hold it all together as a most durable and personalized "book." The materials can be purchased cheaply wherever office supplies are sold.

Once the child is calm in the presence of books and more inclined to listen than to rip, must reading is Dorothy Kunhardt's *Pat the Bunny,* a little book that enables the toddler to interact with the story, using his senses to smell the flowers (perfumed), feel the beard (sandpaper), lift the cloth, pat the bunny (cotton), and see his reflection (mirror). *Pat the Bunny* is never thrown out by a family; it is worn out. Another favorite is *Where's Spot?,* one in a series by Eric Hill, with sturdy movable flaps that hide surprises for the child.

Since familiarity is essential in developing a lasting relationship with books, it's a good idea to purchase your own copies to keep in the home along with those you borrow from the library. Not only does this give you a start in building your children's personal library (see Chapter 6), but you also will avoid the embarrassment of returning torn books to the library.

Many publishers are now marketing "baby board books," durable volumes printed on heavy, laminated pages in nontoxic inks that are easy for little fingers to turn and can be quickly wiped clean (see Helen Oxenbury's books in the Index to Treasury). Place the board books in the high chair, the playpen, and the crib. Let your child see books at least as often as he sees toys and television.

Families accustomed to treasuring every book are sometimes afraid to leave a book in the hands of a baby. Dorothy White, in *Books Before Five,* described those early books as the ones "fated to suffer every indignity that a child's physically expressed affection could devise—a book not only looked at, but licked, sat on, slept on, and at last torn to shreds." The quandary was settled when White and her husband wisely decided "that the enjoyment of personal ownership was a fact of life more worth knowing than how to look after this or that. How can one learn to hold, before one has learnt to have?" she asked.[11] The gentle and affectionate way the *parent* treats the book is far more important.

Frequently the child who is read to regularly can be seen toddling along with his favorite book, looking for someone to read to him.

There are two important elements here. One is to keep in mind that as much as anything else, the child is looking for attention, he wants his body cuddled as much as his mind. The other factor is the idea of a "favorite" book. He has already developed literary tastes, and between now and when he is six, he'll have many favorites, books he asks for often, nightly, for months on end. The more frequently you read and the greater the variety of titles, the broader will be the child's appetite. But too frequently, any kind of favoritism by the child for a particular title will irritate parents who are tired of reading the same book.

However, Dr. Bruno Bettelheim believes that such a book fills a personal need of the child. Some fear or concern is being allayed by the book, a kind of paper security blanket. He finds nightly courage or comfort in its characters or setting. Don't try and reveal this secret to the child; allow him those important self-discoveries. And Bettelheim offers this hope to weary parents: When a child has gotten all he can from the book or when the problems that directed him to the book have been outgrown, he'll be ready to move on to something else.[12]

A wonderful example of how firmly attached a child can become to a certain book is provided by *Mike's House* by Julia Sauer. She tells the story of a boy who only wants to hear the story *Mike Mulligan and His Steam Shovel* by Virginia Lee Burton. It's the only book he'll take out of the library. He comes to associate the library and the book so closely that he thinks of the library as Mike's House. Children who have heard and enjoyed *Mike Mulligan and His Steam Shovel* will find a new favorite in Mrs. Sauer's book.

Mike Mulligan and His Steam Shovel offers a perfect example of how long-lasting the love of books can be when we plant it at the right time in a child's mind. "I had no idea how deep those roots went," a nursery-school teacher told me one day after a workshop, "until last year when I was hiking the Appalachian Trail with my husband, my 19-year-old college freshman son, and a group of friends. We'd been climbing for about three hours and had just taken a rest by the side of the trail when I heard my son begin to recite some familiar words.

"I couldn't believe it," she told me. "Sitting there on a log, he regaled the group with a verbatim recitation of the entire story of Mike Mulligan—at age 19."

How deep do the roots grow? Very deep and very strong when you take the time to plant the seeds correctly.

———

During these early years and even later, your read-aloud effort should be balanced by the outside experiences you bring to the child. It simply is not enough to just read to the child—except in extreme cases like Cushla Yeoman's.

"Reading begins with that first recorded experience," says Phyllis Halloran, first-grade teacher and a national reading consultant for the Learning Institute. "It is that experience, together with all the others to follow, that allows the child to react and respond to ideas in a book."

Pictures of a flower, a plane, or a puppy hold little attraction for the child who has never seen a flower or a plane or puppy. They are, instead, obstacles to overcome on the page. But having played and romped with a puppy, having picked and smelled a flower, "the child now has an experience bank from which he can draw interpretations and appreciations," Mrs. Halloran explains.

I saw firsthand the importance of experience when I was reading *Slake's Limbo* to Elizabeth when she was 11. The novel tells of a young boy chased by a gang into the New York City subway system. In his desperation, he stumbles on an old construction mistake in the tunneling and for the next 120 days lives in the subterranean cave surrounded by the grime, noise, and danger of the speeding trains.

A child in Idaho who has never stood clutching her parent's hand on a subway platform will enjoy this story but most certainly she cannot bring to it the same personal interpretation that Elizabeth could. She was introduced to subways when she was 7 years old and found them frightening almost beyond reassurance. No one knew better than Elizabeth how much courage it took for Aremis Slake to walk those rails each day. Experience, says the axiom, is the best teacher, and no one knows that better than reading teachers. (Elizabeth, by the way, has long since lost those fears and now happily travels the subway as a student at Fordham University in New York City.)

As the child's concept of books begins to evolve, I recommend you begin an important but subtle reading lesson: labeling the book. Point out the title of the story each time you read it, begin to use words like author, pages, pictures, cover, front, and back of the book. Disregard that old third-grade rule about using your finger when you read. Let your finger do the walking and the talking by lightly running your finger under the text as you read. All these efforts gradually teach the child about the meaning of those black squiggly lines on the page, that reading begins in the front, at the top, and moves left to right. These are essential steps in the act of reading, steps we adults take for granted because they're second nature to us now. But they are not second nature to a child. Given these subtle learning advantages now, he'll have an easier time later on.

No parent of young children needs to be told how incredibly active they are or how short are their attention spans. Bearing this in mind, we cannot expect young children to be interested in reading a book whenever *we* happen to be. After all, there's a whole new world out there waiting to be explored by them; that book can wait. And it will. Let it wait until the child is calm and unwound.

Most of us who have read to children for a long time have found it helpful to establish a flexible routine for reading—a time when the child has few other distractions, a time toward which the child can look forward, from which he can gather security, a time as dependable as lunch time, nap time or bath time.

The time of day my family usually chose was bedtime—both in the afternoon before naps and in the evening. These are the times when the child looks for security, appreciates the physical closeness, and is tired enough to stay in one place. This is an appropriate time to introduce children to the various "bedtime" books—stories like the classic *Goodnight Moon* by Margaret Wise Brown (for toddlers) and *Bedtime for Frances* by Russell Hoban (for older children). Other bedtime books are listed under these titles in the Treasury of Read-Alouds at the back of this book.

As you increase the number of picture books you read to the child, keep in mind that between the ages of 1 and 3 children will continue to respond best to illustrations that are easily viewed, like those in the *Harry the Dirty Dog* series by Gene Zion.

As the child grows, if you stay tuned to his moods and needs, you'll know when he needs his books. When Jamie reached nursery-school age he wanted to be read to before leaving for school each day. Obviously he found some support in the reading which he carried with him into the day. This practice continued until he was in third grade, and it was in addition to our nightly bedtime sessions.

The physical growth of the child also means that his interests and needs are growing. He'll be asking millions of questions over the next few years and his capacity for language from age 2 until age 5 has been described by Kornei Chukovsky, the Russian poet and literary historian, as "near-genius." [13] As the principal architect of this building stage, your reading material should keep pace with the child's growth.

Because of this high-level curiosity, many children enjoy nonfiction books as much as fiction at this point. As the "label-the-environment" stage moves into high gear, think of all the things that fascinate children: holes, cars, snow, birds, bugs, stars, trucks, dogs, rain, planes, cats, storms, babies, Mommies and Daddies. Beginning around age 2, they are interested in everything and have a built-in need to have names for those things. I have only a lukewarm feeling for "Sesame Street" as a TV program, but *The Sesame Street Word Book* is excellent in scope, clarity, and concepts. *The Baby's Catalogue* by Janet and Allan Ahlberg is also good.

For nearly every subject of interest to a child, there is a corresponding book. For example, when last I looked there were more than thirty-seven different books—fiction and nonfiction—published on the subject of snow. You haven't seen what books can do for children's imaginations until you've read Virginia Lee Burton's *Katy and the Big Snow* or Wendy Watson's *Has Winter Come?* to a child or class as the winter's first snowflakes fall outside your window. What excitement!

When you see that your child or class has developed a fascination for a particular subject, check your neighborhood library for a book on it. The subject listing in the card catalogue will show what the library has on its shelves, and a handy reference guide in all libraries, *Subject Guide to Children's Books in Print,* will show what is available outside the library as well. This volume can be especially helpful with sixth-, seventh- and eighth-grade students who frequently develop strong appetites for one particular subject and are willing to devour any book about it.

A lesser-known but extremely useful resource found in many libraries is *The Bookfinder,* a two-volume listing of tens of thousands of children's titles under 450 developmental, behavioral, and psychological headings—topics such as adoption, belonging, courage, death, divorce, fighting, friendship, imaginary friends, jealousy, teachers, and siblings.

In this day and age, it is no longer a major problem if your library does not own a particular book. The American free public library system is now organized to the point where any book is obtainable free of charge. Even if you live in a small Alabama town whose tiny library is open only three days a week, your written request is forwarded to a regional headquarters where a computer search for the book is made, through the entire state if necessary. If by chance the book is out of print and the only copy of it is on a shelf in the Arcadia, California, public library, it will nonetheless be found and loaned to you. Not another country in the world can boast of such service. In addition, for a nominal fee, used-book stores will advertise your interest in a particular book through their national journals. I've been especially lucky with this resource when I wanted to own an out-of-print book.

During the period between 2 and 5 years of age, your child's desire to imitate his parent will extend to reading books. In some cases, by the time the child is 4, he can recite a book verbatim, page by page. Notice I said "recite" and not "read," because in the majority of cases the child has merely memorized what you've been reading to him. He'll boast that he is reading—and that's fine. Reward and praise his effort. Let him know how much you admire someone who can read. If he keeps it up, his approximations gradually will come closer to the text and eventually he will be reading naturally.

One excellent means of building the confidence, imagination, and vocabulary of prereaders is through the use of "wordless" books—picture books conveying a simple story without using words; pictures tell the whole story. Children quickly realize that in order to follow these stories, the pictures have to be looked at in sequence—and sequencing is one of the cardinal rules of reading. An increasingly sophisticated and popular medium in recent years, there are more than one hundred wordless books currently available (see Wordless Books listing in Treasury). To start, you'll want to obtain Dick Bruna's *A Story to Tell* and Jan Ormerod's two books on a child's evening and morning routines—*Moonlight* and *Sunshine.* From here you can graduate into the wordless books of Mercer Mayer and John Goodall. The wordless classic *The Silver Pony,* by Lynd Ward, is often used by teachers in creative writing classes; children write what they think is happening in the story.

All wordless books afford children—even 3-year-olds—the opportunity to "read" by privately interpreting the sequence of pictures and developing the story through their own experiences and in their own words. Such actions will be essential later when they really begin to read, but for now they build a healthy sense of self-esteem and accomplishment.

As your child becomes more and more at home in the world, his confidence will grow and, in direct proportion, so will his sense of humor and adventure. I doubt there has ever been an author who stimulated these senses in young children as well as Dr. Seuss. And what Mother Goose does for toddlers' sense of sound, Dr. Seuss does for preschoolers and up. Seuss refers to his writings as "logical nonsense": children find the sights and sounds logical while adults find them nonsensical. What matters here, of course, is the child, and the fact that he is drawn into the book by Seuss's verbal gymnastics and humor.

Although Seuss has written a staggering number of books, I feel his most appropriate stories for read-aloud are those with a story line (*If I Ran the Zoo*) and definitely *not* his "controlled vocabulary" books (*Cat in the Hat*). The latter are intended to be read *by* the child, not *to* him. Bear in mind that while the average first-grade student reads from a primer with only 350 vocabulary words in it, his *listening* vocabulary approaches 10,000 words, according to the Council for Basic Education. Frequent reading aloud of "controlled vocabulary" books is an insult to the listening vocabulary of your child. (See Index to Treasury for recommended Dr. Seuss read-alouds).

Did you ever wonder about the purpose of cumulative rhymes and tales? Stories like *Henny Penny,* with its cumulative repetition—Henny Penny, Cocky Locky, Ducky Lucky, Goosey Loosey, and Turkey Lurkey—have a predictable word-play in them that is one of the strongest (and most enjoyable) of all vocabulary builders. From daily exposure, my daughter Elizabeth at age 5 (and even today at age 20) was able to recite easily the name of the honored Chinese son from Arlene Mosel's *Tikki Tikki Tembo:* "Tikki tikki tembo-no sa rembo-chari bari ruchi-pip peri pembo." One of the cleverest and most amusing of the cumulative rhymes is Audrey and Don Wood's *The Napping House,* in which a mouse, cat, dog, child, and grandmother are sleeping precariously atop each other—until a flea appears.

Even before the child is ready for kindergarten, he can pride himself on having a sense of humor—especially if it has been cultivated with some simple joke and riddle books. Start with something simple like *Bennett Cerf's Books of Animal Riddles* or *Bennett Cerf's Book of Laughs.* The child will love memorizing jokes from these books and trying them out on family and friends. Nothing builds self-confidence like a well-told and well-received joke.[14]

The joke book can be an effective tool for all ages. Reading consultant Bill Halloran of the Learning Institute suggests that every teacher begin the day with a joke. "All over the country teachers are starting out the day with, 'Take out your books.' Why can't they ease into the day with an elephant joke? Start the day with some knock-knock jokes and the kids will be with you for the rest of the day. Go to the library and get the joke and riddle books, leave them around your classroom. Before you know it, even the kids who hate to read will be reading them. And that's the beginning. Reading because they *want* to."

Bernard Waber is an author and illustrator who has his finger on every child's laugh pulse. In his four Lyle books, beginning with *The House on East 88th Street,* children are introduced to a lovable alligator who will touch their hearts as well as their funnybones. The most popular of all the Waber books is *Ira Sleeps Over,* the story of a child's first sleep-over and the trauma of deciding whether or not to bring his teddy bear along to his friend's house.

Ira's adventure brings us to the need for adventure stories that support the growing child who is ready, in his own mind at least, to go out and challenge the world. Nothing has served to fill this need in the last two thousand years as well as the fairy tale.

I know what you may be thinking. "Fairy tales? Is he kidding? Why, those things are positively frightening. Nobody tells those to children any more. Children see enough violence on television—they don't need kids pushing witches into ovens, and evil spells and poisoned apples."

Stop for a minute and remind yourself how long the fairy tale has been with us—in every nation and in every civilization. Surely there must be something important here, an insight so important as to transcend time and mountains and cultures to arrive in the twentieth century still intact. There are, for example, nearly four hundred different versions of *Cinderella* from hundreds of cultures. Nevertheless, they all tell the same story—a truly universal story.

What characterizes the fairy tale—sets it apart from the rest of children's literature—is the fact that it speaks to the very heart and soul of the child. It admits to the child what so many parents and teachers spend hours trying to cover up or avoid. The fairy tale confirms what the child has been thinking all along—that it is a cold, cruel world out there and it's waiting to eat him alive.

Now, if that were all the fairy tale said, it would have died out long ago. But it goes one step further. It addresses itself to the child's sense of courage and adventure. The tale advises the child: Take your courage in hand and go out to meet that world head on. According to Bruno Bettelheim, the fairy tale offers this promise: If you have courage and if you persist, you can overcome any obstacle, conquer any foe. And best of all, you can achieve your heart's desire.

By recognizing the child's daily fears, by appealing to his courage and confidence, and by offering him hope, the fairy tale presents the child with a means by which he can understand his world and himself. And those who would deodorize the tales, eliminating the references to dragons or conflict, impose a fearsome lie upon the child. J. R. R. Tolkien wisely cautioned, "It does not pay to leave a dragon out of your calculations if you live near him." Judging from the daily averages, our land is filled with dragons. On a typical American day, someone is robbed every 87 seconds, someone is raped every 8 minutes, someone is murdered every 27 minutes, and at the Los Angeles Olympics, security guards outnumbered the athletes 18,000 to 10,000. To send a child into that world, unprepared, is yet another crime.

The core of the nursery tale, G. K. Chesterton wrote, is the core of ethics: Happiness and peace in life are conditional upon meeting certain requirements. There is no charge card for true happiness; it must be earned—a message that is also at the core of the Book of Genesis. We must expose future generations to the worthiness of heroes and heroines as early as possible. Not that long ago, a Talent Preservation Project in New York City considered the problem of "underachievers"—very bright children who for some reason were wasting away at the bottom of their high school classes. Included among the observations of that investigation was this one made by the staff psychologist: When these 300 teenagers were asked to name their heroes, to indicate those whom they most admired in life, 298 were unable to think of anyone. [15]

We have every reason to believe there is a direct connection between a child's heroes and heroines—his role models and motivators—and that child's self-image and achievements.

If there is one flaw in the fairy tale, it is that most popular tales are top-heavy with heroes and short on heroines. For balance, readers-aloud will want to try Ethel Johnston Phelps' two collections: *The Maid of the North* and *Tatterhood and Other Tales*. These are traditional tales about nontraditional, courageous, resourceful, and witty heroines from a variety of ethnic cultures. You might also try coupling Trina Schart Hyman's excellent version of *Sleeping Beauty* with Jane Yolen's *Sleeping Ugly*. *The Ordinary Princess* by M. M. Kaye and *Once upon a Test: Three Light Tales of Love* by Vivian Vande Velde both take a tongue-in-cheek look at the stereotyping in fairy tales.

When you read fairy tales to young children it is a good idea to choose books that deal with a single tale. Large volumes containing dozens of stories frequently are too heavy (and sometimes too complicated) for the child to handle comfortably. Up until second grade, children are intimidated by heavy books. They prefer books that are light and easy to hold. Later you can move up to the larger books.

I suggest you start with the simple tales as interpreted by artist Paul Galdone: *The Three Bears, Little Red Riding Hood, The Three Billy Goats Gruff, The Three Little Pigs,* and *The Gingerbread Boy* (see Index to Treasury for a list of Paul Galdone books).

From here you can progress gradually in length and complexity as the child's maturity and imagination demand. Two of today's best illustrators, Nancy Ekholm Burkert and Trina Schart Hyman, have done glorious versions of *Snow White* that are not to be missed.

Some may quarrel with the fact that many of these simpler retellings depart from the language of the original Grimm versions. I can only assume that if these two men were writing today they would use the language and idiom of our time and not of a time departed. I am less concerned with the language of the tales than I am with the meanings, particularly when the child is 5 years and older. Too often the modern adaptations emasculate the tale, leaving children with nothing but charming pap. While I don't recommend *Hansel and Gretel* for 3- and 4-year-olds, I most heartily urge it upon children of 5 and older who wonder to themselves: How long could I survive alone out there if nobody loved me? To alter dramatically *Hansel and Gretel* is to rob your child of its essential meaning.

Once your child or class is ready for the longer and more complicated tales, try the collections of Grimm and Andersen—collections where only the language has been modernized; the meanings remain untouched. Certainly one of the best anthologies available today is *The Fairy Tale Treasury,* edited by Virginia Haviland of the Library of Congress and illustrated by Raymond Briggs. This volume includes, among others, the most popular tales by Jacobs, Andersen, Perrault, and the Brothers Grimm, and runs from the simple *Henny Penny* to the more complex *The Ugly Duckling.*

The strong flavor of adventure in fairy tales and their obvious success have been extended and developed by many of today's best writers and illustrators. Edward Ardizzone's series of Little Tim books features children who save floundering ships, subdue runaway locomotives, and rescue drowning friends from the thundering surf. Each calls for children with courage to face enormous odds.

Maurice Sendak's *Where the Wild Things Are,* one of the best-selling children's books of all time, deals with a child's rage at his parent and his subsequent triumphs in the land of monsters. Ludwig Bemelmans allows his heroine Madeline to enter numerous horrendous predicaments, always to emerge devilishly triumphant. In William Steig's *Sylvester and the Magic Pebble* the hero is turned into a stone (talk about predicaments and a cruel world!), but finally emerges triumphant through his own persistence and the unfailing love of his parents.

Even when you go beyond the picture book, some of the best writers for children often follow the lead of the fairy tale. Natalie Babbitt confronts a 10-year-old girl in *Tuck Everlasting* with a kidnapping, a jailbreak, a murder, and a life-or-death decision. No life-leeched pap here! And no adult or child can read this book without coming to terms with some of life's basic issues.

It is this internal struggle to find out how we feel or who we are that is so central to the idea of reading. More than helping them to read better, more than exposing them to good writing, more than developing their imagination, when we read aloud to children we are helping them to find themselves and to discover some meaning in the scheme of things. When Robert Penn Warren wrote, "We turn to fiction for some slight hint about the story in the life we live," he meant children as much as adults. All the best qualities of great adult fiction can be found in great children's literature, but particularly in the fairy tale. When Professor Richard Abrahamson of the University of Houston studied the "Children's Choices for 1979," a list of favorite books chosen by children across the United States, he found most children preferred books with "episodic plots involving confrontation with a problem and characters who have opposing points of view . . ."[16]

Because of the variety involved, fairy tales offer us an excellent opportunity to introduce the child or class to comparative literature. Try reading Paul Galdone's traditional version of *The Three Little Pigs* and then Tony Ross's *The Three Pigs,* in which the pigs build their own homes because the bank refused to loan them the money ("We're not a *piggy bank!*" says the bank manager). *Jim and the Beanstalk* by Raymond Briggs continues the story of *Jack and the Beanstalk* (also by Paul Galdone), this time with the son of the original giant. Compare *Little Red Riding Hood* by Trina Schart Hyman with the little girl in *The Gunniwolf* by Wilhelmina Harper, then compare both with the mischievous Peter Rabbit. In fairness to wolves, compare the wolves in all the above with the one in Harry Allard's *It's So Nice to Have a Wolf Around the House.* Where are the similarities and differences?

Teachers and parents often ask me, "When do you stop the picture books and start with the 'big' books—the novels?" Although I understand their impatience to get on with the business of growing up, I wince whenever I hear them phrase it that way.

First of all, there is no such time as "a time to stop the picture books." I know nursery-school teachers who read Judith Viorst's *Alexander and the Terrible, Horrible, No Good, Very Bad Day* to their classes and I know a high-school English teacher who reads it to his sophomores twice a year—once in September and, by popular demand, again in June.

Shouldn't those 15-year-olds have outgrown a picture book like *Alexander and the Terrible, Horrible, No Good, Very Bad Day?* Not by my standards. I read a picture book *(Ira Sleeps Over)* to every adult group I address and no one ever objects; in fact, it may be the best part of my entire presentation. A good story is a good story. Beautiful and stirring pictures can move 15-year-olds as well as 5-year-olds. The picture book should be on the reading list of every class in every grade through twelve years of school.

You say your eighth-grade class wouldn't sit still for a picture book? They'd be insulted? Not if you picked the right book and matched it with the right moment and the right attitude on the part of the reader. Try reading *The Shrinking of Treehorn* by Florence Parry Heide to teenagers. I can almost guarantee there will be someone at your desk at the end of the class asking, "What was the name of that book again?"

Writing in *The Reading Journal,* William Coughlin, Jr., director of English education at the University of Lowell (Massachusetts), explained the difficulties he encountered in trying to teach literary form (plot, setting, character) to secondary-school students. [17] The complexity and subtlety of the text he was using, Herman Melville's *Moby Dick,* appeared to overwhelm the class. Coughlin began to wonder if the mistake was in trying to teach a simple idea with a complex book. Why not introduce the concepts of plot and point of view through a simple book and then apply them to a complex work?

Coughlin chose to work with Leo Lionni's *Frederick,* a picture book he describes as "a story of less than 600 words, but the beautifully structured craftsmanship with which its elements of form interrelated exhibited perfectly what I wanted my students to see when they read." The response by his class was immediate and the results positive. In the same article, coauthor Brendan Desilets explained how picture books are used in a similar manner at Bedford (Massachusetts) High School. Both authors agree that "to ignore children's literature in the high school classroom is to overlook a valuable resource for teaching advanced reading skills."

Since many elementary-school teachers only have the opportunity to read to a mixture of slow, medium, and fast students, your initial read-aloud plan should call for material that is within the range of *all* the children in the room. In succeeding readings you can increase the caliber of the books and challenge the group's abilities. Of course, if you are teaching a gifted or top-level class you can begin at a much higher level.

One of the first criteria for lengthening the read-aloud session beyond picture books is the attention span of the child or class. It is no secret among teachers that children's attention spans appear to be growing shorter each year. It is in this battle to expand their attention spans that reading aloud can be particularly effective. A good story, peopled by well-developed characters moving in a suspenseful plot, cannot help but hold children's attention. The more this happens—as with an athlete in training—the stronger becomes the child's listening endurance.

The analogy to athletes is appropriate because of the conditioning factor in both. As the runner must accustom himself to self-discipline, so the child must be conditioned to listen for set periods of time if he is to understand and appreciate the story. And just as the runner doesn't achieve endurance overnight, neither do listeners. You must start slowly and build. Let the mental, social, and emotional level of your class or child guide you in your selections.

I believe children should be introduced early to the concept of "chapter" books—books that don't have to end on Monday; they can be stretched into Tuesday and Wednesday. Eventually, the child recognizes that books can be stretched into the rest of his life. Children as young as 4 years old will respond to little picture books that have been divided into chapters, such as *The Foundling Fox* by Irina Korschunow and *Andy and the Lion* by James Dougherty.

If the class has had experience in being read to, you can move quickly to longer books or longer reading sessions. If it is a new experience, keep your readings short. This gradual conditioning process applies to almost all grades and ages.

If I had a second-grade class with a short attention span at the start of the school year, I'd start with picture books like Bernard Waber's *Ira Sleeps Over, The Aminal* by Lorna Balian, *The Biggest Bear* by Lynd Ward, Steven Kellogg's *The Island of the Skog,* and *Sleeping Beauty* by the Brothers Grimm. Then we'd move to picture books with more words—perhaps the Bill Peet books (see Index to Treasury). And then one day I'd read a picture book and tie in a poem from Shel Silverstein's *Where the Sidewalk Ends.* In another week or so, I would add two poems to the end of the picture book, or perhaps a poem in the morning and a poem in the afternoon when we came back from lunch.

As I felt their interest and enthusiasm grow, I'd move to a series of interconnected read-aloud books, such as Bernard Waber's Lyle series. I would also introduce the children to the series by Carol and Donald Carrick about a young boy named Christopher—seven beautiful stories which I'd spread through an entire week. In this series, the class will follow Christopher through his first sleep-out alone with his dog Bodger *(Sleep Out);* they can empathize with Christopher as he worries about Bodger being caught in an electrical storm *(Lost in the Storm);* they can grieve with Christopher when he must come to terms with his loss after Bodger is killed *(The Accident);* they can grow with him as he finds the replacement for Bodger—a dog abandoned on the wharf *(The Foundling);* they can rejoice with him and his new dog, Ben, in their adventure on the river after a flash flood *(The Washout);* they can plot with him to control a neighborhood nuisance *(Ben and the Porcupine);* and nervously explore a lake bottom with him in *Dark and Full of Secrets.* Seven books, seven days, all linked by the common thread of one family and their concern for each other and their pets. From here it is an easy jump to "chapter books" or short novels like *The Littles* (one in a series) by John Peterson or *The Courage of Sarah Noble* by Alice Dalgliesh, books that can be stretched over several days or a week.

My own judgment and the attention span of the child or class would dictate my next move. If the attention span was still short, I'd stay with the shorter stories for a while longer. Soon, though, they will be ready for longer chapter books—short novels, something between 60 and 100 pages. I'd start with one of the most exciting fantasy stories available, *The Iron Giant* by Ted Hughes, or Shel Silverstein's *Lafcadio, the Lion Who Shot Back.* The latter has all the storytelling charm and humor of Silverstein's famous poetry and can be read to experienced kindergarten children as well as to older classes.

I am firmly convinced that some of the blame for children's short attention spans must be placed on the shoulders of parents and teachers who continually underestimate these capacities. "That story would be too long. They'd never sit still that long," says the teacher, forgetting the fact that the children sit still for three hours of television every day. They have no trouble enjoying and understanding the movie *Star Wars* and they'll have no difficulty appreciating lengthy books—if they are exciting and meaningful.

Having been read a few short novels, your class or child may be ready for the full-length novel. Perhaps the biggest difference between reading aloud the short novel and the full-length novel is the amount of description in the latter. The shorter book keeps its description to a minimum, whereas the longer book allows for greater development of character, plot, and setting.

These descriptive passages require the imagination—the right side of the brain—to build a picture of what's being read. However, if the imagination has been shriveling in front of the television for years, then it is going to be weak and unable to do any heavy lifting or building. Like any muscle in the body, the imagination cannot be built in a day or a week. It stands to reason that the child or class that has been read to regularly will have less trouble in using his imagination with these descriptive passages than will beginners.

In our home we began reading to Jamie a year earlier than we did to Elizabeth (largely because he was the second child and we were that much smarter the second time around). As a result, Jamie was ready for his first full-length novel by the time he was in kindergarten. Elizabeth wasn't ready until first grade. The reading and listening experience of the child or class should not be your only guide. Since each child has his or her own development timetable, we cannot expect all children to arrive at the novel stage at the same time, even if they are read to regularly.

How will you know if they are ready for a full-length novel? Does the child ask you each night to keep reading? What kinds of questions does he ask about the stories you read? Are the descriptions or characters confusing for him?

The first novel I read to Jamie would be my first choice a thousand times over, for almost any child or class—*James and the Giant Peach*. I know a kindergarten teacher who ends her year with this book and I know a sixth-grade teacher who has started her September class with it for twenty years. Any book that can hold the attention and lift the imaginations of 6-year-olds as well as 11-year-olds has to have magic in it. And *James and the Giant Peach* has that.

Once a child or class has reached the novel stage, it is increasingly important for the adult to preview the book before reading it aloud. The length of such books allows them to treat subject matter that can be very sensitive, far more so than a picture book could. As the reader, you should first familiarize yourself with the subject and the author's approach. Ask yourself as you read it through, "Can my child or class handle not only the vocabulary and the complexity of this story, but its emotions as well? Is there anything here that will do more harm than good to my child or class? Anything that might embarrass someone?"

Along with enabling you to avoid this kind of damaging situation, reading it ahead of time will enable you to read it the second time to the class or child with more confidence, accenting important passages, leaving out dull ones (I mark these lightly in pencil in the margins), and providing sound effects to dramatize the story line (I'm always ready to knock on a table or wall where the story calls for a "knock at the door").

Let me offer two personal experiences concerning story selection and reading ahead.

When Jamie was in first grade, I picked out a book by Elliott Arnold called *Brave Jimmy Stone*. It is a dramatic and touching story that describes a boy and his father on a hunting trip. They are two days away from civilization when the father falls and breaks a leg and the boy has to travel through a blizzard to get help. It was a short novel, just the right pace for Jamie, and the vocabulary was well within his grasp.

Mistakenly I considered only the intellectual level of the story and ignored the emotional level. It wasn't until Jamie woke up crying for the second straight night that I realized that I had forgotten about the emotional side of the story. Jamie had thought that because this was happening to Jimmy Stone and his father, it probably would happen to Jamie Trelease and his father, also. He was too young to deal with the realistic emotional drama of the scenes and became blind to the difference between fact and fiction. *Brave Jimmy Stone* is worth reading. It is a beautiful book. The mistake was mine in reading it too soon. I should have waited until Jamie was in third grade.

The embarrassing moment avoided by my wife when she was reading *Lafcadio, the Lion Who Shot Back* to her fifth-grade class points out the need for previewing read-alouds and the importance of staying flexible in our readings. Susan had not read the entire book ahead of time but was staying three chapters ahead of the class in her preparation each night. Suddenly one night she stood in front of me exclaiming, "What am I going to do? I just got to the part where Lafcadio goes to Chicago and has a suit made for himself out of marshmallows. What am I going to do?"

When I expressed bewilderment, Susan explained that there was an overweight child in her class whom the children cruelly had nicknamed "Marshmallow." To make matters worse, she said, the word appeared throughout the next chapter, also. "I know that as soon as I read the word 'marshmallow,' every head in the room is going to turn toward that child. He's going to hate this book and he's going to hate me for reading it. I just can't do that to him. But I've already started the book with the class and they love it."

We solved the problem with a little flexibility: Taking a pencil, we crossed out every "marshmallow" in the text and replaced it with "M & M's." She finished the book and the children never knew the difference, though she didn't leave the book around the room for the kids to examine as she normally would have done.

Sooner or later the question of censorship arises, perhaps not over the word "marshmallow" but over others. My own creed is that I censor everything—newspapers, books, billboards, junk mail, what I read to myself and what I read aloud. If I'm bored with something I'm reading for pleasure, I usually skip over it, as most people do. (Incidentally, Charles Dickens did this whenever he read aloud his works.) If there is something in the text that will detract from the book's impact or disturb the class or child, skip it or change it. You're running the program, not the person who wrote the book, who has no idea what the problems are in your classroom or home. I am not suggesting, as one author friend feared, that you rewrite the book to the tastes of the reader. Reason, not revisionism. The business of plodding along word-for-word, never missing a line, said Clifton Fadiman, is "chronic reverence," something that may be good manners but also "a confounded waste of time."

If you edit calmly you can save many books that ordinarily might have to be scrapped for classroom consumption. A teacher in South Hadley, Massachusetts, confirmed this approach in reading Lois Duncan's *Killing Mr. Griffin* to her eighth-grade remedial-reading class. Her students were 13-year-olds reading on a third-grade level. The story of four teenagers who decide to kidnap and frighten their overstrict English teacher is controversial enough, but the occasional four-letter words if read aloud could put the teacher in hot water. Nevertheless, she knew the story was worth saving. In reading it to her class she skipped or changed the swear words and read on. The resulting class attention and enthusiasm were sky-high. By the middle of the book, half the class wanted to find a copy in the school library in order to read it for themselves.

"I choose to read one chapter a day, no more. That way," the teacher explains, "if a child is absent, he doesn't miss too much of the story. I also do the reading at the beginning of the class. As a result, I never have to call for order. They are 'shush-ing' each other as they walk in the door. There is perfect order at the sound of the bell and seldom is there a late arrival."

But more importantly, they became involved in the story. They immediately recognized the peer pressures that fertilized the kidnapping scheme. They took sides and began to form judgments about the characters, putting themselves in their places. These eighth-grade remedial students had become emotionally, intellectually, and socially involved in the story.

"For me," the teacher enthuses, "that is a dream come true."

Several questions often are raised about a book like *Killing Mr. Griffin*. First, what kind of subject matter is that for kids? In reply I refer you to Robert C. O'Brien's speech in accepting his 1972 Newbery Medal for *Mrs. Frisby and the Rats of NIMH*. O'Brien saw the mind as a seed. As the seed grows, it puts down roots, opens its leaves, and looks around. "It learns about love," O'Brien noted, "about hate, fear, sadness, courage, kindness. But all of them come to life in books in a way that is peculiarly suitable for examination, for contemplation, and evaluation . . .

"Did I mention bad guys?" O'Brien asked. "Did I say Long John Silver? Long John Silver is a liar; he is unctious, greedy, tricky; he is a thief. Then why do we like him better than anybody else in the book?

"Here is where examination and evaluation come into play," O'Brien explained. "The mind learns that it is not easy to separate good from bad; they become deviously intertwined. From books it learns that not all doors are simply open and shut . . ."[18]

The second question arising from a book like *Killing Mr. Griffin* is: Won't remedial students reading on a third-grade level miss much of the story's meaning?

Fader and McNeil answer this question in their book, *Hooked on Books*. Dr. Daniel Fader writes of his experiences in turning reluctant readers into willing readers, particularly at the W. J. Maxey Boys' Training School in Michigan. Many of the delinquent boys at the school were semiliterate, but that didn't stop them from reading books that interested them. Fader points to the boy who wanted to read Nathaniel Hawthorne's *The Scarlet Letter*. When the boy was cautioned that the book might be too difficult, he replied, "Ain't this the one about a whore?" When he was told that, indeed, that description came fairly close to the mark, he proceeded to read it. "If it was a book about a whore, it was a book for him," Fader wrote.

The author convincingly points out that his experiences at Maxey show that children definitely can read and understand without knowing every word in the book:

> Semi-literate readers do not need semi-literate books. The simplistic language of much of the life-leeched literature inflicted upon the average schoolchild is not justifiable from any standpoint. Bright, average, dull—however one classified the child—he is immeasurably better off with books that are too difficult for him than books that are too simple. . . . Reading is a peculiarly personal interaction between a reader and a book . . . but *in no case* does this interaction demand an understanding of every word by the reader. The threshold . . . even in many complex books, can be pleasurably crossed by many simple readers.[19]

By citing Dr. Fader's argument here I am not suggesting that every book you read aloud be over the head of your audience. A child hears a story on at least three different levels: intellectual, emotional, and social. In the Maxey and South Hadley incidents, while the students were on a third-grade intellectual level, their emotional and social levels were often those of their own age or older.

While on the subject of junior- and senior-high school students who are reluctant readers, I think it is important to note that they, too, should be conditioned gradually to the reading-aloud process. In working with these slower students you must first consider the kind of class you have and work from there. I remember the remedial-reading teacher who told me about her frustrations in trying to find the right book for the worst class she'd ever had. This happened to be a sixth-grade class but the lesson applies to all grade levels. First she tried *Charlotte's Web;* they thought it was corny. Then she tried *Charlie and the Chocolate Factory* by Roald Dahl; half the class liked it, half didn't. At last she struck upon *J.T.* by Jane Wagner, the story of a black boy straddling the edge of delinquency. The class loved it so much that half of them found extra copies and finished it ahead of her.

The teacher admitted that her mistake was in not tailoring her first selections to the kind of class she had—a group of restless, nonreading, street-wise, inner-city kids. Make your *initial* choices for a group like that something they can relate to, win their interest, catch their hearts and ears. A few selections of this kind and you'll have won their confidence, after which you can broaden the scope of your reading and introduce them to other times and other places than their own.

Contrary to tradition, humor should be a mainstay in the curriculum as well as your read-aloud library. I recall the August day my neighbor Ellie Fernands asked me, "Which book do you think I ought to start off the year reading aloud?" (She was returning to junior high teaching after a fourteen-year hiatus to raise her own children.) We settled on *Be a Perfect Person in Just Three Days!* by Stephen Manes, a funny short novel about early adolescence.

At the end of that first week of school she confided, "I don't know what I would have done without *Perfect Person* those first few days. I was so nervous that they wouldn't like me and I guess they were nervous that I wouldn't like them. Our shared laughter was the icebreaker, and it won their confidence." Since then, she notes, reading aloud has become the best part of the day.

For older reluctant readers, try beginning each day with a poem from *Where the Sidewalk Ends,* a reading from an anthology like *Best-Loved Folktales of the World* by Joanna Cole, or a selection from *Paul Harvey's The Rest of the Story.* The latter book (and its two successors) contains nearly 100 historic and contemporary tales. Originally used on Harvey's national radio program and written by his son, Paul Aurandt, the stories are only four minutes in length, and each is highlighted by an O. Henry ending: the famous person about whom the story is woven is usually not revealed until the last sentence. A few weeks of these short selections should condition older students to the listening experience.

Please keep in mind that all your selections should not be complete works of literature. If, in your leisure reading, you find a magazine piece, or a book chapter that you think the class would enjoy, read it to them. For example, read the first 16 pages from Dennis Smith's account of life and death at the busiest firehouse in America, *Report from Engine Co. 82.* It might whet their appetites enough to read the book themselves. Reading aloud an occasional newspaper column may turn a student into a fan of that writer. You'll know you're on the right track when a student stops you in the hall between classes and asks, "Did you read Bob Greene's column last night? Wasn't it great?" (There is a collection of Greene's best newspaper and magazine columns, *American Beat,* that makes wonderful reading aloud on the junior and senior high school level. Like everything you read aloud, though, be selective with *American Beat*—a few of the Greene pieces may be too strong for the classroom.)

The youngster being conditioned to reading aloud is much like a runner in training. One of the problems that faces a runner after he has acquired some proficiency is the boredom associated with repetitive training. Long-distance runners combat this boredom by varying the length and routes of their training runs. Readers-aloud face a similar predicament in conditioning children's listening. To solve this problem, readers should imitate the runner—vary your reading routes. Read a three-sitting story after a week of one-sittings.

Just as you should remember to challenge the mental level of your audience, it also is important to realize that you don't have to challenge them *all* the time. Do *you* choose for your personal reading only those books that challenge you? Do you read only the editorial page of the newspaper or do you read the comics and "Dear Abby" too?

If we are to give our children an overview of the literary spectrum available to them, then we should vary the scenery: animal stories like *Lassie, Come Home* and George Seldon's *Cricket in Times Square;* family stories like *Roll of Thunder, Hear My Cry* by Mildred Taylor and *Us and Uncle Fraud* by Lois Lowry; historical stories like *Caddie Woodlawn* and *My Brother Sam Is Dead* by James and Christopher Collier; funny stories like *Freckle Juice* by Judy Blume and Barbara Robinson's *The Best Christmas Pageant Ever;* sad stories such as *Bridge to Terabithia* by Katherine Paterson and *A Day No Pigs Would Die* by Robert Newton Peck; scary stories like William Sleator's *Among the Dolls* and *Our John Willie* by Catherine Cookson; sports stories like *Winning Kicker* by Thomas Dygard and *Hang Tough, Paul Mather* by Alfred Slote.

A parent may choose to challenge a child's mind with each read-aloud and take care of the child's emotional needs in other ways. But classroom teachers are limited in the ways they reach and touch children. Each day millions of children arrive in American classrooms in search of more than reading and math skills. They are looking for a light in the darkness of their lives, a Good Samaritan who will stop and bandage a bruised heart or ego.

Books can do much to ease those hurts. Katherine Paterson spoke eloquently about the healing salve of books when she accepted the 1979 National Book Award for *The Great Gilly Hopkins,* a book that offers hope and affection to those thousands of children who have found themselves rated "disposable"—foster children.

Mrs. Paterson told her Carnegie Hall audience, "A teacher had read aloud *The Great Gilly Hopkins* to her class and Eddie, another foster child, hearing in the story of Gilly his own story, did something that apparently flabbergasted everyone who knew him. He fell in love with a book. Can you imagine how that made me feel? Here was a 12-year-old who knew far better than I what my story was about, and he did me the honor of claiming it for himself. It seemed to me that anyone who liked a book as much as Eddie did should have a copy of his own, so I sent him one. On Saturday I got this letter:

Dear Mrs. Paterson:
   Thank you for the book, *The Great Gilly Hopkins.* I love the book. I'm on page 16.

Your friend always,
Eddie Young [20]

When considering material to read aloud to children, two areas often overlooked are poetry and comic books.

"Children never hear poetry any more," laments Professor Leland Jacobs of Columbia University. "They come to nursery school and they know the jingles from television but they don't know Mother Goose."

The problem is that most parents and teachers assume that children hate poetry. They are right in such assumptions if they are talking about obscure or long descriptive poetry filled with obsolete figures of speech to which children are introduced by having to memorize or analyze it.

On the other hand, when children are introduced to the right poems in the right manner, they love poetry. This love is easily recognized in children's universal love of song—which is just poetry set to music. A child cannot help but begin life with a love of poetry if you consider that the first sound he hears is a poem: the rhythmic beat of his mother's heart. The love of such rhythm stays until it is driven from the child by unthinking and insensitive teachers in his home or classroom.

In making your poetry selections, it would be helpful to bear in mind what Bernice Cullinan, New York University professor of early childhood and elementary education, says in her book *Literature and the Child:* "Children's poetry choices remain stable and consistent over the years. Many children today, like those of 50 years ago, prefer humorous poems. Most children do not like sentimental and serious poetry, or poems difficult to understand. Poetry with clear-cut rhyme and rhythm is well liked; poetry that depends heavily upon imagery is not."[21]

The rules for retaining or developing a love of poetry within children are: read it aloud; read it often; keep it simple; keep it joyous or spooky or exciting. Remember, poetry appreciation is like a ball. "It is more caught than taught," explains Jacobs. For this purpose, keep an anthology of poetry handy at the bedside or on the teacher's desk. Mother Goose, *Where the Sidewalk Ends,* and *The Random House Book of Poetry for Children* by Jack Prelutsky are outstanding poetry collections and are included in the Treasury in the poetry section.

Using anthologies as resources, you frequently can link an appropriate poem with a book you are reading aloud, either before or after the story, later in the day, or on days when your schedule doesn't leave enough time for the day's chapter. Examples of possible read-aloud titles with their accompanying poems would include: *Call of the Wild* and "The Cremation of Sam McGee" (found in *Best Tales of the Yukon* by Robert W. Service); *The Little House* and "The House With Nobody in It" (*The Best Loved Poems of the American People* edited by Hazel Felleman); *Sing Down the Moon* and "The Indian Hunter" (*The Best Loved Poems of the American People*); *Hang Tough, Paul Mather* and "Casey at the Bat" (*Best Loved Poem of the American People*); *The Reluctant Dragon* and "The Tale of Custard the Dragon" (*The Golden Treasury of Poetry* edited by Louis Untermeyer). By familiarizing yourself with the poetry books noted in the Treasury, you will be able to come up with a limitless list of your own.

Along with accomplishing many of the aims of all good literature, poetry has one aspect that sets it apart from the rest. It is an excellent medium for training the disciplines of listening and reading that are such integral parts of your read-aloud program.

"Poetry," explained Donald Barr while headmaster of the Dalton School, "cannot be skimmed. It must be read word for word." Because it is bound by meter and rhythm, every word and every syllable counts. Children quickly come to sense this and discipline their attention in order to stay tuned. There is no room for the skimming that is so prevalent in prose. Barr adds that such unfortunate habits often rob literature of its subtle meanings. "But poetry will not bear it. It is a great discipline."[22]

The other area commonly overlooked for read-aloud is the comic book, and my first choice would be the incomparable *Tintin.* If you looked closely at Dustin Hoffman while he was reading a bedtime story to his son in *Kramer vs. Kramer,* you would have noticed he was reading *Tintin.* Or if you read the list of favorite read-alouds offered by historian Arthur Schlesinger, Jr., in *The New York Times Book Review,* you would have found Hergé's *Tintin* between *Huckleberry Finn* and the Greek myths.[23]

Begun as a comic strip in Belgium in 1929, *Tintin* now reaches, in comic-book form, thirty countries in twenty-two languages and is sold only in quality bookstores. The subject of this success is a 17-year-old reporter (Tintin) who, along with his dog and a cast of colorful and zany characters, travels around the globe in pursuit of mad scientists, spies, and saboteurs.

Two years were spent researching and drawing the 700 illustrations in each issue. These pictures vary in size, shape, and perspective, and run as many as fifteen panels to a page. This layout, with its minute detail and run-on dialogue, inhibits the child from understanding the book by merely looking at the pictures, as he can with most comics. To be understood, *Tintin* must be read—and that is the key for parents and teachers who care about reading. Each issue contains 8,000 words. The beautiful part of it is that children are unaware they are reading 8,000 words. They are reading for the fun of it—the important first step toward all other kinds of reading.

I am not recommending comic books as a steady diet for reading aloud but as an introduction to the comic format. Young children must be shown how a comic "works": the sequence of the panels; how to tell when a character is thinking and when he is speaking; the meaning of stars, question marks, and exclamation points. A comic can be viewed as an interesting sequential diagram of conversation—a language blueprint. Once the blueprint is understood, the child will be ready and willing to follow it on his own without your reading it aloud.

Parents and teachers who provide a wide variety of reading materials for the child need not fear that the child or class will develop a "comic-book mentality." A recent study showed that more top students (nearly 100 percent), in all grades, read comics or comic books than did lower students.[24]

4
The Do's and Don'ts
of Read-Aloud

Writing begins long before the marriage of pencils and paper. It begins with sounds, that is to say with words and simple clusters of words that are taken in by small children until they find themselves living in a world of vocables. If that world is rich and exciting, the transition to handling it in a new medium— writing—is made smoother. The first and conceivably the most important instructor in composition is the teacher, parent, or older sibling who reads aloud to the small child.

—Clifton Fadiman, from
Empty Pages: A Search for Writing Competence in School and Society

Do's

- Begin reading to children as soon as possible. The younger you start them, the better.
- Use Mother Goose rhymes and songs to stimulate the infant's

language and listening. Simple but boldly colored picture books arouse children's curiosity and visual sense.

- Read as often as you and the child (or class) have time for.
- Try to set aside at least one traditional time each day for a story. In my home, favorite story times are before going to bed and before leaving for school.
- Remember that the art of listening is an acquired one. It must be taught and cultivated gradually—it doesn't happen overnight.
- Picture books can be read easily to a family of children widely separated in age. Novels, however, pose a problem. If there are more than two years between the children, each child would benefit greatly if you read to him or her individually. This requires more effort on the part of the parents but it will reap rewards in direct proportion to the effort expended. You will reinforce the specialness of each child.
- Start with picture books and build to storybooks and novels.
- Vary the length and subject matter of your readings.
- Follow through with your reading. If you start a book, it is your responsibility to continue it—unless it turns out to be a bad book. Don't leave the child or class hanging for three or four days between chapters and expect their interest to be sustained.
- Occasionally read above the children's intellectual level and challenge their minds.
- Avoid long descriptive passages until the child's imagination and attention span are capable of handling them. There is nothing wrong with shortening or eliminating them. Prereading helps to locate such passages and they can then be marked with a pencil in the margin.
- If your chapters are long or if you don't have enough time each day to finish an entire chapter, find a suspenseful spot at which to stop. Leave the audience hanging; they'll be counting the minutes until the next reading.
- Allow your listeners a few minutes to settle down and adjust their feet and minds to the story. If it's a novel, you might begin by asking if anyone remembers what happened when you left off yesterday. Mood is an important factor in listening. An authoritarian "Now stop that and settle down! Sit up straight. Pay attention" is not conducive to a receptive audience.
- If you are reading a picture book, make sure the children can see the pictures easily. In class, with the children in a semicircle around you, seat yourself just slightly above them so that the children

in the back row can see the pictures above the heads of the others.

• In reading a novel, position yourself where both you and the children are comfortable. In the classroom, whether you are sitting on the edge of your desk or standing, your head should be above the heads of your listeners for your voice to carry to the far side of the room. Do not sit at your desk and read or stand in front of brightly lit windows, which strain the eyes of your audience.

• Remember that even sixth-grade students love a good picture book now and then.

• Allow time for class and home discussion after reading a story. Thoughts, hopes, fears, and discoveries are aroused by a book. Allow them to surface and help the child to deal with them through verbal, written, or artistic expression if the child is so inclined. Do not turn discussions into quizzes or insist upon prying story interpretations from the child.

• Remember that reading aloud comes naturally to very few people. To do it successfully and with ease you must practice.

• Use plenty of expression when reading. If possible, change your tone of voice to fit the dialogue.

• Adjust your pace to fit the story. During a suspenseful part, slow down, draw your words out, bring your listeners to the edge of their chairs.

• The most common mistake in reading aloud—whether the reader is a 7-year-old or a 40-year-old—is reading too fast. Read slowly enough for the child to build mental pictures of what he just heard you read. Slow down enough for the children to see the pictures in the book without feeling hurried. Reading quickly allows no time for the reader to use vocal expression.

• Preview the book by reading it to yourself ahead of time. Such advance reading allows you to spot material you may wish to shorten, eliminate, or elaborate on.

• Bring the author to life, as well as his book. Consult *Something About the Author* at the library, and read the information on your book's dust jacket. Either before or during the reading, tell your audience something about the author. Let them know that books are written by people, not by machines. You also can accomplish this by encouraging individual children (not the class collectively—authors hate assembly-line mail) to write and share feelings about the book with the author. *Something About the Author* will provide an address, or you can write care of the publisher. It is important to enclose a self-addressed, stamped envelope *just in case* the author has time to respond. The child should understand from the start that his letter's purpose is not to receive a response.

- Add a third dimension to the book whenever possible. For example: have a bowl of blueberries ready to be eaten during or after the reading of Robert McCloskey's *Blueberries for Sal;* bring a harmonica and a lemon to class before reading McCloskey's *Lentil;* buy a small plastic cowboy and Indian for when you read *The Indian in the Cupboard* by Lynn Reid Banks.
- When children are old enough to distinguish between library books and your own, start reading with a pencil in hand. When you and the child encounter a passage worth remembering, put a small mark—maybe a star—in the margin. Readers should interact with books and one way is to acknowledge beautiful writing.
- Reluctant readers or unusually active children frequently find it difficult to just sit and listen. Paper, crayons, and pencils allow them to keep their hands busy while listening.
- Follow the suggestion of Dr. Caroline Bauer and post a reminder sign by your door: "Don't Forget Your *Flood* Book." Analagous to the emergency rations in case of natural disasters, these books should be taken along in the car, or even stored like spares in the trunk. A few chapters from "flood" books can be squeezed into traffic jams on the way to the beach or long waits at the dentist's office.
- Fathers should make an extra effort to read to their children. Because 98 percent of primary-school teachers are women, young boys often associate reading with women and schoolwork. And just as unfortunately, too many fathers prefer to be seen playing catch in the driveway with their sons than taking them to the library. It is not by chance that most of the students in remedial-reading classes are boys. A father's early involvement with books and reading can do much to elevate books to at least the same status as baseball gloves and hockey sticks in a boy's estimation.
- Regulate the amount of time your children spend in front of the television. Excessive television viewing is habit-forming and damaging to a child's development.
- Arrange for time each day—in the classroom or in the home—for the child to read by himself (even if "read" only means turn-

ing pages and looking at the pictures). All your read-aloud motivation goes for naught if the time is not available to put it into practice.

- Lead by example. Make sure your children see you reading for pleasure other than at read-aloud time. Share with them your enthusiasm for whatever you are reading.

Don'ts

- Don't read stories that you don't enjoy yourself. Your dislike will show in the reading, and that defeats your purpose.
- Don't continue reading a book once it is obvious that it was a poor choice. Admit the mistake and choose another. Make sure, however, that you've given the book a fair chance to get rolling; some start slower than others. (You can avoid the problem by prereading the book yourself.)
- If you are a teacher, don't feel you have to tie every book to classwork. Don't confine the broad spectrum of literature to the narrow limits of the curriculum.
- Consider the intellectual, social, and emotional level of your audience in making a read-aloud selection. Challenge them, but don't overwhelm them.
- Don't read above a child's emotional level.
- Don't select a book that many of the children already have heard or seen on television. Once a novel's plot is known, much of their interest is lost. You can, however, read a book ahead of its appearance on television or at the movies. Afterwards, encourage the children to see the movie. It's a good way for them to see how much more can be portrayed in print than on the screen.
- Don't be fooled by awards. Just because a book won an award doesn't guarantee that it will make a good read-aloud. In most cases, a book award is given for the quality of the writing, not for its read-aloud qualities.
- Don't start a reading if you are not going to have enough time to do it justice. Having to stop after one or two pages only serves to frustrate, rather than stimulate, the child's interest in reading.
- Don't get too comfortable while reading. A reclining position is bound to bring on drowsiness, and a slouching position produces similar effects because the lungs can't easily fill to capacity.

- Don't be unnerved by questions during the reading, particularly from very young children. Answer their questions patiently. Don't put them off. Don't rush your answers. There is no time limit for reading a book but there is a time limit on a child's inquisitiveness. Foster that curiosity with patient answers—then resume your reading.
- Don't impose interpretations of a story upon your audience. A story can be just plain enjoyable, no reason necessary. But encourage conversation about the reading. Only seven minutes out of 150 instructional minutes in the school day are spent on discussions between teacher and student.
- Don't confuse quantity with quality. Reading to your child for ten minutes, given your full attention and enthusiasm, may very well last longer in the child's mind than two hours of solitary television viewing.
- Don't use the book as a threat—"If you don't pick up your room, no story tonight!" As soon as the child or class sees that you've turned the book into a weapon, they'll change their attitude about books from positive to negative.
- Don't try to compete with television. If you say, "Which do you want, a story or TV?" they will usually choose the latter. That is like saying to a 9-year-old, "Which do you want, vegetables or a donut?" Since *you* are the adult, *you* choose. "The television goes off at eight-thirty in this house. If you want a story before bed, that's fine. If not, that's fine, too. But no television after eight-thirty." But don't let books appear to be responsible for depriving the children of viewing time.

5

The Home/School Connection

"The binary computer does not know how to be afraid. It does not know how to say, 'I'm sorry, I nearly blew it.' It does not have a sense of humor, and it does not understand story—story that asks questions, that dares to disturb the universe."

—Madeleine L'Engle,
Speaking at Simmons College, 1983

As you experience the positive benefits of reading aloud to children, it is imperative that you not keep them to yourself. Theories are wonderful but nothing moves people like first-hand practical experiences. Share them with neighbors, relatives, and coworkers. It is the responsibility of people who carry torches to pass them on, Plato reminded us. Such sharing is critically important for the survival and growth of a culture.

The most successful and happiest learning experiences are those in which teachers and parents work together, where teaching is shared.

64

If you are a parent who has experienced success with reading aloud at home and wish to see it done by the classroom teacher, it is incumbent upon you to say so. The same holds true for the teacher who reads aloud. When Jane Boyer, a teacher in Harrisburg, Pennsylvania, experienced a phenomenal response from her twenty-two inner-city kindergarteners after reading *James and the Giant Peach*, she followed up with an enthusiastic three-page letter to each child's parents. If the teacher is going to read *Charlotte's Web*, she could let the parents know about another E. B. White book, *Stuart Little*.

Parents, however, are much more reluctant to pass on suggestions to teachers, and this is unfortunate. Good teachers are not threatened by such well-intentioned suggestions but are heartened by parental support in the teaching process. On the other hand, the teacher who responds negatively to parents' ideas is probably a bad teacher, and therefore your involvement is even more necessary to encourage your child during the school year.

A note to the teacher might begin with a description and the benefits of your home read-aloud program. List some of your child's favorite titles. Then suggest that a similar program might be a good idea for the classroom, that it would develop a positive attitude among beginning readers toward the pleasures and not just the skills in reading, and that you are sure the children would love it. Please be assured that such a note is not trying to interfere with the curriculum—it is a reinforcement. Too often parents find the time to write notes to teachers requesting permission to take the child out of school for vacations, shopping trips, and sports tournaments. It is about time parents found the time to add something to the learning process instead of subtracting from it.

I know parents who give their children a day off from school on their birthday (tell me what that tells the child). I would suggest a more positive approach, like the one used at the Waldorf School in Lexington, Massachusetts, where parents are encouraged to purchase a book for the school library on the occasion of their child's birthday. The program, which has brought hundreds of books to the school, is sponsored by the parents and faculty, with the librarian providing a list of recommended titles.

Incidentally, a day-care or child-care program requires just as much—if not more—concern on your part. There are almost ten million children enrolled in such programs today—a sizable investment in tomorrow. We cannot afford just to assume that the care and feeding of our children's minds is being done every day. We must insure it with our involvement. Such local centers seldom have their own libraries and your initiative to begin one is critical.

Both parents and teachers find the courage to try new approaches if they know of successful examples, such as Ann Taylor, a second-grade teacher in West Chester, Pennsylvania. Mrs. Taylor is aware that many children are quick to assume reading is only for school and women because the only people they see reading are teachers—and 98 percent of those are women. In order to combat such thinking, she provides important alternative role models each year during Children's Book Week. Prior to that week, her students write invitations to parents and community members, inviting them to come and read a story to the class. Along with a strong contingent of parents, positive responses came from the mayor, superintendent of schools, principal, reporters, head custodian, school nurse, social worker, and the teacher's husband. Such a response is especially inspiring to the children, who discover that reading is not just for kids in school but for everyone.

The argument that our overcrowded curricula don't allow enough time for "frills" like reading aloud is a shallow one at best. If we can find room in the school day for banking, collecting bus and lunch money, pep rallies, sex education, fire drills, bicycle safety, fund drives, along with class-free days in honor of Washington, Lincoln, Columbus, and Martin Luther King, Jr., then we can find time for reading aloud.

At Glen Loch Elementary School in The Woodlands, Texas, Principal Bonnie Wilkinson finds the time to read to three groups of two hundred students every day. Perched on the edge of the cafeteria stage with microphone in hand, she reads—and occasionally asks questions—while the children listen, respond, and eat lunch. I talked with her one day during the first week of school and she said, "They're already asking when I'm going to start, what's going to be my first book." But reading aloud isn't confined to the principal or cafeteria in Mrs. Wilkinson's school. The school librarian, Carol Miller, reads to twenty-eight classes a week, and every teacher reads aloud as well. The multi-ethnic student body, drawn from a broad socioeconomic community that runs from very poor to very wealthy, boasts outstanding national reading scores.

Mrs. Wilkinson exemplifies the true meaning of the title "principal"—by example, she is the *principal* teacher in the school. The School District of Philadelphia/Federal Reserve Bank reading study showed that a principal's personal involvement with the reading program is critical to its success in the school.[1] "Personal involvement," though, does not boil down to a "personal obsession" with reading scores. It means the kind of involvement demonstrated by Joel West, a South Carolina principal (now district supervisor) who refused to allow the "drilling and skilling" approach to kill the joy of reading in his students. Reading aloud was a required part of the school day—for him and for every one of his teachers. In looking over his teachers' lesson plans, if no time had been allotted for reading aloud, he would leave a note asking, "What are you going to read aloud?"

Under Joel West, every class had special reading projects that fostered the love of books—they ranged from reading lofts (where the kindergarteners could retreat with their books) to an English tea party put on by the third grade after their principal, teacher, and librarian had all read aloud Michael Bond's *Paddington* books. West reports, "In April the students received invitations (with RSVP's) to attend a Paddington tea party in the library. We always used linen tablecloths and china (over the years not one cup was broken). We had some delightful pre-party language lessons about what took place at an English tea. The librarian provided Earl Grey tea, sugar lumps, English muffins and marmalade, and I made scones—for days and days."

In Spring Branch, Texas, retired teachers and teachers on maternity leave serve as volunteer readers in Landrum Junior High, where the administration is dedicated enough to the concept to provide babysitting funds for those volunteers with children.

An often-overlooked resource is the use of siblings and peers as readers aloud—brothers, sisters, babysitters, older students. After his exhaustive study of American education, John Goodlad commented: "One of the blind spots in American schooling is our almost complete failure to use peer teaching. In British schools you see children helping each other. The teacher has twenty-five assistants, so when a child comes in, a couple of other children take that child over, just as older brothers and sisters in big families used to do."[2] We all know the negatives in peer pressure—but we seldom consider its positive aspects.

The reading department in the Pittston Area Schools in Pennsylvania recognized the advantages of peer learning and started the PAC-Readers program in 1983 (PAC-Reader stands for Pittston-Area-Capable-Reader). Fifth- and sixth-grade student volunteers began reading aloud to first- and second-grade classrooms during the preschool breakfast time. After being trained in reading aloud, discussing an appropriate book choice with a teacher, and rehearsing the book (with a teacher/aide), the PAC-Reader introduces himself and his book to the first grade, says a few words about the author, and begins reading aloud.

"The response was unbelievable," explains principal Ross Scarantino. "We initially thought the sixth-grade boys might feel too sophisticated to go into the lower grades, but were we ever wrong! Boys have been volunteering as often as girls," he notes. Listener reaction has been just as positive. "The appearance of that excited sixth-grader with a book in hand says more to that first-grade beginning reader than the teacher could say in an entire week." The volunteer visits are bi-weekly, thus allowing adequate preparation time. After a community breakfast honoring the year's 420 readers, Scarantino noted that the remedial students, traditionally prone to poor self-image, have especially benefited from the program.

Parents can practice the Pittston idea by encouraging older siblings to read to younger ones when you are busy. Reading aloud should also be included among the tasks of every babysitter. (Make sure you provide the appropriate books.) Why not get your money's worth from the sitter? Watching TV is hardly worth the cost of babysitting today.

The influence of a dedicated individual is best exemplified in a statewide project in Delaware. READ-ALOUD Delaware is the 1984 brainchild of Representative Kevin W. Free, a New Zealand native who is now a member of the Delaware House of Representatives. Rep. Free remembered the achievements of the Plunket Society, a New Zealand health maintenance organization working with parents to insure the physical needs of young children, and he wondered if the same principles couldn't be applied to the intellectual needs of the child.

Why not a kind of Plunket Society for the minds of young children here in the United States? He also reasoned that the best head start for the mind is to be read to. Within months after conceiving the idea, Rep. Free founded READ-ALOUD Delaware in Wilmington, a "nonprofit corporation working to ensure that every preschool child in Delaware has someone to read to him or her." A board of directors was formed that included representatives from the public as well as the private sector (statewide women's clubs, colleges, social agencies dealing with early childhood, and parents) and a search committee hired a full-time director from nearly one hundred applicants.

Parents are not the only targets of the READ-ALOUD Delaware program. Through local libraries, day-care centers, Scout groups, and Red Cross classes, the organization has been able to recruit hundreds of volunteers willing to read to children who might not otherwise have a reader within the family. One such program was established at the West End Neighborhood House in Wilmington, where a resident pediatrician attends to the needs of area families. While parents fill out forms in the waiting room, volunteers from READ-ALOUD Delaware read to the children, demonstrating the pleasure as well as the techniques involved—interaction between reader and child, pointing to pictures, turning pages, asking and answering questions.

For parents without proficient reading skills, the volunteers demonstrate that reading doesn't have to be a threatening experience if you start with simple picture books and allow your own progress to grow with your child.

"This is all well and good," says the achievement-oriented parent (or school administrator), "but how can we immediately *measure* the success of reading aloud?" These are representatives of a new breed of adult bent on producing "superkids"; that is, reading by age three, computing by age six. For a moment, let's look at some of the emotional dangers from "professional parenting," starting with today's computers.

Unlike some of my fellow advocates of the printed word, I have great respect for computerization. This book was written on a word processor, the type was set with computers, and the sales tracked by computer. The computer can supply interminable facts, like so many bricks dumped in your yard. What matters in life is not so much the bricks but what you are able to build with them. Computers will give us stress figures for building a bridge, but what will it do to build a child's self-image? On the other hand, a five-year University of California study of 11- and 12-year-olds showed that minority children are more likely to have a lower self-image than their white peers—except for minority children who read regularly.[3]

But amid all the talk of information explosions ignited by computers, it is too easy to confuse information with wisdom. One need only read today's headlines or a history book to find educated men who, in search of power or money, have sold out their country, their constituents, or their employees. People like that believe they have all the answers. What they don't have are the four things that keep the world on an even keel: love, justice, courage, and compassion— four things no computer in the world can teach them. The only ways to learn them are: (1) through life experience; and (2) through a medium that preserves life experience and allows us to pass it on to succeeding generations—the book.

Literature allows us to visit the heart and soul of humanity; it gives us the opportunity to listen in on what Robert Hutchins called "the great conversation"—thoughts and values spanning thousands of years. The finest, most profound thoughts of the human species are available to us within the covers of books. It doesn't matter that Aesop, Twain, or Longfellow are centuries dead. In books, the thoughts and voices of the dead live.

Thanks to our free public library system, the voices in our books are nondiscriminatory. The child in the ghetto and the child in suburbia can both eavesdrop on the conversation of a black Mississippi farming family during the Depression in Mildred Taylor's *Roll of Thunder, Hear My Cry*. And in hearing the expression of that family's hopes and fears, each listener can come away with the knowledge that we are one family—be it in Alaska or Mississippi, be it white, black, yellow, or red. The world owes a special debt to the parent or teacher who makes the permanent connection that plugs a child into books instead of the herd mentality of soap operas and sitcoms; who understands that man is the only animal that understands the meaning of the word "yesterday" and gives the child a vision of yesterday in *Otto of the Silver Hand* by Howard Pyle, so he can better understand today and plan for tomorrow.

Author/ professor Julius Lester of the University of Massachusetts testifies to that experience. Recalling his childhood in Tennessee and Arkansas, he says: "Although I don't recall any content from my early years of books, there was the more important emotional content which those books represented—the knowledge that the segregated world in which I was forced to live, bounded by the white heat of hatred, was not the only reality. Somewhere beyond that world, somewhere my eyes could not then penetrate, were dreams and possibilities, and I knew this was true because the books I read ravenously, desperately, were voices from that world."[4] (A century ago, most of the slave states feared books that set the mind free, and consequently passed laws that forbade the teaching of reading to slaves. The teacher was fined or jailed; the slave had his ears slit.)

The new wave of school reform has been accompanied by a tide of career parents who, having delayed child-rearing in pursuit of those careers, are now beginning families at a later age. These new parents have proven to be not only more mature and affluent but also more anxious about the achievements of their offspring. The result is what child psychologist David Elkind describes as the "hurried child."

The pressure from such parents, coupled with the accountability mentality of a principal, can drain the human qualities from an entire school. Interest and concern over student achievement is one thing; blind obsession is another.

Consider for a minute the ten-mile strip of communities outside Chicago where the average family income is $60,000 a year—families headed by college-educated, affluent, career-oriented parents. The smudge on this pretty picture, Dr. Elkind tells us, is the communities' 250 percent increase in teenage suicides *every* year for the last ten years.[5]

Parents and educators inclined toward the "braining" of education instead of the "living" of education must be reminded that the smartest people in your business, faculty, or neighborhood are not always the nicest. We all know too many brilliant people who can't get along with others, who can't compromise or sympathize. Moreover, I.Q. is a poor predicter of success in career or life. Studies show the majority of successful people in all fields to be those whose I.Q.s fall in the normal rather than extraordinary range.[6] Given a choice of a mother who has a 145 I.Q. but is unaffectionate and a loving mother with a 110 I.Q., which one would you choose? Who is the teacher you remember most vividly? It is seldom the smartest.

When author/critic Clifton Fadiman was asked about the measurements we use in a culture, he said, "We must have a way of developing better human beings. We don't need smarter people—there are plenty of smart people involved in the mess in Washington—but better people. And I still believe that literacy, the literacy that reaches its highest development in literature—is a prerequisite condition for a society of better people. And if you want better people, it makes sense to start with children." This embraces beautifully my favorite definition of childhood—found in the opening sentence of Neil Postman's *The Disappearance of Childhood:* "Children are the living messages we send to a time we will not see."

Successful, achievement-oriented people, accustomed to immediate responses, are prone to the "impatience syndrome." Having experienced instant photography, instant copies, instant communication, instant pudding, instant coffee, even instant meals via the microwave, it is frustrating to them when they can't make instant adults out of their children. To date the only successful formula requires germination time.

Again and again, I encounter people—in education, business, government, the arts—who blossomed into successful human beings on a time schedule other than the one their parents or teachers intended. Late bloomers, they are called, people who ignored the expiration date someone stamped on their foreheads. Our children are not quarts of milk. And they won't turn sour just because they haven't read *Crime and Punishment* by age 15—as some people claim to have. Nor are they chimpanzees whose brains reach maturity after one year. The human brain is not fully developed until age 23.[7]

"The simple fact is that educational institutions, even at their best, cannot turn out fully educated men and women," writes philosopher Mortimer Adler. "The age at which most human beings attend school prevents that. Youth itself is the most serious impediment—in fact, youth is an insuperable obstacle to being an educated person. No one can be an educated person while immature," Adler declares.[8] It is only the maturing experience of life that allows us to be as understanding and knowledgeable as we are in adulthood—the very things we expect of our immature children. These ambitions often spring from our desire to give our children the gifts we never had as children. But such gift-giving must be spaced over time.

In recent decades, free time has become an increasingly rare commodity in the American family where either both parents or the single parent works. Brevity is one of reading aloud's advantages. It doesn't take anywhere near as much time as a game of bridge, Trivial Pursuit, the week's grocery shopping, a bowling string, or a Little League game. And the memories last longer.

Fathers—and a growing number of mothers—always appear to have enough time when it comes to sports. Don't misunderstand me on this, however. I am a sports fan; I competed in athletics in high school, and in college I did the play-by-play radio broadcasts on all the University of Massachusetts football and basketball games. But I believe we must convince fathers that it doesn't have to be an either/or situation: You either coach your child or teach your child. I say you can do *both*. You can take the child to a hockey game on Saturday and to the library on Monday; you can play catch in the driveway, and, on the same night, read to the child.

Boys constitute 70 percent of the students in remedial reading classes but make up less than 50 percent of the student body. The imbalance is due in large part to fathers who show by their interests and actions that the *really* important things in life are the things you throw and the things you catch. The child may never see his dad getting excited about a book, but he definitely sees him enthralled by the Los Angeles Lakers.

The "instant" qualities in sports make them especially attractive to parents because the child athlete's efforts are immediately measurable: he singled and struck out twice; she had 5 baskets and six rebounds. The child's mind, however, grows painfully slowly, and such growth is rarely immediately measurable. I often ask hurrying parents—that is, those looking for quick measures from tests and who think reading aloud might be too painstaking—to consider the example of my friend, Gracie Peaslee, a Florida kindergarten teacher. Each fall during the first week of school, Gracie asks her students to bring in a pair of oversize socks. She then helps them pull the socks on over their shoes (much to their delight) and leads them out into the field adjacent to the school for recess.

After romping through the grass and weeds, the children return to the classroom. Gracie instructs them to take the socks off their shoes, and gives each child a flower pot, telling the astonished class to bury a sock in each pot. Before they gleefully start to dig, however, she points out the wide variety of seeds picked up by the fabric of their socks. In the weeks that follow, the potted socks on the windowsill beginning growing their own field of weeds and grasses.

If only parents could realize that, figuratively speaking, each child is born with a sock over his heart and mind. And the richness of the fields of experience to which we bring our children will play a significant role in how much eventually grows in those hearts and minds. But unlike Gracie Peaslee's project, our seeds won't blossom in a fortnight. Sometimes it's a case of the watched pot never blossoming. As parents and teachers, we would do better to pay less attention to the blossom and more attention to the seedling.

The parent who needs proof need only look at the statistics on firstborn children. Scientists tells us it is impossible for parents to pass on genetically the bulk of their intelligence to the child, but it *is* possible to spend the bulk of their *time* with the child—which happens most often with firstborn children. Follow-up research indicates that, like a new toy, the firstborn receives all the attention and stimulation, and it bears fruit academically and socially in later years. A study of the National Merit Scholarship finalists showed that 60 percent of them were firstborn children—despite being outnumbered two to one in the general population. Washington, Lincoln, Jefferson, Wilson, F.D.R.—as well as nineteen of the United States' first twenty-three astronauts—were firstborn children.

It is no secret that women have carried the burden of teaching in this culture for the last century. They comprise 98 percent of the classroom teachers and have done the greater part of teaching in the home. But to give modern fathering its due, there are some cheering signs on the horizon. Men still watch too much television (200 minutes a day for the average U.S. male) when compared with one-on-one time with their children, but child-care experts report today's new fathers are more involved in the parenting process. If requirements were to be imposed for fathering, a pediatrician might draw up one set, a teacher another. Looking back on my twenty-year experiences, these would be mine: That every father read to his child daily (and by cassette if he's traveling); and that every new father read (or have read to him) Bob Greene's *Good Morning, Merry Sunshine*. The latter is a new father's journal through the first year of his child's life—from the labor room to delivery, from first sight to sleepless nights, from the first smile to the first tooth. All the anxieties and joys of parenting are covered in one father's stream of consciousness. I'd been a father for nineteen years when I read it, and it made me cry for both the things I'd missed or those I'd forgotten. I know I would have been a better father had this book been available for me two decades ago. But reading it also made me proud to be this special person called a parent.

Some parents and teachers, caught up in academics, feel newspapers and magazines are not challenging enough and therefore don't qualify as reading. But why apply different standards to the child than you have. Do you read only the editorial page in a newspaper or do you also read comics, business, theater, sports, and "Dear Abby"? I recall the mother who said to me, "I just don't know what to do with my 13-year-old. He hates to read."

When I asked what his interests were, she replied, "Sports." But when I suggested a subscription to a sports magazine, she said, "Oh, he already gets *Sports Illustrated*. He reads it cover to cover."

"Excuse me, but I thought you said he hates to read?" I inquired. The woman looked puzzled for a moment and responded, "Well, I didn't think *Sports Illustrated* counted." I quickly explained to her that it did count, that I had read (and saved) every issue of *Sports Illustrated* from the time I was 13 until I was 18 and that was where I first encountered Faulkner, Hemingway, and J. P. Marquand. "A literate person," I said, "reads *everything*. It would help, of course, if occasionally *you* read *Sports Illustrated*."

Another parent may ask, "What happened to the classics? Don't you believe in reading the classics to children?"

Nothing happened to the classics—but something happened to children: their imaginations went to sleep in front of the television set twenty-five years ago. Reading a classic to a child whose imagination is in a state of arrested development will not foster a love of literature. Instead, it may result in boredom and frustration. I believe you should start with good, but not watered-down, stories and build to the classics. The person who claimed 150 years ago that you should read only classics to children, would have missed out on a contemporary young writer named Hans Christian Andersen who was writing some marvelous tales.

What is a classic? There are two schools of thought on this. One defines a classic as any book which ought to be read by (or to) children because: their teacher/principal/superintendent or parent/grandparent read it as a child; the author has been dead for more than fifty years; and the right people will be impressed by its appearance in the curriculum or on the bookshelf.

The more enlightened school prefers Webster's definition: "a work of the highest class and of acknowledged excellence." Within this framework I find two categories: early classics, like the fairy tales of Andersen, Grimm, and Perrault, *Pinnocchio* by Carlo Collodi, and *The Secret Garden* by Frances Hodgson Burnett; and modern classics like *Charlotte's Web* and *The Lion, the Witch, and the Wardrobe*.

Among the early classics I have listed in the Treasury are: *Aladdin* retold by Andrew Lang; *Bambi* by Felix Salten; Jack London's *Call of the Wild; Mother Goose;* Kenneth Grahame's *The Reluctant Dragon; Robin Hood;* Frances Hodgson Burnett's *Sara Crewe* and *The Secret Garden; The Complete Adventures of Peter Rabbit* by Beatrix Potter; *A Wonder Book* by Nathaniel Hawthorne; and L. Frank Baum's *The Wonderful Wizard of Oz*. Numerous others are included among the recommended anthologies in the Treasury, especially *Classics to Read Aloud to Your Children* by William Russell, an excellent collection of classical prose and poetry whose meaning is accessible to young listeners.

6
Home and
Public Libraries

The library is not a shrine for the worship of books. It is not a temple where literary incense must be burned. . . . A library, to modify the famous metaphor of Socrates, should be the delivery room for the birth of ideas.

—Norman Cousins,
ALA *Bulletin* (October 1954)

Long before children are introduced to their neighborhood public library, books should be a part of their lives. Begin a home library as soon as the child is born. If you can provide shelving in the child's room for such books, all the better. The sooner children become accustomed to the sight of the covers, bindings, and pages of books, the sooner they will begin to develop the concept that books are a part of daily life.

Admittedly, we were late in starting our home library for Elizabeth, our first child. Public library books were heavily relied upon until she was about 4 years old—the time when her younger brother, Jamie, was born. Since we had begun to see the positive effects of reading aloud to Elizabeth, my wife and I decided at that point to begin the children's home library. We had no idea, of course, that this library would eventually serve not only the children but their parents as well. Within a few years of Jamie's birth, Susan took a teaching degree in elementary education and used the books every day in her classes. It was the reaction of my own children and of those in my wife's classes to these books that first inspired me to write this handbook.

I'd like to make a few suggestions that may prove helpful to those beginning a home library, particularly if you have children under the age of 4.

Divide your books into two categories: expensive and inexpensive. The higher priced or fragile books should be placed up on shelves out of the reach of sticky fingers, dribbles, and errant crayons. While out of reach, they should still be within sight—as a kind of goal. On lower shelves and within easy reach should be the less expensive and, if possible, more durable books. If the replacement price is low enough, you'll have fewer qualms about the child "playing" with the books. This "playing" is an important factor in a child's attachment to books. He must have ample opportunity to feel them, taste them, and see them.

At the same time, parents act as role models in the way they treat books (carefully and affectionately) and the way they speak of books ("And here's our old friend Little Toot. We haven't seen him in a long time.") Children should be encouraged to become as affectionate with a book as they are with a teddy bear.

Where space permits, have many of the home library's books positioned on the shelf with the cover facing out. These covers serve as stimulants to the child's imagination, causing him to wonder what is happening both in the picture and inside the book. This inspires one of the foundation stones for all learning—a sense of curiosity.

This sense of curiosity will become even more acute as the child grows older. When Jamie was around 9 or 10 years old, I remember finding him lying in bed one morning, staring at the top shelf of his bookcase. Because of space limitations, all but a few of the books were shelved with bindings facing outward, thus obscuring the covers.

"See that book up there, Dad? The one named *Trigger John's Son?* What's it about?" he asked.

"I haven't read it myself," I said, "but I think it's about an orphan boy who constantly gets himself into mischief. A little like *Homer Price,* I think. Why do you ask?"

"Oh, I was just thinking about it," Jamie explained. "Sometimes when I wake up, I just look up at the titles and, if it's a book I haven't seen or read, I try to figure what it's about from the title."

This incident also shows one of the advantages of having a home library as well as a public library. These periods of idleness and daydreaming most often strike children at times when they are far removed from distractions—in their own room or home. The buzz of activity in many public libraries is not especially conducive to daydreaming, and school libraries (many of which are now bastardized into "media centers") are often the least conducive of all. It's important to remember that during these intervals of unoccupied leisure the child's imagination does its window shopping. How much it eventually buys depends on how much you have on display.

I know of no greater testament to the home library than the career of Lester Del Rey, author of more than forty books and one of the most respected science fiction writers. The son of poor northern sharecroppers, Del Rey and his family moved from one poor farm to the next in areas where the public library system had not established itself. Fortunately for him, his father had invested in the complete works of Darwin, Gibbon's *Decline and Fall,* Jules Verne, and H. G. Wells. Once he learned to read, the books were available for Del Rey to plow through each evening. "In 1927, when I was barely 12," he recalled, "my father moved to a small town where I could have a chance to attend high school, and my horizons were suddenly broadened by the availability of books and magazines from quite a good local library."

Del Rey's story illustrates that money is no obstacle in compiling a home library. In today's world, his father would have haunted weekend garage sales in building his library. Obviously, they were poor—but not poor in spirit or dedication. The Del Rey home library served as a "greenhouse" until Lester was introduced to the limitless wonders of the public library.

Before discussing further the role of the public library, I would like to offer several ideas I have used in building a good home library for children. The principal problems are cost, where to buy the books, and which books to buy. (The solutions I offer should also be of help to patrons who cannot locate a particular book in their local library or are puzzled by which of the "new arrivals" in children's fiction are worth reading.)

While inflation has more than doubled the cost of children's books in the last five years, it is not an insurmountable obstacle to a good home library if you combine the following information with a little ingenuity.

On the bright side of the financial ledger is the cheering fact that more and more children's publishers are issuing their own books in paperback, usually within a year of hardcover publication. Some are published simultaneously in paperback. The hardcover is aimed at schools and libraries while the softcover is aimed at parents and school book clubs. The paperback editions are at least half the price of the hardcover.

Over the years I've made it a habit never to visit a new city or town without checking the Yellow Pages for a secondhand bookstore. These shops frequently are gold mines for book-shopping parents or teachers. I shopped in the secondhand department of Johnson's Bookstore (in Springfield, Massachusetts) so often that many of the customers, and even some of the employees, thought I worked there. Your local Salvation Army thrift shop is another good source for children's book bargains. It also pays to check in advance with your local public library, as well as those in surrounding communities, for the date of its annual "discard" sale.

I fully recognize the qualities of a brand-new book—it's bright, crisp pages, its clean smell. But in an age of daily inflation, such books are a luxury that is often unaffordable to parents. If that is the case, remember that the words and story and pictures are the same in a used book as they are in a new book. Barring damage, one reads as well as the other.

Most schools today subscribe to one of several young people's paperback book clubs. These clubs offer nearly forty monthly selections at half price. The paperback your child pays $1.50 for in class will cost $3.00 in the bookstore and $9.95 in hardcover. Not only are many excellent books available through these clubs, but they are being offered in paperback sometimes within a year of their hardback publication as well. Encourage your child's school to belong to one of these clubs and look over the selection sheets each month. By adding your choices for the family library to the child's selections, you'll be saving a considerable expense as well as showing the child your interest in books.

The question of durability frequently arises in discussing paperbacks. If the book is to be used only as a read-aloud by a teacher or parent, then this is not a problem. But if it is going to be handled by a family of children or circulated through a classroom, its durability becomes important. My own solution, and one which has had considerable testing, is to protect the paperback with clear plastic self-sticking shelf paper, which can be bought in your local supermarket or discount department store.

Because our books are used not only by the immediate family but also by neighborhood children and by students, they must stand up to constant wear. This laminating system gives paperbacks a strength that even some hardcovers don't possess.

I first open the book fully so that both its front and back covers are spread out on the plastic sheet. This enables me to gauge the amount I'll need to cut from the roll. Allowing for an inch overlap all around the book, I cut the plastic. This piece is then peeled and rolled gently onto the book's cover, wrapping the overlapping inch around the edges. I also cut strips (or use scraps) to cover the area inside the book where the cover and pages meet at the spine, front and back.

This procedure prevents attractive covers from picking up kitchen-table stains or becoming torn, and greatly reduces the most frequent damage to children's paperbacks—separation at the spine.

Nearly every city in America now has a bookstore that specializes in paperbacks, and a juvenile section usually is included. Make a habit of visiting this section at least every two weeks to review new arrivals. If your bookseller does not carry a particular line or book, badger him until he does. "Why don't you have any Bill Peet books? You certainly are missing out on a great author and illustrator. When are you going to order some?" In addition, most major publishing houses in the juvenile market will send you their catalogues of titles upon request. These can then be ordered through your bookstore or directly from the publisher.

Another often-neglected source of savings for the teacher is the book wholesaler (or jobber) who supplies your school library. A handsome discount is given for nearly every purchase your school makes from that jobber. When you want to order a book for yourself, ask your school librarian to add it to her regular order and pay her accordingly. Although jobbers most often deal in hardcover, some handle paperbacks as well. Take advantage of the discounts available to you, which can run from 25 percent to as much as 45 percent. If the book is for your classroom, you are entitled to a sales tax exemption, and if you are paying for it out of your own pocket you can write off the entire cost on your personal income tax as a business (teaching) expense.

If you are searching for a particular book that is unavailable at your local bookstore, I recommend you write to the publisher. There will be no discount but at least you will avoid the handling costs that retail stores frequently charge.

Parents who are looking for the best literary bargain available should consider a subscription to *Cricket: The Magazine for Children*. Geared for children between ages 3 and 12, *Cricket*'s monthly offering includes more than twenty stories and features from many of today's finest artists and writers, a potpourri of literature: poetry, fiction, nonfiction, humor, fables, mystery, and sports. The price of each issue represents a substantial savings for a family when you consider that many of its features have previously appeared in book form at five times the price of the magazine. If you haven't seen a copy, check the children's department of your local library or bookstore.

How should you decide which books to buy? This handbook, with its list of read-alouds, should solve at least part of that problem. You'll also find that neighbors, friends, librarians, and teachers who read aloud are eager to share the names of their favorites.

If your child's teacher reads aloud, she probably has a long list of choices she can't possibly get to in the course of the year. At your next parent-teacher conference, ask her for some recommendations. She may even have one she thinks is particularly pertinent to your child.

Most libraries have a variety of outstanding resource books on children's literature, books like Betsy Hearne's *Choosing Books for Children*, and Bernice Cullinan's *Literature and the Child*, a comprehensive collection of specific teaching ideas and activities centered on hundreds of wonderful children's books.

Your neighborhood library subscribes to several journals that regularly review new children's books, including *The Horn Book, Kirkus Reviews, Publishers Weekly, School Library Journal*, and *Booklist*. These will give you an excellent sense of what is new, good, bad, or indifferent in children's literature. Unfortunately, many people are unaware of these periodicals, but librarians will be happy to share them with you.

Additionally, there are several inexpensive newsletters on children's books:

• Published each fall, winter and spring, *T'N'T (Tips and Titles of Books for Grades K-6)* is a newsletter for busy parents and teachers, covering more than a hundred books each year. Written by Jan Lieberman, a former elementary teacher who understands children and their reading appetites, each issue covers a cross-section of literature—old and new, fiction, nonfiction, and poetry—with creative tips on related activities. Subscribers are free to make copies for faculties and PTA groups at no extra charge. Send only three self-addressed, stamped envelopes (legal size) with $1.00 in cash or stamps to: Jan Lieberman, Department of Education, University of Santa Clara, Santa Clara, CA 95053.

• *THE WEB (Wonderfully Exciting Books),* aimed primarily at teachers, is published quarterly out of the College of Education at Ohio State under the direction of Charlotte Huck, a leading authority in children's literature. Subscribers should send a check or money order for $6.00 to: *THE WEB,* The Ohio State University, Room 200 Ramseyer Hall, 29 West Woodruff, Columbus, OH 43210.

• *Why Children's Books?,* a quarterly newsletter for parents, is less a reviewing service than a happy conversation about wonderful books and children, grouped under topical headings. Written by Amy Cohn and published by *The Horn Book,* America's most distinguished journal for children's literature, it costs $4.00 (bulk rates are available for PTA groups and libraries). Check or money order to: The Horn Book Inc., 31 St. James Avenue, Boston, MA 02116.

In addition to professional journals and newsletters, here are some of the easiest and least time-consuming methods for staying abreast of new titles.

Check the "new arrivals" section in the children's department of your local library. If no such section exists, ask the librarian to start one. It saves patrons much time.

Many large metropolitan newspapers publish reviews of new juvenile books, and some, like *The New York Times,* publish special supplements each spring and fall, reviewing the best in recent publications.

One of my favorites, but an unsung resource for parents and teachers, is the fall and spring Children's Book issues of *Publishers Weekly.* These special issues can be purchased individually without subscriptions. Every new children's book is listed, plot synopses are offered, and the major publishers heavily advertise their biggest authors' new titles. In addition, there's a sneak preview of what's coming up next. These issues must be requested separately each fall or spring. Send a check or money order for $3.00 to: Magazine Circulation Department, R. R. Bowker Co., 205 East 42nd Street, New York, NY 10017.

Several year-end lists of the best from each year's children's books are available. "Children's Books (year)" is published by the Library of Congress and covers preschool through junior high. It is available for $1.00 from the Superintendent of Documents, U.S. Government Printing Office, Washington, D.C. 20402 (Library of Congress Catalog Card Number: 65–60015).

The American Library Association's "Notable Children's Books (year)" is available for 25 cents (and a self-addressed mailing label) from: Association for Library Service to Children, ALA, 50 East Huron Street, Chicago, IL 60611.

The longest list (400 titles divided into twenty subject categories for four age groups) is published each year by the Child Study Children's Book Committee at a cost of $3.50. Send check or money order to the Committee at Bank Street College of Education, 610 West 112th Street, New York, NY 10025.

In your search for which books to buy for your home or classroom library and which books to read aloud to children, look to guidebooks, friends, teachers, librarians, and reviews. But always reserve the final decision for yourself. Only *you* know the level and interests of your children. Only you can appreciate their special needs and capacities.

Occasionally you will make a mistake. The book will be boring or too far above or below the child. The best thing to do in that case is to admit the mistake and go on to another book. But such mistakes will occur less frequently when you take the time to seek the advice of experts in the field.

As important and convenient as a home library is, it cannot replace a public library. The home library should act as an appetizer, stimulating the child's taste for the vast riches offered by the free public library. It is a town's or city's most important cultural and intellectual asset. Nevertheless, in this age of declining literacy and skyrocketing inflation, libraries face increasingly difficult times.

"What can be done to turn things around for library circulations?" the chairman asked the library director at a trustees' meeting I attended.

"Well," the director hedged for a moment, "a good Depression might help . . ."

There were chuckles around the table (although the banker and two business owners laughed least), but the truth of the statement was lost on none of us. It is only in hard times that we appreciate the community services we receive for free. America's free public library systems received unprecedented use during the Depression years when other forms of entertainment or enlightenment were too costly.

Dollar for dollar, the greatest bargain in America today is still the free public library system—yet less than 10 percent of the American people are regular patrons. I can't begin to estimate the number of times I've heard parents (rich and poor) say they'd like to bring their children to the library more often but there just isn't time. And to each of them I reply, "Would you estimate that you've taken your child to the shopping mall ten times more often than the library or one hundred times more often?" What does this say to your child about your priorities in life? When Cabbage Patch Dolls held center stage during the 1983 Christmas shopping season, I couldn't help but wonder whether those same dedicated parents would have driven as far, stood in line as long, or paid as much for a library card as they did for those dolls. It is a terrible indictment of our time and culture that the majority of those parents would *not* have been willing to make the same sacrifices for the library card. Saddest of all is the fact that those children's priorities invariably will someday reflect those of their parents.

Some libraries are attempting to survive the cultural and economic pressures by shedding old habits in favor of new vigor and aggressive marketing. Sadly, not all libraries are able to do so; there are still some who don't have either the money, the community support, or the staff leadership to initiate such changes.

If, as a parent or teacher, you feel your local library is not adjusting to the times, protect your rights as a taxpayer and become involved. Join with your friends to form a "Friends of the Library" group which can, among other things, lobby local government or the library administration for positive change. In the majority of cases, however, it is not the staff but the community that needs prodding.

In such cases libraries cannot afford to stand by and wring their hands over the decline in reading habits. If they are to survive they must:

1. Shed the image of "Marian the Librarian," who governs the stacks with a rule of silence, in favor of an image that shouts to the community, "Hey! Come on in—look what we've got for free!"
2. Sell the healthful advantages of its services to the community in much the same way we sell the United Way, Catholic Charities, United Jewish Appeal, and the March of Dimes.
3. Become competitive with television.

Here are specific examples of how and where this approach has worked. If these are within the fiscal and personnel budgets of your library, write to these institutions for more information (be sure to enclose a self-addressed No. 10 envelope).

The Orlando (Florida) Public Library, like its counterparts in Cleveland (Ohio), and Harrisburg (Pennsylvania), doesn't waste time in making the parent/child connection. Following an aggressive and creative line of thinking, it supplies thirteen area hospitals with packets that contain: a cover letter on the importance of early language exchanges with infants; a list of available books on parenting, child care, and children's literature; a list of books for very young children; a brochure on getting books by mail from the library; an invitation to attend the library's program "You, Your Baby, and the Library"; and an invitation to enroll children in the library's toddler story hours.

The Cuyahoga County Public Library in Cleveland sends new parents a diaper-shaped packet of twenty family-related brochures and flyers about library services—including a map noting all 27 branches. Harrisburg area hospitals were more than happy to print and distribute a pamphlet, "A Stitch in Time," compiled by Dauphin County Library Children's Director Steven Herb and his wife, Sara, an assistant professor of early childhood education. In conjunction with the pamphlet, the library offers a course showing new parents how to interact with infants in ways that stimulate the babys' social, intellectual, and motor development.

Reaching the community's poor requires more effort than connecting with its affluent and educated, but Baltimore County Public Library doesn't shy away from the task. One of the nation's most progressive systems, Baltimore operates "Growing Day-By-Day," a monthly program that delivers (and collects) packages of books and records to the homes of day-care affiliated parents who often have no transportation to libraries.

Judging from my experiences in traveling and lecturing throughout the United States, the best libraries:

- Offer storytimes for more than just preschoolers. More than fifty libraries throughout the nation now offer toddler programs for children 18–24 months. The Mountain View (California) Public Library runs story programs for four different age groups—with just one full-time and one part-time librarian.
- Provide registration tables at nursery and elementary schools in the first week of school to distribute library information and register parents and children for cards.
- Maintain a constant campaign to stress reading aloud to children, in the home and in the classroom—like Los Angeles County's Rose Diaz Piñan Reading Aloud Collection, a $64,000 program that is instructional and inspirational, and operates year-round. Parents and teachers are a library's "sales representatives," and the product line's success largely depends on how well the reps are motivated and trained.
- Fight fire with fire. If 70 percent of the community's parents are watching television each evening, they are a captive audience for this fifteen-second commercial: "The Springfield Public Library wants to know—Did you read to your child tonight?" (The voice-over image on the screen is a reading parent nestled with his children.)
- Instruct parents and teachers on read-aloud by offering demonstrations and "talking book" tapes as models. Many of today's adults were raised on television; they need to see or hear an example of how to read to children—the expression, the pace, how to tie the pictures into the story, and how to discuss a book when it is finished.
- Sponsor "foster grandparent" programs, which connect senior citizens with children and allow the "grandparent" an opportunity to read to, talk to, and listen to the child.
- Use the local newspaper to print the list of new books acquired each month. The large metropolitan newspapers are usually unwilling, but the smaller dailies and local weeklies are happy to receive such notices. Semiannual listings of new acquisitions are printed on recycled paper and left in beauty parlors, barber shops,

shopping malls, pediatricians' offices, nursery schools, and supermarkets.

- Know that children are motivated in much the same way as adults—most of them initially pick their books by the appearance of the cover. (Paperback publishers realized this thirty years ago.) The library staff clears enough shelf space to display 150 to 200 children's books with the covers face out. By the end of the day all are usually in circulation, and they are replaced on the shelf by fresh ones the next day. This library staff—like its bookstore counterpart—realizes it is burying a major selling factor every time a book is shelved with only the spine showing. Write to B. Dalton Booksellers (Marketing Department, 7505 Metro Boulevard, Minneapolis, MN 55435) for a copy of their faceout merchandising booklet, "Let's Face It."
- Create a climate that welcomes children with open arms. Its walls festooned with colorful posters, the library brings books alive with tanks of fish and cages of gerbils, hamsters, and rabbits. It offers an outlet for the imagination that books inspire by having pencils, crayons, and paper readily available for children who want to come in and draw.
- Schedule their service hours for the convenience of the patrons and not the convenience of the staff or labor union. In this day and age, the idea of a library being closed on Sundays makes about as much sense as scheduling a picnic in January. Twice as many people in the community are free to use the library on Sunday as on Monday. Nevertheless, the vast majority of American libraries are closed on Sundays. In the last two decades, such tradition-bound institutions as the Roman Catholic Church and the YMCA have adjusted their long-standing service schedules to fit the changing American weekend lifestyle. And they have accomplished these changes while facing many of the personnel and financial shortages that confront today's libraries.
- Enlist the aid of the private sector to advertise library programs. The library—with its "Friends" committee—convinces paper companies and printers to donate paper and printing costs for fliers and pamphlets. It persuades sign companies, mass-transit authorities, and the news media to donate advertising space for a yearly campaign that portrays the free public library as the best and most important bargain in town.
- Design children's departments not to win architecture awards but

to win friends. The Kansas City (KS) Public Library demonstrates that a good children's department also includes the parent; they keep the books and cassettes on child care and family life near the children's books. Kansas City also provides a glass-fronted crying room for parents with babes-in-arms who have older children in the story hour.

Library systems are beginning to realize what fast-food chains and billboard advertisers learned long ago: If you want business, you go where the people are. And the largest collection of people on any given day in any community in America will invariably be found in the shopping mall. With that in mind, a handful of pioneering libraries have opened branches in shopping malls. One such is the Clackamas County branch in the Town Center Mall in Milwaukee, Oregon. A deal struck by the county commissioners with the initial mall petitioners allows the library to rent space for a token $1 a year. Nestled among the indoor ice rink and eighty stores, the branch is open seven days a week and has been circulating five hundred books a day since opening in 1982.

"We are not a reference library," explains Clackamas Librarian Katharine Jorgensen. "We're set up like a bookstore—no Dewey Decimal System—and our stock in trade is paperbacks. Situated as we are, we've issued new cards to a remarkable number of former patrons who had lost the reading habit—including many tired husbands who come in now to relax and read." The three mall bookstores, instead of viewing the branch as a competitor, recognized it as a valuable partner in the reading business and donated shelving, display racks, and signs. The spinoff effect has been a marked increase in circulation within the two other Clackamas branches.

Realizing that French subway commuters spend upwards of an hour a day on the subway system, the Paris library now has a branch in the Metro System that is open during rush hours.

Parents can profit from such examples. If your child can read but chooses not to, then it may be a case of "out of sight, out of mind." If all the reading material in your home is neatly ensconced in living-room bookcases or magazine racks while all the daily traffic is in the kitchen and bathroom, the answer is obvious. Put a magazine rack in the bathroom with the issues of *Reader's Digest*, *Seventeen*, *Time*, and *Sports Illustrated*. With the majority of American parents now working, more children eat meals alone than at any time in history. And what do you, as an adult, do when you are eating alone? You read the newspaper, your mail, magazines, or, if need be, the dessert menu. Your children will follow suit if you stop *shelving* all the books and magazines. Leave those books and magazines in the kitchen and bathroom, as well as in the bedrooms and living room.

Reading is one area where the private and public sectors can and should join hands in cooperative ventures. When it is done right, in places like Wyoming County, New York, the results can be spectacular. In that northern New York county, Project Read was initiated in 1978 under the inspired leadership of Mrs. Mardi VanArsdale of Castile, New York, with the cooperation of principals, teachers, public and school librarians, reading specialists, United Way, the Departments of Social Services and Health, and parents.

Project Read's primary aim is to foster parental involvement with children's leisure reading. This is done on a long-term daily basis and can be summed up neatly by the phrase "family reading," that is, parents reading to children as well as parents and children reading to themselves. What has made Project Read so successful over the years is not its concept but its members' indefatigable efforts to market it: story hours in libraries and on local radio stations, booths at all school Open Houses and kindergarten registrations, workshops for parents taking court-mandated parenting courses, two booths at the week-long County Fair (staffed by hundreds of volunteers) where children's books are both sold and read aloud, along with thousands of school recognition awards to children whose families were involved in the program, and the compilation/distribution of recommended reading lists to guide both parent and child. That is dynamic leadership and promotion.

One day somebody at the Minneapolis Public Library stopped to think how much of the gross national product is dependent upon gift-giving. The toy industry markets toys as the perfect gift. Why don't libraries and bookstores market just as creatively? Conceding that many adults don't know the appropriate books for certain age groups, the Minneapolis library—as well as numerous other libraries—publishes pamphlets that list titles and synopses, grouped by age, for both book buying and borrowing.

Books do make the perfect gift, and we badly need an ongoing national campaign saying so. Under the direction of the Library of Congress' Center for the Book and financially supported by the publishing industry, libraries and bookstores, it should be a public awareness campaign that sells books like we sell political candidates or jeans. Unlike toys, books can't break. They're ready-made and powerful, but with no assembling or batteries necessary. They're the one gift you can reopen all the time, and they last longer than candy or flowers. Portable and noiseless, they can be enjoyed anywhere at any time of day by any age group. Unlike clothes, books never go out of style but do become more valuable with age. As author/illustrator Steven Kellogg says, "One book can do what even the greatest toy cannot do: inspire a child to laugh, imagine, appreciate art, and understand human nature."

Knowing that people prefer giving gifts before money, the Upton-Mendon Public Schools in Massachusetts made a community plea for books with a project called "Sponsor-a-Book" when Proposition 2 ½ required drastic library budget cuts for the middle school. Despite having one of the state's highest unemployment rates, the community responded with enough money to purchase more than two hundred paperbacks and have them Permabound. Families and friends were able to choose specific titles from a master list provided by the school librarian, and the donors' names were placed in the books.

A valuable but largely overlooked link in the child-family-library connection is the pediatrician. With the deterioration of the extended American family, who is left to teach the business of parenting, to provide the common-sense instructions formerly passed along by grandparents? Librarian and pediatrician are a natural alliance and should have a much closer working relationship than they presently have. Many of the brochures promoting the library's programs and benefits should be available in the waiting rooms of pediatricians, dentists, and health clinics. Several pediatricians in Ohio complained to me recently about the absence of video cassettes that could be used in their reception areas—story cassettes that would instruct parents on reading aloud to children while at the same time holding the attention of the child patient. Here is something that libraries can and should be providing locally to the community's pediatricians.

While it is not true in every case, in all honesty I must say that pediatricians could be contributing more toward making this a truly literate nation. These men and women are among the prime beneficiaries of the printed word, yet the average pediatrician neither encourages reading aloud as a family practice, nor urges the curtailment of television viewing.

Mention of doctors' waiting rooms reminds me that the most dog-eared and mangled collection of books in any community is invariably found in doctors' offices. For the pediatrician looking for a tax write-off, I suggest investing in better books. If they are stolen or borrowed by his patients, it only affords the opportunity for another write-off. Incidentally, the second worst collection of children's titles can be found in hospital gift shops. The nation's airlines are also remiss; while offering dozens of magazines to adults, they ignore the minds of bored child passengers. At least two copies of *Cricket: The Magazine for Children,* and several picture books should be aboard every plane.

One doesn't have to dream up fantastic schemes. Books for kids on planes is common sense. Here's another: Have you noticed how often brand name products are popping up in motion pictures? "E.T." didn't start eating Reese's Pieces by accident; it was carefully negotiated by people whose sole job is the "casting" of brand names in movies—and thus into the public's awareness. Why not a similar committee of librarians and publishers bent on "casting" books in the cultural marketplace? The Cabbage Patch Dolls each came with a set of adoption papers. Candice Morris of the El Paso, Texas, Public Library said to me, "Why don't they also come with a little list of books for children to read aloud to the dolls?" (For such a list, see *Ira Sleeps Over* in the Treasury.) The Public Library of Columbus and Franklin counties (Ohio) saw an opportunity immediately in the Cabbage Patch craze and printed up 5,000 "doll-baby library cards" for children who wanted to introduce their dolls to the world of books. Needless to say, the project was a great success.

Kevin Blanton, a school librarian in Aldine, Texas, had been reading about school systems that have writers-in-residence—authors who will inspire children to write. "Why not *readers*-in-residence?" he asks. "Schools should model on the idea of an Alan a'Dale, a traveling bard. Employ someone whose sole task is to turn on kids to the joys of reading, someone who knows which stories to read to which age group." Not a far-fetched idea. Joanne Busalacchi, a dynamic language arts supervisor in Montgomery County (Maryland) public schools dresses up as an absent-minded *Mother Goose* each month and visits elementary grades to question them on their rhymes. For the older grades, she arrives as that mixed-up purveyor of homonyms, *Amelia Bedelia.*

Watching my children eat breakfast one morning several years ago, it occurred to me that if we want to send book messages to the largest number of children in one place at one time, all we have to do is put them on the back of a cereal box. Judging from my classroom discussions with thousands of school children, I strongly suspect that more children voluntarily read the back of cereal boxes each day than any other form of print. And what is on these boxes? Advertisements for ballpoint pens, T-shirts, and model trains. That is not very exciting stuff, but at a time when more American children are eating breakfast alone than at any other time in the last hundred years, anything to read is better than staring at what is in the bowl.

What would happen, I wonder, if the back of the cereal box contained an advertisement for libraries? To my way of thinking, the best kind of library advertisement would be a chapter from a children's book; a chapter so funny, so intriguing, or so exciting that it would bring those young breakfast readers to the library door first thing after school. Imagine how the publishers would compete to have their book chosen; imagine how authors would love it. Moms would go out of their way to buy that particular brand—not because it had less sugar, not because it was cheaper, but because it sent their children to the library.

But what about the pens and the T-shirts? Alternate them every month with book chapters, if need be. But I don't think you'd have to. The largest cereal manufacturer in America, controlling 38 percent of the U.S. cereal market, netted $243 million in 1983. I don't believe they need those T-shirts and pens but I *do* think they would love to be known as the cereal company that lured one million kids into libraries so they could finish *Freckle Juice* by Judy Blume.

Impossible? Not if you make literacy—the ability to read, write, and communicate clearly—the business of *all* America and not just that of teachers and librarians. If all sectors of the community work together to bring the excitement of books into our homes early enough and to develop libraries that are truly "delivery rooms for ideas," then we need not fear an electronic Pied Piper stealing our children's minds and imaginations.

7
Television

I believe television is going to be the test of the modern world, and that in this new opportunity to see beyond the range of our vision we shall discover either a new and unbearable disturbance of the general peace or a saving radiance in the sky. We shall stand or fall by television—of that I am quite sure.

　　　　　　　　　　　—E. B. White
　　　　　　　　　　　　from "Removal from Town,"
　　　　　　　　　　　　Harper's Magazine (October 1938)

In its short lifetime, television has become the most pervasive influence on the human family and, at the same time, the major stumbling block to literacy in America. The A.C. Nielsen Company reports the average television set ran for 4 hours, 35 minutes each day in 1950; by 1984, the daily total had risen to 7 hours, 2 minutes.[1]

During that span of time, television's negative impact on children's reading habits—and, therefore, their thinking—has been enormous. In this chapter I suggest a method for dealing with television. As this approach is used in my own home and as I have seen it used in countless other homes, it is a reasonable and workable solution to the problem. However, in order to make it work, parents must believe in it, must understand fully why they are using it, and what the consequences are to family and child if it is not used.

This understanding is just as important for teachers as it is for parents. True, the classroom teacher, principal, and guidance counselor have no immediate control over the television sets in pupils' homes. But they *are* in the education business, and television is the prime educator in the world today. It is the school's primary competitor for children's minds.

Educators spend millions of dollars and thousand of classroom hours teaching children how to cope with the hard-core drugs that come into their lives. But they spend no time or money, relatively, in teaching children how to cope with the soft-core drug in their living room: television.

TV has been described by author Marie Winn as the "plug-in drug," and not without reason. Its control of children is demanding and extensive. It will largely determine what they wear and what they won't wear, what they eat and what they won't eat, what they play and what they won't play, what they will read and what they will not read. Our children must be taught in the home and in the classroom how to cope with television. They must be taught to control *it* instead of letting it control *them*.

I do not think of television as a totally negative influence. As a tool for educating, informing, and entertaining it has unlimited potential. Unfortunately, current programming devotes itself almost exclusively to entertaining, thereby falling far short of its natural potential. As entertainment it should be treated as dessert and not be allowed to become the principal meal in our children's lives.

The first serious alarm was sounded by a small cluster of educators in 1964 when the scores were computed for that year's college admission tests. That year's high-school seniors, born in the late 1940s, were the first generation to be raised on a steady television diet. Their Scholastic Aptitude Test (SAT) scores showed an unprecedented decline from previous years. From an average verbal score of 478 in 1963, U.S. students dropped to a low of 424 in 1981. By 1984, they had risen slightly, only to 426.[2]

Naturally there are those in the television industry who claim that these lowered standards have nothing to do with their medium. Social scientists, educators, and psychologists respond loudly that there is every connection between the two. Television, they declare, interrupts the largest and most instructive class in childhood: life experience.

Paul Copperman, president of the Institute of Reading Development and author of *The Literacy Hoax,* sees the interruption in these terms: "Consider what a child misses during the 15,000 hours [from birth to age 17] he spends in front of the TV screen. He is not working in the garage with his father, or in the garden with his mother. He is not doing homework, or reading, or collecting stamps. He is not cleaning his room, washing the supper dishes, or cutting the lawn. He is not listening to a discussion about community politics among his parents and their friends. He is not playing baseball or going fishing, or painting pictures. Exactly what does television offer that is so valuable that it can replace all of these activities?"[3]

A recent alarm was sounded by the state of California's Department of Education with the announcement of its findings from a scholastic achievement test in reading, writing, and mathematics that was administered to sixth- and twelfth-grade students in 1980. (One of the factors which lends great significance and credibility to this test is the number of students involved: half a million children.) Buried in the test was a question that appeared to have nothing to do with the students' classwork but in actuality had very much to do with it. The question was: How much time do you spend watching TV each day? It was the one question that more students (99 percent) chose to answer than any other in the exam.

When the educators finished compiling the scores on the 500,000 exams, they began to correlate each child's grade with the number of hours the student spent watching television. Their findings showed conclusively that the more time the student spent watching TV, the lower the achievement score; the less time, the higher the score. Interestingly, these statistics proved true regardless of the child's IQ, social background, or study practices (all of which were queried in the exam process).[4]

Tannis Macbeth Williams of the University of British Columbia studied three Canadian towns—two with television and one without. Children in the community without television had higher reading scores—until television was introduced to the town. Not surprisingly, the scores then declined.[5]

Today's television programming is a serious impediment to children's personal growth because of both what it offers and what it does *not* offer:

1. *Television is the direct opposite of reading.* In breaking its program into eight-minute commercial segments (shorter for shows like *Sesame Street*), it requires and fosters a short attention span. Reading, on the other hand, requires and encourages longer attention spans in children. Good children's books are written to hold children's attention, not interrupt it. Because of the need to hold viewers until the next commercial message, the content of television shows is almost constant action. Reading also offers action but not nearly as much, and reading fills the considerable space between action scenes with subtle character development. Television is relentless; no time is allowed to ponder characters' thoughts or to recall their words because the dialogue and film move too quickly. The need to scrutinize is a critical need among young children and it is constantly ignored by television. Books, however, encourage a critical reaction; the reader moves at his own pace as opposed to that of the director or sponsor. The reader can stop to ponder the character's next move, the feathers in his hat, or the meaning of a sentence. Having done so, he can resume where he left off without having missed any part of the story.

2. *For young children television is an antisocial experience, while reading is a social experience.* The 3-year-old sits passively in front of the screen, oblivious to what is going on around him. Conversation during the program is seldom if ever encouraged by the child or by the parents. On the other hand, the 3-year-old with a book must be read to by another person—parent, sibling, or grandparent. The child is a participant as well as a receiver when he engages in discussion during and after the story. This process continues to an even greater degree when the child attends school and compares his own reactions to a story with those of his classmates.

3. *Television deprives the child of his most important learning tool: his questions.* Children learn the most by questioning. For the thirty-three hours a week that the average 5-year-old spends in front of the set, he can neither ask a question nor receive an answer.

4. *Television interrupts the most important language lesson in a child's life: family conversation.* Studies show that the average kindergarten graduate has already seen 5,000 hours of television in his young lifetime. Those are 5,000 hours during which he engaged in little or no conversation.

5. *Much of young children's television viewing is mindless watching, requiring little or no thinking.* When two dozen 3- to 5-year-olds were shown a "Scooby Doo" cartoon, the soundtrack of which had been

replaced by the soundtrack from a "Fangface" cartoon, only three of the twenty-four children realized the soundtrack did not match the pictures.[6]

6. *Television presents material in a manner that is the direct opposite of the classroom's.* Television's messages are based almost entirely on pictures and our emotions in response to those pictures. Conversely, the classroom relies heavily on reading, the spoken word, and a critical response to those words, not just raw emotion. School also requires large amounts of time to be spent on a task. These minutes spent doing things like multiplication tables and spelling can often be boring and repetitious when compared with watching "The Dukes of Hazzard," but they are critical for learning.

7. *Television is unable to portray the most intelligent act known to man: thinking.* In 1980 Squire Rushnell, vice-president in charge of ABC's children's programming, said that certain fine children's books cannot be adapted for television. Much of the character development in these books, Rushnell noted, takes place inside the character's head. He said, "You simply can't put thinking on the screen." As a result, a child almost never sees a TV performer thinking through a problem.[7]

8. *Television encourages deceptive thinking.* In *Teaching as a Conserving Activity,* educator Neil Postman points out that it is implicit in every one of television's commercials that there is no problem which cannot be solved by simple artificial means.[8] Whether the problem is anxiety or common diarrhea, nervous tension or the common cold, a simple tablet or spray solves the problem. Seldom is mention ever made of headaches being a sign of more serious illness, nor is the suggestion ever made that elbow grease and hard work are viable alternatives to stains and boredom. Instead of thinking through our problems, television promotes the "easy way." The cumulative effect of such thinking is enormous when you consider that between ages 1 and 17 the average child is exposed to 350,000 commercials promoting simple solutions to problems.

9. *Television, by vying for children's time and attention with a constant diet of unchallenging simplistic entertainment, stimulates antischool and antireading feeling among children.* A 1977 study showed that the majority of the preschool and primary-school students examined felt that school and books were a waste of time.[9] Offered the same story on television and in book form, 69 percent of the second-grade students chose television. That figure increased to 86 percent among the third-

grade pupils—the grade where national reading skills begin to decline.

10. *Television has a negative effect on children's vital knowledge after age 10, according to the Schramm study of 6,000 school children.*[10] It does help, the report goes on to say, in building vocabulary for younger children, but this stops by age 10. This finding is supported by the fact that today's kindergarteners have the highest reading-readiness scores ever achieved at that level and yet these same students tail off dismally by fourth and fifth grades.

11. *Television stifles the imagination.* Consider for a moment this single paragraph from Eric Knight's classic, *Lassie, Come Home:*

> Yet, if it were almost a miracle, in his heart Joe Carraclough tried to believe in that miracle—that somehow, wonderfully, inexplicably, his dog would be there some day; there, waiting by the school gate. Each day as he came out of school, his eyes would turn to the spot where Lassie had always waited. And each day there was nothing there, and Joe Carraclough would walk home slowly, silently, stolidly as did the people of his country.

If a dozen people were to read or hear those words, they would have a dozen different images of the scene, what the boy looked like, the school, the gate, the lonely road home. As soon as the story is placed on film there is no longer any room for imagination. The director does all your imagining for you.

12. *Television overpowers and desensitizes a child's sense of sympathy for suffering, while books heighten the reader's sense of sympathy.* Extensive research in the past ten years clearly shows that television's bombardment of the child with continual acts of violence (18,000 acts viewed between ages of 3 and 17) makes the child insensitive to violence and its victims—most of whom he is conditioned to believe die cleanly or crawl inconsequently offstage.[11]

Though literature could never be labeled a nonviolent medium, it cannot begin to approach television's extreme. Frank Mankiewicz and Joel Swerdlow noted in *Remote Control: Television and the Manipulation of American Life* that you would have to see all thirty-seven of Shakespeare's plays in order to see the same number of acts of human violence (fifty-four) that you would see in just three evenings of prime-time television.

13. *Television is a passive activity and discourages creative play.* The virtual disappearance of neighborhood games like I spy, kick the can, spud, hopscotch, Johnny-jump-the-pony, stickball, red light, Simon says, flies up, giant steps, and statue attests to that.

Compared to reading, television is still the more passive of the two activities. In reading, educators point out, a child must actively use a variety of skills involving sounds, spelling rules, blendings, as well as constructing mental images of the scene described in the book. Television requires no such mental activity.

14. *Television is psychologically addictive.* In schools and homes where students voluntarily have removed themselves from TV viewing, their subsequent class discussions and journals report the addictive nature of their attachment to television: it draws upon their idle time and there is an urgency to watch it in order to fulfill peer and family pressure.

15. *Television has been described by former First Lady Betty Ford as "the greatest babysitter of all time," but it also is reported to be the nation's second largest obstacle to family harmony.* In a 1980 survey by the Roper Organization, 4,000 men and women listed money as the most frequent subject of fights between husband and wife. Television and children tied for second, and produced three times as many arguments as did sex.

16. *Television's conception of childhood, rather than being progressive, is regressive—a throwback, in fact, to the Middle Ages.* In *Teaching as a Conserving Activity,* Postman points to Philippe Ariès's research, which shows that until the 1600s children over the age of 5 were treated and governed as though they were adults.[12] After the seventeenth century, society developed a concept of childhood which insulated children from the shock of instant adulthood until they were mature enough to meet it. "Television," Postman declares, "all by itself, may bring an end to childhood." Present-day TV programming offers its nightly messages on incest, murder, abortion, rape, moral and political corruption, and general physical mayhem to 85 million people—including 5.6 million children between ages 2 and 11 who are still watching at 10:30 p.m.[13] The afternoon soap operas offer a similar message to still another young audience. Of the twenty-one children (ages 7 to 9) in my wife's second-grade class one year, all but four of them were *daily* soap opera viewers.

17. *Television presents a continuous distortion of physical and social realities, thus reinforcing false stereotypes.* Extensive studies by major research firms[14] have produced these warps:

- TV shows are populated by three times as many men than women, and men are usually ten years older than women. (In reality, women outnumber men, 52 percent to 48 percent, with a median age two years older than men's.)
- Children make up only one-tenth of the TV population. (In reality, 27 percent.)
- Only 4 percent of TV characters suffer from obesity. (In reality, 30 percent.)
- Only 6 to 10 percent of TV characters hold blue-collar or service jobs. (In reality, 60 percent.)
- TV characters seldom wear glasses. Fifty percent of the population wears them.
- Two out of every three TV businessmen are portrayed as foolish, greedy, or criminal.
- TV characters seldom wear seat belts, yet never sustain crippling injuries from TV car crashes.
- Murder is 200 percent more prevalent as a TV crime than it is in reality.

Children's television is just as heavily distorted. A study funded by the Ford and Carnegie Foundations showed thirty-eight hours of Boston children's programming contained these misrepresentations: Of the 1145 characters, 3.7 percent were black; 3.1 percent were Spanish-speaking; only 16 percent were women. In reality, the following statistics hold true: blacks—11 percent; Spanish-speaking—6 percent; women—52 percent.

Bob Keeshan, most often heard in the role of his TV character Captain Kangaroo, places the prime responsibility for television's negative influence upon the parent. In a 1979 interview with John Merrow on National Public Radio's *Options in Education,* Keeshan said, "Television is the great national babysitter. It's not the disease in itself, but a symptom of a greater disease that exists between parent and child and the parent-child relationship. A parent today simply doesn't have time for the child, and the child is a very low priority item, and there's this magic box that flickers pictures all day long, and it's a convenient babysitter. I'm busy, go watch television. . . . The most direct answer to all our problems with television and children is the parent, because if the parent is an effective parent, we're not going to have it." [15]

Keeshan, along with Fred Rogers ("Mr. Rogers' Neighborhood"), has represented one of the few bright spots in television's thirty-four-year association with children. Dedicated to stretching children's imaginations and attention spans with shows that always included the reading of at least one children's book each morning, "Captain Kangaroo" was an example of what could be accomplished when television is used as both a teacher and an entertainer. While many were shocked when CBS dropped "Captain Kangaroo" in December 1984 after a distinguished twenty-nine-year span, I was not surprised. What else could you expect from the network executives who brought us "The Dukes of Hazzard"?

Keeshan's call for parental control of the television set is more easily said than done, as any parent can tell you who has ever tried it. I know firsthand.

My family's restricted viewing began in 1974, at about the time I'd begun to notice a growing television addiction in my fourth-grader daughter and kindergarten-age son. There had even begun a deterioration of our long-standing read-aloud time each night because, in their words, it "took too much time away from the TV."

One evening while visiting Marty and Joan Wood of Longmeadow, Massachusetts, I noticed that their four teenage children went right to their homework after excusing themselves from the dinner table.

I asked the parents, "Your television broken?"

"No," replied Marty. "Why?"

"Well, it's only six forty-five and the kids are already doing homework."

Joan explained, "Oh, we don't allow television on school nights."

"That's a noble philosophy—but how in the world do you enforce it?" I asked.

"It is a house *law*," stated Marty. And for the next hour and a half, husband and wife detailed for me the positive changes that had occurred in their family and home since they put that "law" into effect.

That evening was a turning point for my family. After hearing the details of the plan, my wife, Susan, agreed wholeheartedly to back it. "On one condition," she added.

"What's that?" I asked.

"*You* be the one to tell them," she said.

After supper the next night we brought the children into our bedroom, surrounded them with pillows and quilts, and I calmly began,

"Jamie . . . Elizabeth . . . Mom and I have decided that there will be no more television on school nights in this house—forever."

Their reaction was predictable: they started to cry. What came as a shock to us was that they cried for four solid months. Every night, despite explanations on our part, they cried. We tried to impress upon them that the rule was not meant as a punishment; we listed all the positive reasons for such a rule. They cried louder.

The peer group pressure was enormous, particularly for Elizabeth. "There's nothing to talk about in school anymore," she sobbed. "All the kids were talking about "Starsky and Hutch" at lunch today and I didn't even see it."

There was even peer pressure from other parents directed at Susan and me. "But, Jim," they would ask, "not even for an hour after supper?" in a tone that suggested our plan was a new form of child abuse. "And what about all the National Geographic specials? Aren't you going to let the kids watch *those?*" they'd ask.

It should be pointed out that a great many parents use National Geographic specials, Jacques Cousteau specials, and "Sesame Street" as the salve on their consciences. I can count on one hand the number of children I know who actually like those specials. Given the choice, as the vast majority are, they'll choose "Dukes of Hazzard" or MTV every time.

As difficult as it was at first, we persevered and resisted both kinds of peer pressure. We lived with the tears, the pleadings, the conniving. "Dad, my teacher says there is a special show on tonight that I have to watch. She said don't come to school tomorrow if you haven't seen the show," Elizabeth would say after supper.

After three months my wife and I began to see the things happen that the Woods had predicted. Suddenly we had the time each night as a family to read aloud, to read to ourselves, to do homework at an unhurried pace, to learn how to play chess and checkers and Scrabble, to make the plastic models that had been collecting dust in the closet for two years, to bake cakes and cookies, to write thank-you notes to aunts and uncles, to do household chores and take baths and showers without World War III breaking out, to play on all the parish sports teams, to draw and paint and color, and—best of all—to talk with each other, ask questions and answer questions.

Our children's imaginations were coming back to life again.

For the first year, the decision was a heavy one for all of us. With time it grew lighter. Jamie, being younger, had never developed the acute taste for television that Elizabeth had, and he lost the habit fairly easily. It took Elizabeth longer to adjust, largely because she'd been allowed such a steady dose for so long.

Over the years the plan was modified until it worked like this:

1. The television is turned off at supper time and not turned on again until the children are in bed, Monday through Thursday.

2. Each child is allowed to watch one school night show a week (subject to parents' approval). Homework, chores, et cetera must be finished beforehand.

3. Weekend television is limited to any two of the three nights. The remaining night is reserved for homework and other activities. The children make their selections separately.

The suggestion to modify the original diet and allow one school night show a week came from my wife during the third year of the plan and it met with my immediate resistance. Only reluctantly did I agree to give it a try.

As it turned out, it was an excellent addition. By limiting the choice to one show a week, we forced the child to be discriminating in his or her selections, to distinguish worth from trash. They became very choosy, refusing to waste the privilege, and began using a critical eye in evaluating shows.

The habit of watching, however, continued to decrease while other interests expanded. By the time Elizabeth was a ninth-grade student, she didn't bother to use her school-night option more than three or four times in the course of the entire year. More than half the time Jamie forgot until the week was over. "Hey!" he'd say on Saturday. "I never watched my show this week. Why didn't somebody remind me?"

We structured the diet to allow the family to control the television and not the other way around. Perhaps this particular diet won't work for your family, but a similar one would—if you have the courage and determination to make it work.

If you are going to require your children to curtail their TV viewing, if you are going to create a three-hour void in their daily lives, then *you* must make a commitment to fill that void. *You* have to produce the crayons and paper, *you* have to teach them how to play checkers, *you* have to help with the cookie mix. And most importantly, *you* must pick up those books—books to be read to the child, books to be read by the child, books to be read to yourself—even when you have a headache, even when you're tired, even when you're worried about your checkbook. You'll be surprised. Just as that book will take your child's mind off television, it also will take your mind off the headache or checkbook.

A short time after the release of the fifty-two American hostages by the Iranian government in January 1981, I had the opportunity to address the children's librarians of the Massachusetts Library Association. As the fourth member of a panel on "Children's Television: Friend or Foe?" I was preceded by three speakers who went to great lengths to praise the medium and its efforts in stimulating children's minds, both in the classroom and at home.

In my opening remarks I reminded the audience of the recent events in Iran and the unprecedented worldwide daily coverage by the media throughout the 444 days.

Isn't it interesting that with all the marvelous computerized and transistorized accomplishments of TV—including those you've heard espoused by the previous speakers today—we've yet to hear any of the hostages say, "Thank God we had TV! It got us through our darkest hours. We could never have survived without it."

We have, however, heard hostage after hostage pay tribute to the one element that appears to be the savior of the hostages' sanity: their imaginations. Upon their release they . . . detailed for State Department doctors the intricate "daydreaming" which allowed them to escape their tormentors many times a day. One captive fantasized a train trip from India to England, including a mental script for seating arrangements, passenger descriptions— even a dining car menu. Another remodeled his parents' home— inch by inch, making mental notes of what he would use for wallpaper, paneling and flooring.[16]

And nearly all the hostages [I reminded the librarians] made daily fantasy trips home to their families—walking through their children's rooms, mowing lawns, hosting backyard barbecues. Psychologists have been studying such "daydreaming" since the Korean War and they have found it serves two immediate purposes: it allows the prisoner momentary escape and it serves as a constant reminder of who they are and why they are there.

My point in mentioning this is to remind you that a great many of our children face a future in which they will someday be hostages: hostages to bad marriages, hostages to unhappy jobs and

careers, hostages to illnesses or neighborhoods. How well they survive their captivity—however long it may be—may well be determined by their imaginations, their ability to dream and hold fast
to those dreams.[17]

From this capacity to dream springs the very progress of the human race. Without the willingness to wonder, notes the great Russian children's poet Kornei Chukovsky, there would be no new
hypotheses, inventions, or experiments.[18] Science and technology would
be at a standstill. Albert Einstein reaffirmed this when he stated: "The
gift of fantasy has meant more to me than my talent for absorbing
positive knowledge."

Several years ago Sylvia Ashton-Warner, an internationally recognized authority on teaching and learning, spent a year teaching and
observing in an American community. Afterwards, in *Spearpoint:
"Teacher" in America,* she wrote of her concern about what television
was doing to the human condition here. In stripping them of a third
dimension, she noted, television leaves us with children who are daily
less capable of dreaming. "You don't get far without a dream to lure.
A dream keeps you looking forward. . . . Man does not live by bread
alone but by dreams also. . . . Man does not die from breadlessness
but from dreamlessness also."[19]

The substitute for dreams is boredom—bored children, bored parents, an entire culture held hostage by boredom. The growing national awareness of this is evidenced in the number of communities
sponsoring "Pull the Plug" programs.

Two of the most famous efforts occurred in the exclusive communities of Ridgewood, New Jersey, and Farmington, Connecticut. The
Ridgewood program was initiated by the Home and School Association at Hawes Elementary School and centered on 142 fourth-, fifth-,
and sixth-graders, who were asked to keep journals while abstaining
from television for a week. The object of the program was to make
families aware of television's addictive qualities and its dominance of
leisure time. The shocking results (parents proved to be as addicted
as the children) received front-page coverage in *The Wall Street Journal* and should be required reading for every parent in America.[20]

When the Farmington Library Council joined forces with the Farmington Public Schools to ask the town's 17,000 residents to turn
off their televisions for the month of January 1984, they never dreamed
it would receive coast-to-coast media coverage that ranged from *USA*

Today to CBS Radio News and *Entertainment Tonight.* Such attention is yet another indicator of national concern. The results heightened the entire community's awareness to television's pervasiveness in family and student life.

One of the best television awareness and assertiveness efforts I have seen is a pamphlet, "Caution! Children Watching," produced by the Baltimore County Public Library. Designed so it can be unfolded into a poster, its excellent graphics note the frightening statistics in children's viewing habits, alternative activities for parent and child, as well as addresses and phone numbers of local stations and networks for viewers to register suggestions and complaints.

I think every television awareness effort should adopt as its official mascot David McPhail's delightful picture book *Fix-It,* which details the trauma and eventual discoveries of a little girl bear whose television breaks. Also especially effective is Florence Parry Heide's *The Problem with Pulcifer.*

With the arrival of cable television and video cassette recorders, the concept of prime-time viewing has become antiquated, and television is causing even greater concern among educators and parent groups trying to keep track of how much and what children should watch. In that direction, I recommend Lynn Minton's *Movie Guide for Puzzled Parents,* a common-sense guide to more than 1500 films that may be coming into your home.

Although the current wave of VCR madness might lead one to believe otherwise, I'm somewhat optimistic about the outcome. One positive factor already evident is the concern being shown by Madison Avenue that VCR owners are becoming more discriminating in their viewing habits: they're "zapping" the commercials on taped shows. This wreaks havoc with advertising dollars when you realize the average 10-year-old (prior to VCRs) was exposed to four hundred commercials a week.

If anything, the VCR poses a viable alternative to the "mindless" viewing that composes much of our video hours and forces us to think about our choices. In fact, the choice of what and when we watch is no longer in the hands of the networks and Madison Avenue—with a VCR the choice is ours.

You don't have to throw out the television. All you have to do is control it. When it is used correctly, it can inform, entertain and, occasionally, even inspire. Used incorrectly, television will control your family. It will limit its language, its dreams, its achievements. The choice is yours.

Many of today's educators have become increasingly concerned over the condition of children's listening skills. "It is *the* most important communications skill and very little is done with it at any educational level," states educator Rhoderick J. Elen in *Elementary English.*[21] Since reading comprehension stems directly from listening comprehension, it stands to reason that many of our current reading problems can be attributed to a breakdown in children's listening skills.

There is little argument that reading aloud is one of the best stimulants for listening skills, but there are several others which deserve the attention of parents, teachers, and librarians: records, radio drama, and tape recorders. While these devices lack the immediacy of a live person (who can answer a child's questions), they do fill the gap when an adult is unavailable.

Records of children's songs, rhymes, and stories should be among the family's first purchases after books. They offer rhythms and distinct vocalizing, both of which fill important needs in young children. Neighborhood libraries and record shops have extensive children's record collections from which to choose. Most producers of quality story records and cassettes based on children's literature are more than happy to send you their catalogues. Four of the best, with hundreds of available titles, are:

- Caedmon Inc., 1995 Broadway, New York, NY 06883
- The Mind's Eye, P.O. Box 6727, San Francisco, CA 94101
- Weston Woods Studios, Department CAS, Weston, CT 06883
- Listening Library, Inc., One Park Ave., Old Greenwich, CT 06870

Many libraries and recording companies now offer copies of old radio dramas, such as *Superman, The Green Hornet, The Lone Ranger, Sergeant Preston of the Yukon,* and *Inner Sanctum.* These are excellent stimulants to listening and imagining for 9-year-olds and older.

In *Remote Control: Television and the Manipulation of American Life,* Mankiewicz and Swerdlow describe how much more mental exercise is demanded by the reader or radio listener than by the television viewer: "[The reader or listener] must give all the characters faces and features, they must be tall or short, pretty or plain. He must provide clothes, mannerisms and modes of expression. . . . He must be an architect and an interior decorator."

Most children today have never heard radio drama and will be amazed at how much they can "see" in such recordings once the curtain lifts on their imaginations and listening skills. After you explain how the various sound effects were achieved for the shows, or listened to sound effects recordings, their ambitions will grow. They'll be asking, "Can we try making our own show with a tape recorder?"

That is when the learning swings into high gear—with script writers, directors, performers, sound technicians, and musicians. You'll see firsthand how listening skills lead to better speaking, writing, and reading.

Most public libraries now boast a large collection of long-playing records and cassettes featuring great literature read aloud. The readers include not only featured names of the theater like Alexander Scourby, Orson Welles, and James Earl Jones but a host of literary figures reading their own work: Eudora Welty, John Cheever, John Updike, Shirley Jackson, William Saroyan, and Howard Fast. As one listens to James Earl Jones read Richard Wright's description of fear from *Native Son,* one cannot help but want to read or reread the book. Since most library collections of the spoken word are strong in the field of adult literature, these records can be especially pertinent to the curriculum of the junior and senior high school teachers.[22]

The cassette tape recorder could be the handiest listening device known to man, barring, of course, the human ear. Its low cost and simple operation make it a must item for every classroom and home, as a source of both instruction and entertainment. One of its obvious but often overlooked uses is for "talking books," similar to those used by the blind. In recent years, classroom teachers have begun to incorporate the recorder into their learning centers, but parents still haven't realized its enormous potential. Dr. Marie Carbo, now a reading consultant and professor at St. John's University in New York, taped stories and books for her students and achieved "phenomenal" results while working as a learning disabilities specialist. Her students had severe learning handicaps: they were disabled, educable-retarded, emotionally disturbed, and severly speech-impaired children.

By listening to Dr. Carbo's tape and following in the book, each child was free to move at his own pace and had a constant language model as a companion—the tape. There was also the additional reinforcement from repeated playing of the tape. The pace of the reader's voice was slow enough for the child to follow and indicated when the page should be turned. As the child's reading ability improved, Dr. Carbo increased the pace of the story and the size of the word groupings.[23]

Describing a particular case, Dr. Carbo says, "The greatest gain in word recognition was made by Tommy, a sixth-grade boy reading on a 2.2 level. Prior to working with the tapes he had faltered and stumbled over second-grade words while his body actually shook with fear and discomfort. Understandably, he hated to read. Because a beloved teacher had once read *Charlotte's Web* to him, he asked me to record his favorite chapter from this book. I recorded one paragraph on each cassette side so that Tommy could choose to read either one or two paragraphs daily. The first time that he listened to a recording (five times) and then read the passage silently to himself (twice), he was able to read the passage to me perfectly with excellent expression and without fear. After this momentous event, Tommy worked hard. At last he knew he was capable of learning to read and was willing to give it all he could. The result was a fifteen-month gain in word recognition at the end of only three months. Every learning-disabled child in the program experienced immediate success with her or his individually recorded books," explains Dr. Carbo.

If such remarkable results are possible with learning-disabled children, imagine what can be done with children who have fewer disadvantages.

Although many commercial recordings are available, the sound of a parent or teacher reading at an unhurried pace will carry far more meaning than will listening to a stranger's voice. In fact, some professional recordings move too quickly in trying to squeeze in more of the story. Tape-record those Mother Goose rhymes and have them playing during the day when you are busy.

For the traveling parent (or absentee grandparent), the tape recorder is an excellent surrogate storyteller. During a job change several years ago, Barry Lein of Sterling, Massachusetts, was separated from his wife, Cheryll, and two sons for long periods of time. Cheryll tells how "he used to read stories to Adam [age 4] and Matthew [age 2] on cassettes and mail them home. Each night the boys would listen to their dad's voice, and they would be together—at least in spirit. When a new tape arrived, all play stopped until it was heard— not just by our sons but also by their cousins with whom we were staying."

She also recalls when, during this period, Adam was hospitalized with a severe asthma attack. "He was in an oxygen tent with his tape recorder playing when his doctor came. 'What's this?' he asked. When I told him that it was Adam's daddy reading stories to him, the doctor seemed amazed—and impressed."

It is important to remember, however, the cassette recorder is not an unqualified replacement for the personal touch of a live parent or teacher. As a substitute, it is better than nothing, but far short of the living, responsive voice and the person behind it. They've yet to invent the recorder or television set that can hug a child.

8
Sustained
Silent Reading:
Reading-Aloud's Natural Partner

With the tests, with the "methods," with the class structures, with the teacher's determination to teach . . . no one had ever had much time in school to just read the damn books. They were always practicing up to read, and the practice itself was so unnecessary, or so difficult, or so boring you were likely to figure that the task you were practicing for must combine those qualities and so reject it or be afraid of it.

—James Herndon, from
How to Survive in Your Native Land

After finishing my forty-five-minute career talk to the fourth-grade students at Brunton School in Springfield, Massachusetts, I debated whether to ask my usual question: What have you read lately? A week before, I'd asked the question of a fifth-grade class in the same school system and came away depressed by the lack of response. Only four children in the room had been able to think of anything they had

111

read lately. I was embarrassed for the class, the teacher, the system, and the city. Reluctantly, I now asked the question again, dreading another disappointing response.

But those wonderful fourth-grade pupils surprised me. For forty-five minutes they spouted the names of the books they had been reading. I could barely get a word in edgewise as their enthusiasm and excitement flooded the room.

Later, as I was leaving, I asked the teacher, Terri Cullinane, "What have you done to those kids? I haven't seen a class this excited by books in years."

"Two things," she answered. "We—the other teachers and I—read aloud to them every day, and SSR." (SSR is an acronym for Sustained Silent Reading.) "Every day when we go to lunch, each child leaves his library book on his desk. It is ready and waiting for him when he returns after lunch. We read quietly for ten minutes, close our books, and go on with classwork."

Terri explained that the SSR program had been in effect only a few months but already the faculty had seen a dramatic change in reading habits and attitude among the children.

"Ten minutes a day may not seem like much time but think of it this way: ten minutes a day for five days. That's almost a solid hour of reading and it puts the child well into the book, much further, by the way, then most of them would be if they were left to read it on their own time."

SSR is one of those common-sense ideas that is so obvious and un-complicated that it is easily overlooked in today's complex educational scheme. Sadly, 99 percent of our school systems (and nearly 100 percent of our homes) either haven't heard about it or can't spare the time to try it.

Its basic principle is simple. Reading is, among other things, a skill, and like all skills, the more you use it the better you become at it. Conversely, the less reading you do, the more difficult it is. It is no secret among educators that today's students are assigned 50 percent less reading than their counterparts in the early 1960s. In *The Literacy Hoax,* Copperman points out that the average Soviet high-school student is required to read more English literature than the average American student. He also reports that the decline in reading skills has required twenty of the largest textbook publishers to down-grade the reading level of their books to two full grades below the grade in which they are to be used.

When reading and writing skills decline, schools increase the hours of skills instruction, search for new methods, change textbooks, and wring their hands in despair. We invest time in teaching reading skills to our children, then fail to provide them with the time to use the skills—either in the home or in the classroom. Goodlad's comprehensive study of American schooling showed that only 6 percent of class time is occupied by the act of reading in the elementary-school day and 3 percent and 2 percent at junior and senior high school levels.[1] SSR is the logical answer.

Originally proposed in the early 1960s by Lyman C. Hunt, Jr., of the University of Vermont, SSR has received its biggest boost from reading experts Robert and Marlene McCracken.[2] Experimenting with a variety of techniques and schools, the McCrackens recommend the following procedures for SSR programs:

1. Children should read to themselves for a *limited* amount of time. Teachers and parents should adapt this to their individual class or family and adjust it with increasing maturity. Ten or fifteen minutes are the frequent choices for the classroom.

2. Each student should select his own book, magazine, or newspaper. No changing during the period is permitted. All materials must be chosen before the SSR period begins.

3. The teacher or parent must read also, setting an example. This cannot be stressed too strongly.

4. No reports are required of the student. No records are kept.

Along with the obvious opportunity to practice reading skills in an informal manner, SSR provides the student with a new perspective on reading—as a form of recreation. There appears to be a desperate need for such an example (see Chapter 1).

Nearly all SSR studies done to date report immediate attitude changes. Junior and senior high schools show significant changes in students' feelings toward the library, voluntary reading, assigned reading, and the importance of reading. While there is no marked improvement in reading skills at this secondary level, there is no decline either, despite the loss of reading instruction time. Since by age 13 children usually have reached their language development peak, attitudes are more apt to improve than are skills during adolescence.[3]

Younger readers, however, show significant improvement in both attitude and skills with SSR.[4] "Poor readers," points out Professor

Allington of the State University of New York, "when given 10 minutes a day to read, initially will achieve 500 words and quickly increase that amount in the same period as proficiency grows."

In a School District of Philadelphia—Federal Reserve Bank study made to determine which reading methods "worked," it was shown that among 1,800 Philadelphia fourth-grade students "the more minutes a week of sustained silent reading, the better the pupils achieved." The same study also indicated that the number of minutes a day of reading instruction that might be lost through SSR did not affect pupil achievement.[5]

Martha Efta offers a special example of SSR's worth. Ms. Efta teaches a primary-level class of educable mentally retarded children in Westlake, Ohio. The children, ranging in age from 7 to 10, are frequently hyperactive and nonreaders. When she heard of the SSR procedure in a graduate course, she was cautious about the idea despite the professor's wholehearted support for it. After all, she thought, the experts were talking about normal children, not the retarded.

With some trepidation, she explained the procedures to her students and reshaped the rules to fit her classroom. Because of their short attention spans, she allowed each student to choose as many as three books or magazines for the period. Students were allowed to sit any way and in any place they chose in the room. Ms. Efta initially kept the program to three minutes in length, then gradually increased it to thirteen minutes over a period of weeks. This was the class's limit.

"From the onset [of SSR]," Ms. Efta explains, "the students have demonstrated some exciting and favorable behavior changes—such as independent decision making, self discipline, sharing . . . and broadened reading interests. The enthusiastic rush to select their day's reading materials following noon recess is indicative of the children's interest and eagerness for SSR. The children seem to delight in the adult-like responsibility of selecting their own reading matter."[6]

The McCrackens' extensive studies of SSR show conclusively that best results are achieved when the program is schoolwide, as in the case of Gateway Regional Middle School in Huntington, Massachusetts. This school instituted a twenty-five minute sustained silent reading program in 1978 on Monday and Friday mornings. During these periods, the entire school (this includes the principals, secretaries, and teachers, as well as the students) puts its "work" aside and picks up something to read. The choice of material is up to the individual.

"We instituted it to show the children just how important and how enjoyable reading is for *everyone*—not just for students," explained principal James Lutat. "Now it's become one of the most popular features of the week. We all look forward to it. We don't allow any work during those twenty-five-minute periods. Why, we don't even answer the phone if we can help it."

At 10:30 a.m. on Mondays and Fridays the only sound in Gateway School is the sound of turning pages—pages that are turned eagerly instead of reluctantly.

The McCrackens report that most of the instances where SSR fails are due to teachers (or aides) who are supervising instead of reading. The other problem area is where classes lack enough SSR materials from which to choose.

Writing in *The Reading Teacher,* the McCrackens called attention to the overwhelming part the teacher plays as a role model in SSR.[7] Teachers reported widespread imitation by students of the teacher's reading habits.

Students in one class noticed the teacher interrupting her reading to look up a word in the dictionary and began doing the same. When a junior-high teacher began to read the daily newspaper each day, the class began doing the same.

But of all the role model examples, the most moving for me was the retarded child in Martha Efta's class. This nonreader found it impossible to settle down with his books until he noticed his friend reading silently and intently. So transfixed was he by his friend's concentration, he spent an entire SSR period just watching the boy scanning the sentences with his finger. Within several days he, too, settled into "reading"—by imitating the behavior of his friend.

When teachers talk about what they are reading or describe a spine-tingling section of their book, students are quick to follow suit and share their reaction. By doing this, the McCrackens write, "they are teaching attitudes and skills; they are teaching children that reading is communication with an author, an assimilation and reaction to an author's ideas."

SSR works as well in the home as in the classroom. The same rules apply, though I recommend they be tailored to fit your family. For children who are not used to reading for more than brief periods of time it is important at first to limit SSR to ten or fifteen minutes. Later, when they are used to reading in this manner and are more involved in books, the period can be extended—often at the child's request. As in the classroom, it is important to have a variety of reading material—magazines, newspapers, novels, picture books. A weekly family trip to the library can do much to solve this need.

The time selected for family SSR is also important. Involve the child in the decision, if possible. Bedtime seems to be the most popular SSR time, perhaps because the child does not have to give up any activity for it except sleeping—and most children gladly surrender that.

9
How to Use
the Treasury

The success we have in helping children become readers will depend not so much on our technical skills but upon the spirit we transmit of ourselves as readers. Next in importance comes the breadth and depth of our knowledge of the books we offer. Only out of such a ready catalogue can we match child and book with the sort of spontaneous accuracy that is wanted time and again during a working day.

—Aidan Chambers, from
"Talking About Reading,"
The Horn Book (October 1977)

Approximately 2,000 new children's books are published each year. Of that number, 60 percent could be categorized as "fast food for the mind" and of minimum lasting value. Only about 10 percent of the year's crop of books could be rated Grade A.

This is not to say that fast-food books are worthless. On the contrary, they serve as hors d'oeuvres and build appetites (to say nothing of reading skills) for more nourishing books later. They also serve as valuable transition steps between textbook reading and leisure reading. Jacques Barzun, most recently a consultant to the Council for Basic Education, is the author of *Teacher in America* (written while he was professor of history and later provost of Columbia University), in which he comments on so-called junk reading by children: "Let me say at once that all books are good and that consequently a child be allowed to read everything he lays his hands on. Trash is excellent; great works . . . are admirable. . . . The ravenous appetite will digest stones unharmed. Never mind the need to discriminate; it comes in its own time."[1] (In using the word "trash," Barzun was referring to formula fiction like the Hardy Boys and Nancy Drew.)

The reader-aloud, however, offers an alternative for the child, allowing him to sample the "Grade A" books which may be beyond either his skills or his surface appetites. We should, therefore, in reading aloud concern ourselves primarily (though not exclusively) with books that will stimulate children's emotions, minds, and imaginations, stories that will stay with them for years to come, literature that will serve as a harbor light toward which a child can navigate.

Few parents have the time to wade through the vast numbers of newly published books, not to mention the previous years' volumes. Librarians can be a big help in this chore, at least in the picture book category. They know the patrons' favorites from over the years and their story-hour experience is invaluable. But when you are looking for read-aloud novels, the forest begins to thicken and it is much harder to find your way. Not all librarians—and few teachers and parents—have a strong background in this area of read-aloud. It is my hope that the Treasury of Read-Alouds included in this book will help to alleviate this problem.

I make no boast of the Treasury being a comprehensive list. It is intended only as a starter and time-saver. (I'd be willing to wager, in fact, that I've left your all-time favorite off the list.) Some books, like *Treasure Island* or *Tom Sawyer* have not been listed here because they already are included in most school reading curricula. Another obvious choice, the Bible, is omitted. As the world's greatest collection of stories, it is an obvious choice for reading aloud, but the multiplicity of sects makes the choice of one or even several texts impossible. Fortunately there is no shortage of books containing Bible stories for children and their selection best rests in the hands of the individual parent or teacher.

As much as the Treasury appears to be a potpourri of titles, I do admit to some rhyme and reason for my selections. I required the following for each selection:

1. I must have read and enjoyed the book.

2. The book must have a proven track record of success as a read-aloud with children. I noted the reactions of my own children, neighbors' and friends' children, and school classes.

3. The book must be the kind of book that will inspire children to want to read another one just like it, or even the same book over again.

I did not require that the book be a classic, although some of the books on the list are classics. Nor did I ask that the book be acclaimed previously by the critics, though many on the list own that distinction. Nearly all the books are strong on narrative. They have a story to tell in which there is a conflict, some drama, and a conclusion. I have purposely avoided the new wave of novels now being published that are top-heavy with dialogue; they have little or no setting and character development, but plenty of one-line retorts by the children. With all that dialogue, they are difficult to read aloud and probably would be better labeled television scripts than books.

The grade recommendations with each book are meant to be flexible. If you stop to think about it, there is no such thing as a "fourth-grade book" any more than there is a "middle-age book." Many sixth-grade students are fully capable of enjoying the same book a third-grade child is enjoying. The grade numbers are intended only as general read-aloud guidelines, not as rules. In addition to the numbered grade levels, the following codes are included:

Tod.—Infants and toddlers up to 3-year-olds
Pre S.—From 3-year-olds to 5-year-olds
K—Kindergarteners

Wherever possible I have included the names of hardcover and paperback publishers. This information, however, is subject to change as books go out of print or are made available in paperback for the first time. I offer it only as a reference for those readers wishing to obtain a personal copy or, if it is unavailable, a copy through a school or public library. If the book is still in print, it usually can be ordered directly from the publisher. *Children's Books in Print,* available in all libraries, includes a complete listing of publishers' addresses, their different imprint names, and the books that are available. *Paperback Books in Print* does the same for all paperbacks, children and adult. In the Treasury, those books out of print as of 1984 carry (OP) after the publisher's name, though readers should not be discouraged by such a notation—it most probably is still available on library shelves.

In my listing of publishers, the paperback publisher always follows the hardcover publisher, separated by a semicolon, for example: Harper, 1960; Bantam, 1971. Where a particular publisher handles both the hardcover and paperback editions, the notation will be, for example: Harper (both), 1962; 1975.

The Treasury is divided into six categories, arranged as follows: a brief listing of Wordless Books, Picture Books (p), Short Novels (s), Novels (n), Poetry (po), and Anthologies (a). All books in the respective categories are listed alphabetically by title. The Author-Illustrator Index to Treasury will also help you locate books in different categories.

At the end of the book synopses in the Treasury, I often have noted other read-alouds by the same author or referred the reader to related titles listed elsewhere in the Treasury. In these instances, the letter that follows the title—*Ira Sleeps Over* (p)—indicates the section of the Treasury that contains that particular book: (p) for Picture Books. If no letter appears after the recommended title, its synopsis is not available in the Treasury because of space limitations. Such references allow for the inclusion of several hundred titles over and above the more than three hundred separate synopses. Any listing of other books by the author is not meant to be all-inclusive. The author may have written other books but they may not lend themselves to reading aloud or the limitations of space prohibit their inclusion. In addition, the category of Short Novels is an umbrella term, generally referring to books with more text than picture books but generally less than one hundred pages. To avoid overcomplicating the Treasury, I have included what sometimes are called "chapter books" in this category.

In the synopses, I have tried to indicate wherever I thought certain books needed special attention from the reader-aloud. For example, Harry Mazer's *Snow-Bound* is a compelling novel about two teenagers fighting for their lives in a snowstorm. Many of my teacher friends read it to their middle-school classes each year and skip over the occasional four-letter words in the text. The story is one of the children's favorites and it would be a shame to deprive them of its excitement and values because of a dozen strong words. Nevertheless, the reader-aloud should be alerted to the situation.

I have noted "for experienced listeners" to indicate those books I feel would be poor choices for children just beginning the listening experience. These books should be read aloud only after the children's attention and listening spans have been developed with shorter books and stories.

The number of pages noted for each book should indicate to the reader the number of sittings the book requires. A children's book of thirty-two pages can be completed easily in one session.

All of these books, when they are read aloud in the right manner and with the right attitude by the reader, will go a long way toward turning children into book lovers; they will help to turn on the turned-off reader; and they will reach children in ways far beyond our dreams.

10 Treasury of Read-Alouds

Wordless Books

Picture Books (pages 123–166) are often written and illustrated by the same person. Books marked with an * are described in the Picture Books section of the Treasury.

The Adventures of Paddy Pork, John Goodall (Harcourt, 1968)
Ah-Choo!, Mercer Mayer (Dial, 1976)
Amanda and the Mysterious Carpet, Fernando Krahn (Clarion, 1985)
Apples, Nonny Hogrogian (Macmillan, 1972)
April Fools, Fernando Krahn (Dutton, 1974)
The Ballooning Adventures of Paddy Pork, John Goodall (Harcourt, 1968)
Beach Day, Helen Oxenbury (Dial, 1982)
The Bear and the Fly, Paula Winter (Crown, 1976)
A Birthday Wish, Ed Emberley (Little, Brown, 1977)
Bobo's Dream, Martha Alexander (Dial, 1970)
A Boy, a Dog, and a Frog, Mercer Mayer (Dial, 1967)

Bubble, Bubble, Mercer Mayer (Parents, 1973)
Catch That Car, Fernando Krahn (Dutton, 1978)
Changes, Changes, Pat Hutchins (Macmillan, 1971)
Charlie-Bob's Fan, W. B. Park (Harcourt, 1981)
Creepy Castle, John Goodall (Atheneum, 1975)
The Creepy Thing, Fernando Krahn (Clarion, 1982)
*Deep in the Forest, Brinton Turkle (Dutton, 1976)
Do You Want to Be My Friend?, Eric Carle (Crowell, 1971)
Frog Goes to Dinner, Mercer Mayer (Dial, 1974)
Frog on His Own, Mercer Mayer (Dial, 1973)
Frog, Where Are You?, Mercer Mayer (Dial, 1969)
Good Night, Good Morning, Helen Oxenbury (Dial, 1982)
The Great Ape, Fernando Krahn (Viking, 1978)
The Great Cat Chase, Mercer Mayer (Four Winds, 1974)
Here Comes Alex Pumpernickel, Fernando Krahn (Little, 1981)
The Hunter and the Animals, Tomie dePaola (Holiday House, 1981)
Jacko, John Goodall (Harcourt, 1972)
Lilly at the Table, Linda Heller (Macmillan, 1979)
Little John and Me, Yutaka Sugita (McGraw-Hill, 1973)
Look What I Can Do, Jose Aruego (Scribner, 1971)
Lost, Sonia Lisker (Harcourt, 1978)
The Midnight Adventures of Kelly, Dot, and Esmeralda, John Goodall
(Atheneum, 1972)
Monkey See, Monkey Do, Helen Oxenbury (Dial, 1982)
* *Moonlight,* Jan Ormerod (Lothrop 1982; Puffin, 1983)
Mother's Helper, Helen Oxenbury (Dial, 1982)
The Mystery of the Giant Footprints, Fernando Krahn (Dutton, 1977)
Naughty Nancy, John Goodall (Atheneum, 1975)
Noah's Ark, Peter Spier (Doubleday, 1977)
One Frog Too Many, Mercer Mayer (Dial, 1975)
The Other Bone, Ed Young (Harper, 1984)
Out! Out! Out!, Martha Alexander (Dial, 1968)
Paddy Finds a Job, John Goodall (Atheneum, 1981)
Paddy Goes Traveling, John Goodall (Atheneum, 1982)
Paddy Pork's Holiday, John Goodall (Atheneum, 1975)
Paddy's Evening Out, John Goodall (Atheneum, 1973)
Paddy's New Hat, John Goodall (Atheneum, 1980)
Pancakes for Breakfast, Tomie dePaola (Harcourt, 1978)
Peter Spier's Christmas, Peter Spier (Doubleday, 1982)
*Peter Spier's Rain, Peter Spier (Doubleday, 1982)
Rosie's Walk, Pat Hutchins (Macmillan, 1968)
Sebastian and the Mushroom, Fernando Krahn (Delacorte, 1976)
The Self-Made Snowman, Fernando Krahn (Lippincott, 1974)
Shopping Trip, Helen Oxenbury (Dial, 1982)

Shrewbettina Goes to Work, John Goodall (Atheneum, 1981)
Shrewbettina's Birthday, John Goodall (Harcourt, 1970)
*The Silver Pony, Lynd Ward (Houghton Mifflin, 1973)
Skates, Ezra Jack Keats (Franklin Watts, 1973)
Sleep Tight, Alex Pumpernickel, Fernando Krahn (Little, 1982)
The Snowman, Raymond Briggs (Random, 1978)
The Sticky Child, Malcolm Bird (Harcourt, 1981)
A Story to Tell, Dick Bruna (Dick Bruna Books, 1968)
Sunshine, Jan Ormerod (Lothrop, 1981; Puffin, 1983)
The Train, Witold Generowicz (Dial, 1983)
Truck, Donald Crews (Greenwillow, 1980)
Two Moral Tales, Mercer Mayer (Four Winds, 1974)
Two More Moral Tales, Mercer Mayer (Four Winds, 1974)
Up a Tree, Ed Young, (Harper, 1983)
Up and Up, Shirley Hughes (Prentice-Hall, 1979)

Picture Books

THE ADVENTURES OF PADDY PORK
by John S. Goodall
Harcourt, 1968
Pre S.−2   60 (small) pages
This is the British counterpart (but more sophisticated in concept) of America's successful Boy and Frog series by Mercer Mayer. It is a series of wordless books that detail the adventures of a naughty pig and his bottom-less curiosity. Because of the small format, it is best read with no more than three children at once. Sequels: *Ballooning Adventures of Paddy Pork; Creepy Castle; Jacko; The Midnight Adventures of Kelly, Dot, and Esmeralda; Naughty Nancy; Paddy Finds a Job; Paddy Goes Traveling; Paddy's Evening Out; Paddy's New Hat; Paddy Pork—Odd Jobs; Paddy Pork's Holiday; Shrewbettina Goes to Work; Shrewbettina's Birthday.*

ALADDIN
Retold by Andrew Lang • Illustrated by Errol Le Cain
Puffin, 1983 (paperback only)
Gr. 2 and up   30 pages
Here is the world-famous tale about the magic lamp that brings the poor Persian boy his heart's desire—but only after great trials. More such tales can be found in an excellent new edition of *One Thousand and One Arabian Nights* by Geraldine McCaughrean (Oxford). Other giant or jinni tales: *Inside My Feet* (s); *Giant Kippernose and Other Stories* (a); *Jim and the Beanstalk* by Raymond Briggs.

ALEXANDER AND THE TERRIBLE, HORRIBLE, NO GOOD, VERY BAD DAY
by Judith Viorst • Illustrated by Ray Cruz
Atheneum (both), 1972; 1976
K and up   34 pages
Everyone has a bad day once in a while but Alexander has the worst of all. Follow him from a cereal box without a prize to a burned-out night light. A modern classic for all ages to chuckle over and admit, "I guess we're all entitled to a terrible, horrible, no good . . ." Sequel: *Alexander Who Used to Be Rich Last Sunday.* Also by the author: *If I Were in Charge of the World and Other Worries* (po); *I'll Fix Anthony.*

AMELIA BEDELIA
by Peggy Parish • Illustrated by Fritz Seibel
Harper, 1963; Scholastic, 1970
K–4   24 pages
America's most lovable maid since "Hazel," Amelia is a walking disaster— thanks to her insistence on taking directions literally. She "dusts the furniture" with dusting powder; "dresses the turkey" in shorts; "puts the lights out" on the clothesline. She makes for a hilarious exploration of homonyms and idioms. Sequels: *Amelia Bedelia and the Baby; Amelia Bedelia and the Surprise Shower; Amelia Bedelia Goes Camping; Amelia Bedelia Goes Shopping; Amelia Bedelia Helps Out; Come Back, Amelia Bedelia; Good Work, Amelia Bedelia; Play Ball, Amelia Bedelia; Teach Us, Amelia Bedelia; Thank You, Amelia Bedelia.* Related books: *The Stupids Step Out* (p); *Punnidles* by Bruce McMillan; *The King Who Rained* by Fred Gwynne.

THE AMINAL
by Lorna Balian
Abingdon, 1972
K–5   26 pages
A picture book story of how children's imaginations often run ahead of reality, particularly when accompanied by their fears. Also by the author: *The Sweet Touch; Humbug Rabbit.* Related books: *How I Hunted the Little Fellows* (p); *Sam, Bangs and Moonshine* by Evaline Ness; *Wolf! Wolf!* (p).

BABUSHKA
Retold and illustrated by Charles Mikolaycak
Holiday House, 1984
K–4   32 pages
Throughout the Christian world, in many different forms, there lives the legend of one who missed out on a chance to join the Three Kings in their visit to the child Jesus. This is the Russian version describing the woman who claimed to be too busy with chores, then a day later realizes her mis-

take and begins a lifetime journey in search of the child, leaving behind in each place a small gift or candy. In such legends St. Nicholas and Santa Claus were born. Also illustrated by Mikolaycak: *Child Is Born; I Am Joseph; Peter and the Wolf.* Other Christmas books: *A Certain Small Shepherd* (s); *The Christmas Cookie Sprinkle Snitcher* by Vip; *The Christmas Strangers* by Marjorie Thayer; *The Elves and the Shoemaker* retold by Freya Littledale; *Father Christmas* by Raymond Briggs; *The Fir Tree* by Hans Christian Andersen; *The Friendly Beasts* by Tomie dePaola; *The Legend of Old Befana* by Tomie de-Paola; *The Little Juggler* by Barbara Cooney; *Karin's Christmas Walk* by Susan Pearson; *The Night Before Christmas* illustrated by Tomie dePaola; *The Night After Christmas* by James Stevenson; *Peter Spier's Christmas* by Peter Spier; *The Polar Express* by Chris Van Allsburg; *Star Mother's Youngest Child* by Louise Moeri; *The Story of the Three Wise Kings* by Tomie dePaola; *Why the Chimes Rang* by Raymond M. Alden; *The Story of Holly and Ivy* by Rumer Godden.

BEA AND MR. JONES
by Amy Schwartz
Bradbury Press, 1982; Puffin, 1983
K–3   30 pages
Little Bea is tired of kindergarten and her father is tired of his advertising job. So they switch jobs—with hilarious results. Children love role reversals and they'll enjoy these: *One Day at School* (student becomes the teacher) by Ida Lutrell; *Your Turn, Doctor* (girl patient examines the pediatrician) by Dr. Carla Perez and Deborah Robison.

BEDTIME FOR FRANCES
by Russell Hoban • Illustrated by Garth Williams
Harper (both), 1960; 1976
Pre S.–2   28 pages
Frances the badger cannot get to sleep. All the ploys of little children to avoid bedtime, all the fears of nighttime, are treated with gentle humor here. Sequels: *A Baby Sister for Frances; Best Friends for Frances; A Birthday for Frances; Bread and Jam for Frances* (illustrated by Lillian Hoban). Related books on bedtime theme: *Corduroy* (p); *Ira Sleeps Over* (p); *What's Under My Bed?* (p); *When the Dark Comes Dancing* (po); for younger children, see listing under *Good Night Moon* (p).

BENNET CERF'S BOOK OF ANIMAL RIDDLES
by Bennett Cerf • Illustrated by Roy McKie
Random, 1959
Pre S.–2   62 pages
Joke books are an instant favorite with children. Because jokes are easily and willingly committed to memory, they offer the child an opportunity

to display his cleverness when he recites them, thus building self-confidence and a sense of humor. Sequels: *Bennett Cerf's Book of Laughs; Bennett Cerf's Book of Riddles; More Riddles.* Related book: *Spooky Riddles* by Marc Brown. For older children: *Puns, Gags, Quips and Riddles* by Roy Doty (one of a series); *How Do You Get a Horse Out of the Bathtub?* by Louis Phillips.

THE BICYCLE MAN
by Allen Say
Houghton Mifflin, 1982
K–3   40 pages
Shortly after the end of World War II, two Americans from the occupying forces show up unexpectedly at a Japanese mountain school. The tall black soldier borrows the principal's bicycle, treats everyone to a fancy cycling show, and wins the hearts and cheers of young and old. Also by the author: *The Feast of Lanterns;* Related books: *Crow Boy* (p); *Bicycle Rider* by Mary Scioscia; *How My Parents Learned to Eat* by Ina Friedman.

THE BIG ORANGE SPLOT
by Daniel Manus Pinkwater
Hastings, 1977; Scholastic, 1981
Pre S.–2   30 pages
Mr. Plumbean is a nonconformist at heart but he also lives in a neighborhood where all the houses are exactly the same. When the opportunity presents itself, he listens to his heart and paints his house in the most bizarre combination of colors—much to the consternation of his tradition-bound neighbors. But his one act of individuality is all it takes to plant similar seeds in the minds of his neighbors—who suddenly discover independence. Also by the author: *The Magic Moscow.* Related books: *Crow Boy* (p); *The Story of Ferdinand* (p); *Lafcadio the Lion Who Shot Back* (s); *Nice Little Girls* (p); *The Hill and the Rock* by David McKee; *Nicholas Bentley Stoningpot III* by Ann McGovern; *Oliver Button Is a Sissy* by Tomie dePaola; *The Visitors Who Came to Stay* by Annalena McAfee and Anthony Browne.

THE BIG RED BARN
by Eve Bunting • Illustrated by Howard Knotts
Harcourt (both), 1979
Gr. 1–4   32 pages
An old family barn serves as an emotional refuge for a little farm boy. He hides there when his mother dies and again later when his dad brings home a new wife. When the barn accidentally burns, the child and his grandfather talk about new beginnings, and how families and barns can be rebuilt. Also by the author: *Goose Dinner; The Man Who Could Call Down Owls; One More Flight; The Valentine Bears; Winter's Coming.* For a list of books on grief, see *Nadia the Willful* (p).

THE BIGGEST BEAR
by Lynd Ward
Houghton Mifflin (both), 1952; 1973
K–3   80 pages

Johnny adopts a bear cub fresh out of the woods and its growth presents problem after problem—the crises we invite when we tame what is meant to be wild. Also by the author: *My Friend Mac; Nic of the Woods; The Silver Pony* (p). Related books: *The Carp in the Bathtub* (p); *Do You Love Me?* (p); *Storm Boy* (s); *Black Bear Baby* by Berniece Freschet; *Capyboppy* by Bill Peet; *Pelican* by Brian Wildsmith.

BLUEBERRIES FOR SAL
by Robert McCloskey
Viking, 1948; Puffin, 1976
Tod.–K   56 pages

While blueberry picking one day, a little girl mistakes a bear for her mother and mom mistakes a bear cub for Sal. A realistic and happy story with bold drawings against a plain white background make this one of the best books for that toddler through kindergarten age group. For other books by the author, see *Make Way for Ducklings*. Related books: *Deep in the Forest* (p); *Are You My Mother?* by P. D. Eastman; *Black Bear Baby* by Berniece Freschet; *The Blueberry Bears* by Eleanor Lapp; *Jamberry* by Bruce Degen.

THE BOOK OF GIANT STORIES
by David Harrison   ·   Illustrated by Philippe Fix
American Heritage, 1972
K–3   44 pages

Three delightful stories about giants: a giant who throws tantrums (because he can't whistle); a giant who is afraid of butterflies (because he needs glasses); and giants who are frightened by a little boy (because he has measles). To make the "measle" story a bit more accessible for today's child, change the word "measles" to "chicken pox" when reading it aloud. Nowadays few children are aware of the word "measles." Related books: *The Fairy Tale Treasury* (Jack and the Beanstalk) (a); *The Foolish Giant; Giant Kippernose and Other Stories* (a); *Inside My Feet* (s); *The Iron Giant* (s); *The Selfish Giant* by Oscar Wilde (illustrated by Lizbeth Zwerger); *Tom Thumb* by Charles Perrault (illustrated by Linda Postma).

BRIAN WILDSMITH'S ABC
by Brian Wildsmith
Watts, 1963
Pre S.–1   54 pages

With all the awards this book has collected over the years, there is little doubt that it is the best alphabet book available today. Upper- and lower-case letters form the names of familiar objects that are colorfully portrayed one to a page. Another excellent alphabet book, using photographs of mostly household objects, is *ABC: An Alphabet Book* by Thomas Matthesen (Platt).

An excellent numbers concept book is *Helen Oxenbury's Numbers of Things;* see also toddler books by Peter Spier under *Peter Spier's Rain* (p). Other related concept books: *The Napping House* (p); *The Tomorrow Book* (p); *The Baby's Catalogue* by Janet and Allan Ahlberg; *But Where Is the Green Parrot?* by Thomas and Wanda Zacharias; *Here a Chick, There a Chick* by Bruce McMillan; *Push Pull, Empty Full: A Book of Opposites* by Tana Hoban; *The Sesame Street Word Book* (Golden); Alice and Martin Provensen's three books— *The Year at Maple Hill Farm, Our Animal Friends,* and *A Horse and a Hound, A Goat and a Gander.*

BRODERICK
by Edward Ormondroyd • Illustrated by John Larrecq
Parnassus, 1969; Houghton Mifflin, 1984
Pre S.–2   32 pages
Because they share mutual problems in a world preoccupied with bigness, children seem to have an affinity for mice and their stories. Broderick is one of the best of the lot. Nestled away in a library where he searches for the meaning of his life while eating the bindings, he finally discovers the purpose of books—and the world opens up for him. He develops ambition and, after much hard work, becomes world-famous. In old age he retires to write his memoirs, lectures to young mice, and donates money to the library. Also by the author: *Theodore* and *Theodore's Rival.* Other mouse books: *Frederick* (p); *Island of the Skog* (p); *Amos and Boris* and *Doctor De Soto* (p), both by William Steig; *The Good Mousekeeper* by Robert Kraus; *If You Give a Mouse a Cookie* by Laura Numeroff; *Loudmouse* by Richard Wilbur; *Mouse Soup* and *Mouse Tales,* both by Arnold Lobel; *The Mousewife* by Rumer Godden; *Norman the Doorman* by Don Freeman; *The School Mouse* by Dorothy Harris; *The Tale of Two Bad Mice* by Beatrix Potter; *Walter the Lazy Mouse* by Marjorie Flack. For mice novels, see *Pearl's Promise* (n).

BROWN BEAR, BROWN BEAR, WHAT DO YOU SEE?
by Bill Martin, Jr. • Illustrated by Eric Carle
Holt, 1967
Tod.–1   26 pages
For years one of the most popular books in early reading classes, this colorful volume by a world-renowned educator is now available to the general public. Colors and animals are shown in bold double-page spreads with a rhyming text. For a list of related books, see *Brian Wildsmith's ABC* (p).

THE CARP IN THE BATHTUB
by Barbara Cohen • Illustrated by Joan Halpern
Lothrop, 1972
Gr. 1–4   48 pages

When Leah and Harry's mother brings a live carp home (to cook for Passover) and temporarily stores it in the bathtub, she never anticipates their adopting it as their best friend. With bittersweet humor, the story offers a nostalgic view of Passover customs. Also by the author: *Molly's Pilgrim;* for older children: *R, My Name Is Rosie* (n); *Thank You, Jackie Robinson* (n); *Benny; King of the Seventh Grade.* Related books: *The Biggest Bear* (p); *The Golem* and *Stories for Children* both by Isaac Bashevis Singer.

THE CARROT SEED
by Ruth Krauss • Illustrated by Crockett Johnson
Harper, 1945; Scholastic, 1971
Tod.–Pre S.   22 pages
Simple pictures against a plain background depict a child's faith in the carrot seed he plants, despite the fact that no one else believes it will grow. And what a carrot it becomes! Also by the author: *A Hole Is to Dig* (p); *The Happy Day; Open House for Butterflies.* Related books: *Harold and the Purple Crayon* (series) by Crockett Johnson.

A CHAIR FOR MY MOTHER
by Vera B. Williams
Greenwillow, 1982
K–3   30 pages
This is the first book in a trilogy of tender picture books about a family of three women: Grandma, Mama, and daughter Rosa (all written in the first person by the child). In this story, they struggle to save their loose change (in a glass jar) in order to buy a chair for the child's mother—something she can collapse into after her waitressing job. In *Something for Me*, the glass jar's contents are to be spent on the child's birthday present. What an important decision for a little girl to make! After much soul-searching, she settles on a used accordion. In *Music, Music for Everyone*, the jar is empty again. With all the loose change going for Grandma's medical expenses now, little Rosa searches for a way to make money and cheer up her grandma. The family radiates determination and love in a way that leaves you wishing they lived next door to you. It might be a good idea to have a fat glass jar ready for change after reading the first book. Also by the author: *Three Days on a River in a Red Canoe.* Related books: *The Giving Tree* (p); *The Witch of Fourth Street* (s); *A Royal Gift* by Marietta Moskin; see also Index to Treasury for the books by Ezra Jack Keats.

CINDERELLA
Retold by John Fowles • Illustrated by Sheila Beckett
Little, Brown, 1976
Gr. 2–5   32 pages
A highly acclaimed writer for adults has skillfully translated Perrault's classic fairy tale. It is accompanied by 25 exquisite drawings by Sheila Beckett.

You will also want to read Trina Schart Hyman's prize-winning version of *Little Red Riding Hood*. Other related books: see listing with *Household Stories of the Brothers Grimm* (p).

CLOUDY WITH A CHANCE OF MEATBALLS
by Judi Barrett • Illustrated by Ron Barrett
Atheneum (both), 1978; 1982
Pre S.–5   28 pages
In the fantasy land of Chewandswallow, the weather changes three times a day (at breakfast, lunch, and supper), supplying all the residents with food out of the sky. But suddenly the weather takes a turn for the worse; instead of normal size meatballs, it rains meatballs the size of basketballs; pancakes and syrup smother the streets. Something must be done! Also by the author: *Animals Should Definitely Not Act Like People; Animals Should Definitely Not Wear Clothing; Benjamin's 365 Birthdays; Old McDonald Had an Apartment House.* Also by the illustrator: *Hi-Yo Fido.* Related books: *The Great Green Turkey Creek Monster* (p); *The Giant Jam Sandwich* by John Lord; *Gregory the Terrible Eater* by Mitchell Sharmat.

THE COMPLETE ADVENTURES OF PETER RABBIT
by Beatrix Potter
Warne, 1982; Puffin, 1984
Tod.–1   96 pages
Here in one volume are the four original tales involving one of the most famous animals of all time—Peter Rabbit. In a vicarious way children identify with his naughty sense of adventure, and then thrill at his narrow escape from the clutches of Mr. McGregor. Much of the success of Beatrix Potter's books is due to her sensitive illustrations as much as to the story line. For this reason I feel the recent editions of *The Tale of Peter Rabbit* illustrated by others fail by comparison. All the Potter books come in a small format, which young children feel very comfortable holding. This combined volume offers the original art in a slightly larger format (8½ × 11). The stories run from uncomplicated—*The Tale of Peter Rabbit*—to complex—*The Tale of Mr. Tod.* Also included are: *The Tale of Benjamin Bunny* and *The Tale of Flopsy Bunnies.*

THE CONTESTS AT COWLICK
by Richard Kennedy • Illustrated by Marc Simont
Little, Brown, 1975
Pre S.–1   48 pages
When outlaws ride into town one day while the sheriff and his men are off fishing, it falls to little Wally to save the town by arranging an ingenious and amusing series of contests with the outlaws. The scruffy outlaws offer the reader-aloud a wonderful opportunity for loud, grouchy voices. Also by the author: *Inside My Feet* (s); *The Blue Stone; Come Again in the Spring.* Re-

lated books: *Henry the Explorer* (p); *How Tom Beat Captain Najork and His Hired Sportsmen* (p); *Nicholas Bentley Stoningpot III* by Ann McGovern.

CORDUROY
by Don Freeman
Viking, 1968; Puffin, 1976
Tod.–2   32 pages
The story of a teddy bear's search through a department store for a friend. His quest ends when a little girl buys him with her piggybank savings. Sequel: *A Pocket for Corduroy*. Also by the author: *Norman the Doorman* (p). Toddlers will enjoy the board books *Corduroy's Day; Corduroy's Party;* and *Corduroy's Toys*. For list of related books, see *Ira Sleeps Over* (p).

THE COUNTRY BUNNY AND THE LITTLE GOLD SHOES
by DuBose Heyward   •   Illustrated by Marjorie Hock
Houghton Mifflin (both), 1939; 1974
Pre S.–3   48 pages
One of the classic holiday stories, this tells of the struggles of a little country bunny to achieve her lifelong dream—to become an Easter Bunny. No one gives her much of a chance, but her persistence and courage carry her not only to her dream but also to the greatest honor a bunny can receive. Related books: *Mr. Rabbit and the Lovely Present* by Charlotte Zolotow.

CRANBERRY THANKSGIVING
by Wende and Harry Devlin
Four Winds, 1971
K–4   30 pages
The first of a series of mystery–adventure tales set on the cranberry bog shores of Cape Cod. A regular cast of young Becky, her grandmother, and a retired old sea captain are supported by a variety of pratfalling villains and sheriffs. If possible, read the series in this order: *Cranberry Thanksgiving; Cranberry Christmas; Cranberry Mystery*.

The Devlins also have done a Halloween picture book series that is excellent for read-aloud: *Old Black Witch; Old Witch and the Polka-Dot Ribbon; Old Witch Rescues Halloween*. Also by the authors: *How Fletcher Was Hatched; The Knobby Boys to the Rescue*.

CROW BOY
by Taro Yashima
Viking, 1955; Puffin, 1976
K–4   38 pages
The story of a shy little schoolboy, ignored or taunted by classmates, who marches to a different and slower drummer. His silent gifts go unnoticed

until a special teacher brings them to the surface, and everyone sees that it is our differences that make life so exciting. Here is a message for every child, parent, and teacher. Also by the author: *The Village Tree*; *Umbrella*; *Momo's Kitten*. Related books on school: *First Grade Takes a Test* and *When Will I Read* both by Miriam Cohen; *Oliver Button Is a Sissy* by Tomie dePaola; *The Other Emily* by Gibbs Davis; *Timothy Goes to School* by Rosemary Wells.

CURIOUS GEORGE
by H. A. Rey
Houghton Mifflin, (both); 1941; 1973
Pre S.–1   48 pages
One of the classic figures in children's books, George is the funny little monkey whose curiosity gets the best of him and wins the hearts of his millions of fans. Also in the series: *Curious George and the Dump Truck*; *Curious George Flies a Kite*; *Curious George Gets a Medal*; *Curious George Goes to the Aquarium*; *Curious George Goes to the Circus*; *Curious George Goes Sledding*; *Curious George Goes to the Hospital*; *Curious George Learns the Alphabet*; *Curious George Rides a Bike*; *Curious George Takes a Job*.

DAWN
by Molly Bang
Morrow, 1983
K–4   30 pages
In this modern adaptation of a Japanese fairy tale ("The Crane Wife"), a shipbuilder marries a mysterious woman who weaves magnificent sails for him. Her only demand is that he never watch her while she weaves. All is well until he breaks his vow. The incorporation of a child and an upbeat ending make this adaptation especially successful. Also by the author: *The Gray Lady and the Strawberry Snatcher*; *Ten, Nine, Eight*; *Tye May and the Magic Brush*; *Wiley and the Hairy Man*. Related books: *The Wreck of the Zephyr* (p); *The Crane Wife* retold by Sumiko Yagawa.

DEEP IN THE FOREST
by Brinton Turkle
Dutton, 1976
Pre S.–2   30 pages
A wordless book reversing the conventional Goldilocks/Three Bears tale. This time the bear cub visits Goldilock's family cabin with hilarious and plausible results. Also by the author: *Thy Friend, Obadiah* (p); *Do Not Open;* for older children, *The Fiddler on High Lonesome*. Related books: *Blueberries for Sal* (p); *The Blueberry Bears* by Eleanor Lapp; *Jamberry* by Bruce Degen; *Picnic* by Emily McCully.

DOCTOR DE SOTO
by William Steig
Farrar, 1982; Scholastic, 1985
Pre S.–3   30 pages
The dentist Dr. De Soto is in a quandary: the sly fox is in pain from a toothache—but foxes eat mice. Should he risk entering that hungry mouth in the name of medicine? Where does trust end and common sense begin? The doctor and his wife solve the problem with the cleverness that has become a trademark of the author. For other books by the author, see Index to Treasury. Related books: *Anna and the Seven Swans* by Maida Silverman; *It's So Nice to Have A Wolf Around the House* by Harry Allard; *Mr. and Mrs. Pig's Evening Out* by Mary Rayner; *Peter and the Wolf* by Charles Mikolaycak; *The Sorcerer's Apprentice* by Wanda Gag. For a listing of picture books on mice, see *Broderick* (p).

DON'T FORGET THE BACON
by Pat Hutchins
Greenwillow, 1976; Puffin, 1978
K–5   32 pages
A humorous tale for every child and adult who has ever been sent to the store to pick up grocery items—only to forget the names of the items along the way. An excellent listening lesson. Other versions of this tale are: *That Noodle-head Epaminondas* by Eve Merriam and *The Cat Who Wore a Pot on Her Head* by Jan Slepian and Ann Seidler.

DO YOU LOVE ME?
by Dick Gackenbach
Clarion, 1975; Dell, 1978
Pre S.–2   46 pages
When young Walter is traumatized by the accidental killing of a hummingbird he tried to capture, his mother eases his pain by showing that not all creatures want us to love and hug them. A simple book about death, love, and our fragile relationship with nature. For other books by the author, see Index to Treasury. Related books: *The Biggest Bear* (p); *The Tenth Good Thing About Barney* (p); *Pelican* by Brian Wildsmith.

EAST OF THE SUN AND
WEST OF THE MOON
by Mercer Mayer
Four Winds, 1980
K–6   48 pages
The trouble with most retellings of classic fairy tales is that they tend to sap the original tale of its strength, leaving the listener with hollow stories. Not so with this retelling and combination of the Grimms' *Frog Prince* and

Norway's *East O' the Sun and West O' the Moon*. The author-illustrator has used the originals only as a seed in bringing forth a magnificent tale of evil, magic, and courage. See Index to Treasury for other Mercer Mayer books.

AN EVENING AT ALFIE'S
by Shirley Hughes
Lothrop, 1985
Pre S.–2   28 pages
This is the classic "babysitter" story, describing the excitement for little Alfie, his baby sister and the babysitter on the night the water pipe burst. (This book and Peter Spier's *Noah's Ark* are a wonderful combination—read *Noah* first.) Other books in the Alfie series: *Alfie Gives a Hand; Alfie Gets in First; Alfie's Feet*. Also by the author/illustrator: *Bathwater's Hot; David and Dog; Noisey; Up and Up* (wordless).

FABLES
by Arnold Lobel
Harper, 1980
Gr. 2–6   42 pages
An award-winning author-artist offers twenty short fables coupled with an equal number of large illustrations, offering both comic and serious commentary on the human condition. Any of these fables is the perfect opening (or closing) note for a school day. If the audience responds to this collection, pick up James Reeves' retold *Fables* from Aesop, Eric Carle's *Twelve Tales from Aesop*, or *Aesop's Fables* illustrated by Heidi Holder. Albert Cullum's *Aesop in the Afternoon*, an excellent teacher's guide to sixty-six fables, shows how easily fables can be made into short plays for the classroom. Also by the author, see listing under *Frog and Toad Are Friends* (p).

FAIR IS FAIR
by Leon Garfield   •   Illustrated by S. D. Schindler
Doubleday, 1983
K–5   28 pages
Two street orphans follow a stray dog into an old English mansion where their meals are mysteriously provided each day. Set in eighteenth-century England in winter, the story brims with secrets, friendship, beautiful language, and dramatic illustrations—topped with a surprise ending. Related books: *Sara Crewe* (s); *A Lion to Guard Us* (s); *Little Tim and the Brave Sea Captain* series (p); *Wilfred the Rat* (p).

FAMILY
by Helen Oxenbury
Wanderer, 1981
Tod.   14 laminated pages

In a 5" × 6" boardbook format, we see a child relating to important items in daily life; in this case members of immediate and extended family labeled only by one word. Other books in the Wanderer (Simon and Schuster) series deal with household toys, animals, eating, bathing, and toilet training under the titles: *Friends*; *Playing*; *Working*. Oxenbury continues the series (this time wordless) with Dial: *Beach Day*; *Good Night, Good Morning*; *Monkey See, Monkey Do*; *Mother's Helper*; *Shopping Trip*. Also by the author: *Tiny Tim* (nursery rhymes). Related books: *Pat the Bunny* (p); *The Early Words Picture Book* and *The First Words Picture Book* both by Bill Gillham; *Mother Goose* by Watty Piper; For other related toddler books, see Index to Treasury for these authors: Dick Bruna; Eric Hill; Barbro Lindgren; Peggy Parish; Peter Spier; Rosemary Wells.

THE FOUNDLING FOX
by Irina Korschunow • Illustrated by Reinhard Michl
Harper & Row, 1984
Pre S.–2   48 pages
The poignant story, told in six very short chapters in a realistic manner, of a young motherless fox and the vixen who finds him whimpering in the woods. She saves him from predators and raises him as one of her own. This, along with *Andy and the Lion* by James Dougherty, is an excellent introduction to the concept of "chapters" in a book. It is also a poignant treatment of adoption.

FREDERICK
by Leo Lionni
Pantheon (both), 1966
Pre S. and up   28 pages
Frederick is a tiny gray field mouse. He is also an allegorical figure representing the poets, artists, and dreamers of the world. While his brothers and sisters gather food against the oncoming winter, Frederick gathers the colors and stories and dreams they will need to sustain their hearts and souls in the winter darkness. Also by the author: *Alexander and the Wind-Up Mouse; The Biggest House in the World; Fish Is Fish; Little Blue and Little Yellow; Pezzetino; Swimmy*. For related books, see listing under *Broderick* (p).

FROG AND TOAD ARE FRIENDS
by Arnold Lobel
Harper (both), 1970; 1979
Pre S.–2   64 pages
Using a simple early-reader vocabulary and fablelike story lines, the author-artist has developed an award-winning series that is a must for young children. Generous helpings of humor and warm personal relationships are the trademarks of the series, each book containing 5 individual stories relating

to childhood. Sequels: *Days with Frog and Toad; Frog and Toad All Year; Frog and Toad Together.* Also by the author: *Fables* (p); *The Great Blueness and Other Predicaments; Mouse Soup; Mouse Tales; Owl at Home; Uncle Elephant.*

THE GIVING TREE
by Shel Silverstein
Harper, 1964
K–4   52 pages
A tender look at friendship, love, and sharing in a simple but unorthodox fashion. Excellent for class discussion about values. Also by the author: *Where the Sidewalk Ends* (po). Related books on giving: *Babushka* (p); *A Chair for My Mother* (p) and *Something for Me* both by Vera B. Williams; *The Silver Pony* (p); *Wilfred the Rat* (p); *McGoogin Moves the Mighty Rock* by Dick Gackenbach; *Mr. Rabbit and the Lovely Present* by Charlotte Zolotow.

GOODNIGHT MOON
by Margaret Wise Brown
Harper (both), 1947; 1977
Tod.–Pre S.   30 pages
A classic tale for very young children on the bedtime ritual, sure to be copied by every child who hears it. Also by the author: *The Important Book; Little Fur Family; Margaret Wise Brown's Wonderful Storybook; The Runaway Bunny; The Sailor Dog; When the Wind Blew.* Related books on bedtime: *Moonlight* (p); *The Napping House* (p); *The Tomorrow Book* (p); *At This Very Minute* by Kathleen Rice Bowers; *Goodnight, Goodnight* and *What Sadie Sang* both by Eve Rice; *Hush Little Baby* by Jeanette Winter; *A Story to Tell* by Dick Bruna; *Sleepy Time* by Gyo Fujikawa; *The Sun's Asleep Behind the Hill* by Mirra Ginsburg; *Ten, Nine, Eight* by Molly Bang. For older children, see *Ira Sleeps Over.*

THE GREAT GREEN TURKEY CREEK MONSTER
by James Flora
Atheneum (both), 1976; 1979
Pre S.–3   32 pages
A mix-up in the seed bin at the general store results in the sprouting of a Great Green Hooligan Vine which wreaks havoc and laughter throughout the town as it grows and grows in a modern "bean stalk" tale. Since the vine is finally subdued by trombone music, one suggestion would be to have a copy of the music of "76 Trombones" from *The Music Man* available to listen to afterwards. Also by the author: *The Day the Cow Sneezed; Grandpa's Ghost Stories; Grandpa's Witched-Up Christmas; Wanda and the Bumbly Wizard.* Related books: *Cloudy With a Chance of Meatballs* (p); *Grasshopper and the Unwise Owl* (s); *The Shrinking of Treehorn* (p); *A Special Trick* (p); *The Boy Who Was Followed Home* by Margaret Mahy; *Jack and the Beanstalk* by

Paul Galdone; *Ralph's Secret Weapon* by Steven Kellogg; *Tattie's River Journey* by Shirley Murphy.

HANS ANDERSEN–HIS CLASSIC FAIRY TALES
Translated by Erik Haugaard   •   Illustrated by Michael Foreman
Doubleday, 1978
K and up   188 pages
This collection of 18 tales taken from Haugaard's *The Complete Fairy Tales and Stories of Hans Christian Andersen* is handsomely illustrated and includes the most popular stories. (For further discussion on the merits of fairy tales, see Chapter 3.)

The following picture books of his individual stories are recommended:
The Emperor's New Clothes, illustrated by Virginia Lee Burton (Houghton, 1949; Scholastic, 1971), 42 pages.
The Fir Tree, illustrated by Nancy Ekholm Burkert (Harper, 1970), 36 pages.
The Little Match Girl, illustrated by Blair Lent (Houghton, 1968), 44 pages.
The Little Mermaid, translated by Eva Le Gallienne, illustrated by Edward Frascino (Harper, 1971), 50 pages.
The Nightingale, translated by Eva Le Gallienne, illustrated by Nancy Ekholm Burket (Harper, 1965), 48 pages.
The Snow Queen, adapted by Naomi Lewis, illustrated by Toma Bogdanovic (Scroll, 1968), 30 pages.
The Steadfast Tin Soldier, illustrated by Thomas DiGrazia (Prentice, 1981), 30 pages.
Thumbelina, translated by Richard and Clara Winston, illustrated by Lisbeth Zwerger (Morrow, 1980), 30 pages.
The Ugly Duckling, retold and illustrated by Lorinda Bryan Cauley (Harcourt [both], 1979), 44 pages.
The Wild Swans, retold by Amy Ehrlich, illustrated by Susan Jeffers (Dial, 1981), 40 pages.

For preschool children being introduced to fairy tales for the first time, see Index to Treasury for Paul Galdone books. For other fairy tale titles, see listing at the end of *Household Stories of the Brothers Grimm* (p).

HARRY AND THE TERRIBLE WHATZIT
by Dick Gackenbach
Clarion (both), 1977; 1984
Pre S.–3   32 pages
When his mother doesn't return immediately from her errand in the cellar, little Harry is positive she's been captured by the monsters he thinks live down there. A gentle lesson in courage and the need to confront our fears before they get out of hand. Also by the author: *Annie and the Mud Monster*; *A Bag Full of Pups*; *Claude the Dog*; *McGoogin Moves the Mighty Rock*; *The Princess and the Pea.* Related books: *Where the Wild Things Are* (p); *The Beast*

in the Bed by Barbara Dillon; *It's Only Arnold* by Brinton Turkle; *Spiders in the Fruit Cellar* by Barbara Joosse; *There's a Nightmare in My Closet* by Mercer Mayer.

HARRY THE DIRTY DOG
by Gene Zion • Illustrated by Margaret B. Graham
Harper (both), 1956; 1976
Tod.–2   28 pages
This little white dog with black spots just might be the most famous dog in all of children's literature. All children identify with Harry—partly for his size, partly for his aversion to soap and water, partly for his escapades. The sentences are simple and expressive but it is the artwork that triumphs in the Harry books. The bold black outline of the characters easily enables very young children to see and understand the progress of the story. Sequels: *Harry and the Lady Next-Door; Harry by the Sea; No Roses for Harry.*

HENRY BEAR'S PARK
by David McPhail
Little, Brown, 1976; Puffin, 1978
Gr. 1–5   48 pages
This is so original, so dramatic, and so beautifully told and illustrated that few children will forget it. When Henry Bear's well-to-do father leaves suddenly on a ballooning adventure, he leaves Henry in charge of his newly purchased park. Henry, feeling the importance of filling in for his father, moves into the park as superintendent and excels in the position until the loneliness for his father begins to wear him down. In one little book, the author has made some poignant observations about the feelings we all have for "special places," the longing for our loved ones when they are away, the sadness when friends disappoint us, and the joy of being loved.

In the sequel, *Stanley: Henry Bear's Friend,* we are introduced to a little raccoon who eventually becomes Henry's assistant at the park. Driven away from his home by bruising brothers, Stanley sets out to seek his fortune. He runs into a con man, ends up in jail, is vindicated in court, finds a job and a friend and eventually his self-confidence. Here are all the charms of the first book but with even more drama in the story line. Also by the author: *Alligators Are Awful and They Have Terrible Manners; Andrew's Bath; Fix-It; Great Cat; Pig Pig Goes to Camp; Pig Pig Grows Up; Pig Pig Rides; Sisters; The Train.* Related books: *My Father's Dragon* (s); *Just Me and My Dad* by Mercer Mayer; *Uncle Elephant* by Arnold Lobel.

HENRY THE EXPLORER
by Mark Taylor • Illustrated by Graham Booth
Atheneum (paperback only), 1976
Pre S.–3   46 pages

Little Henry personifies the need and drive for independence existing in all children. While he climbs mountains, blazes trails, explores jungles, and braves the seas, Henry is Every Child, he is the stuff of which dreams are made. Sequels: *The Case of the Missing Kittens* and *The Case of the Purloined Compass* (two books with Henry's dog, Angus, in a central role); *Henry Explores the Jungle; Henry Explores the Mountains; Henry the Castaway.* Related books: *How Tom Beat Captain Najork and His Hired Sportsmen* (p); *Little Tim and the Brave Sea Captain* (p); *The Wild Baby* (po); *Arnold of the Ducks* by Mordicai Gerstein; *Nicholas Bentley Stoningpot III* by Ann McGovern.

THE HOLE IN THE DIKE
Retold by Norma Green · Illustrated by Eric Carle
Crowell, 1974
Pre S.−2   30 pages
The legend of the brave little Dutch boy who discovered the hole in the dike and plugged it with his finger until help arrived at dawn. A tale that should be in the core curriculum of every school system in the nation. Related books: *The Courage of Sarah Noble* (s); *The Legend of the Bluebonnet* (p); *Little Tim and the Brave Sea Captain* (p); *The Bell Ringer and the Pirates* by Eleanor Coerr; *Hansy's Mermaid* by Trinka Noble.

A HOLE IS TO DIG
by Ruth Krauss · Illustrated by Maurice Sendak
Harper, 1952
Tod.−K   44 pages
A little book of little pictures and definitions for little people. The simplicity of the ink drawings against a plain white background as well as that of the text makes this ideal for toddlers and up. Also by the author: *The Carrot Seed; Open House for Butterflies.* Related books: *The Sesame Street Word Book; The Tomorrow Book* (p); *The Picture in Harold's Room* (series) by Crockett Johnson; *Some Things Go Together* by Charlotte Zolotow.

HOUSEHOLD STORIES OF THE BROTHERS GRIMM
Translated by Lucy Crane · Illustrated by Walter Crane
Dover (paperback only), 1963
K and up   270 pages
This collection of 53 tales contains the Grimms' most popular works in a translation that is easily read aloud and includes more than 100 illustrations. The maturity and listening experience of your children should determine their readiness to handle the subject matter, complexity of plot, and language of these unexpurgated versions. Among the many picture books of tales of the Brothers Grimm are:
The Elves and the Shoemaker, retold by Freya Littledale, illustrated by Brinton Turkle (Four Winds, 1975; Scholastic, 1977), 30 pages.

Hansel and Gretel, translated by Charles Scribner, Jr., illustrated by Adrienne Adams (Scribner [both], 1975; 1978), 28 pages.

King Grisly-Beard, translated by Edgar Taylor, illustrated by Maurice Sendak (Farrar, 1973; Puffin, 1978), 22 pages.

Little Red Riding Hood, retold and illustrated by Trina Schart Hyman (Holiday, 1984), 32 pages.

Rapunzel, retold by Barbara Rogasky, illustrated by Trina Schart Hyman (Holiday, 1982), 32 pages.

Sleeping Beauty, retold and illustrated by Trina Schart Hyman (Little, 1977), 48 pages. See also: *Sleeping Ugly* by Jane Yolen, illustrated by Diane Stanley (Coward, 1981).

Snow White, translated by Randall Jarrell, illustrated by Nancy Ekholm Burkert (Farrar, 1972), 26 pages.

For preschool children being introduced to the fairy tale for the first time, see Index to Treasury for books by Paul Galdone and (K–4) Tomie dePaola, nearly all of which are based on folk/fairy tales. For fairy tale collections, see Anthology section of Treasury. Novels written in the fairy tale/fantasy format are listed under *The Lion, the Witch and the Wardrobe* (n).

THE HOUSE ON EAST 88th STREET
by Bernard Waber
Houghton Mifflin (both), 1962; 1975
Pre S.–3   48 pages
When the Primm family discovers a gigantic crocodile in the bathtub of their new apartment, it signals the beginning of a wonderful picture book series. As soon as the Primms overcome their fright, they see him as your children will—as the most lovable and human of crocodiles. Sequels: *Lyle and the Birthday Party; Lyle Finds His Mother; Lyle, Lyle, Crocodile.* Also by the author: *Ira Sleeps Over* (p). Related book: *The Story of the Dancing Frog* by Quentin Blake.

HOW I HUNTED THE LITTLE FELLOWS
by Boris Zhitkov • Illustrated by Paul O. Zelinsky
Dodd, 1979
Gr. 1–6   48 pages
This is a dramatic and unconventional story that deals with a child's overactive imagination. Forbidden to touch the ship model on his grandmother's mantle, the child begins to imagine there is a tiny crew living aboard the ship. Finally he is so convinced of this that he breaks open the ship to catch them. The unconventional part of the tale is in its ending—it leaves off almost in midair. This edition was translated from the 1930s Russian story by Djemma Bider. The sequel that the author wrote to tie it together was eventually lost. Along with being an excellent book about values, the story offers children the opportunity to imagine what might have happened

in the sequel. Related books: *The Aminal* (p); *The Indian in the Cupboard* (n); *The Island of the Skog* (p); *The Wreck of the Zephyr* (p); *George Shrinks* by William Joyce; *Poor Stainless* by Mary Norton.

HOW TOM BEAT CAPTAIN NAJORK AND HIS HIRED SPORTSMEN
by Russel Hoban   ·   Illustrated by Quentin Blake
Atheneum (both), 1974; 1978
Pre S.−2   32 pages
Dirty-faced little Tom likes to fool around—much to the consternation of his humorless maiden aunt. So she sends for stuffy Captain Najork and his crew to teach the boy a lesson. But the Captain meets his match in wirey Tom. Related books: *The Contests at Cowlick* (p); *Liza Lou and the Yeller Belly Swamp* (p); *Madeline* (p); *Nicholas Bentley Stoningpot III* by Ann McGovern; *Ralph's Secret Weapon* by Steven Kellogg; *Tales for the Perfect Child* by Florence Parry Heide; *When the Wind Changed* by Ruth Park.

I CAN—CAN YOU?
by Peggy Parish
Greenwillow, 1980
Tod.   10 laminated pages
This is one in a series (See and Do Books) that stimulates a baby's language, motor, and social skills through activities suggested by the text. For example, in this book children (multi-ethnic) are pictured touching toes, wiggling fingers, sticking out tongues—and the child is asked if he can do that activity. All the books in the series have the same title, the difference being a "level" number (1–4) on the cover that refers to the child's maturity level. Related books: *The Early Words Picture Book* and *The First Words Picture Book* both by Bill Gillham. For other related toddler books, see the listing of authors at the end of *Family* (p) by Helen Oxenbury.

IF I RAN THE ZOO
by Dr. Seuss
Random (both), 1950; 1980
Pre S.−4   54 pages
Little Gerald McGrew finds the animals in the local zoo pretty boring when compared with the wonderfully zany and exotic creatures that populate the zoo of his imagination. Children love to follow in the wake of Gerald's madcap safari around the world in search of Thwerlls, Chuggs, Gussets, Gherkins, and Seersuckers, species so rare only the words and pen of Dr. Seuss could describe them. Be sure to tell your audience that, in real life, Dr. Seuss's father was the zoo director in Seuss's hometown, Springfield, Massachusetts. Sequel: *If I Ran the Circus*.

Dr. Seuss is the best-selling author of children's books for the most deserving of reasons: children love his books. Whether it is because of the verbal gymnastics or the unbounded imagination evident in his drawings, the affection and excitement between child and book is unmistakable. Though Seuss's "limited vocabulary" books like *The Cat in the Hat* are excellent beginning readers, it is his storybooks that should receive the attention of readers-aloud. These include (in rhyming verse): *I Can Lick 30 Tigers Today and Other Stories; I Had Trouble in Getting to Solla Sollew; On Beyond Zebra; Scrambled Eggs Super;* and *Thidwick, the Big-Hearted Moose*. These five, along with *If I Ran the Zoo* and *If I Ran the Circus,* are now available in large-format paperback.

Other Dr. Suess books which make excellent read-alouds include: *And to Think That I Saw It on Mulberry Street; Bartholomew and the Oobleck; The Butter Battle Book; Did I Ever Tell You How Lucky You Are?; Dr. Seuss's Sleep Book; The 500 Hats of Bartholomew Cubbins; How the Grinch Stole Christmas; Horton Hatches the Egg; Horton Hears a Who; Hunches in Bunches; The King's Stilts; The Lorax; McElligot's Pool; The Shape of Me and Other Stuff; The Sneetches and Other Stories;* and *Yertle the Turtle*.

Dr. Seuss fans will also enjoy Bill Peet books (see Index to Treasury).

IRA SLEEPS OVER
by Bernard Waber
Houghton Mifflin (both), 1972; 1975
K–6   48 pages
This is a warm, sensitive, and funny look at a boy's overnight visit to a friend's house. The tale centers on the child's personal struggle over whether or not to bring along his teddy bear. It makes for lively discussion about individual sleeping habits, peer pressures, and the things we all hold on to—even as grownups. Also by the author: *The House on East 88th Street* (p). Related books on teddy bears, dolls, etc.: *Corduroy* (p); *The Legend of the Bluebonnet* (p); *William's Doll* (p); *David and Dog* by Shirley Hughes; *The Story of Holly and Ivy* by Rumer Godden; *Ghost Doll* by Bruce McMillan; *Good as New* by Barbara Douglas; *The Hand-Me-Down Doll* by Steven Kroll; *I'll Protect You From the Jungle Beasts* by Martha Alexander; *Katharine's Doll* by Elizabeth Enright; *Our Teddies, Ourselves* by Margaret and Douglas Palau; *Theodore* and *Theodore's Rival* both by Edward Ormondroyd.

THE ISLAND OF THE SKOG
by Steven Kellogg
Dial (both), 1973; 1976
Pre S.–2   32 pages
Sailing away from city life, a boatload of mice discover the island of their dreams, only to be pulled up short by the appearance of a fearful monster already dwelling on the island. How imaginations can run away with us and how obstacles can be overcome if we'll just talk with others are central

issues in this tale. Also by the author: *The Mysterious Tadpole* (p); *Can I Keep Him?*; *Paul Bunyan*; *The Mystery Beast of Ostergeest*; *The Mystery of the Flying Pumpkin*; *The Mystery of the Magic Green Ball*; *The Mystery of the Missing Mitten*; *Chicken Little*; *Pinkerton, Behave!*; *Ralph's Secret Weapon*; *A Rose for Pinkerton*; *Tallyho, Pinkerton!*; *Won't Somebody Play with Me?* Related books: *The Aminal* (p); *How I Hunted the Little Fellows* (p); *Nicholas Bentley Stoningpot III* by Ann McGovern.

KATY AND THE BIG SNOW
by Virginia Lee Burton
Houghton Mifflin (both), 1943; 1974
Pre S.–2   40 pages
The modern picture book classic about the brave, untiring tractor whose round-the-clock snowplowing saves the blizzard-bound city of Geoppolis. As much as this is the story of persistence, it is also a lesson in civics as Katy assists the local authorities in pursuing their duties. Also by the author: *The Little House* (p); *Mike Mulligan and His Steam Shovel* (p); *Choo Choo— the Runaway Engine*. Related books: *The Little Engine That Could* (p); *Little Toot* (p); *Anna, Grandpa, and the Big Storm* by Carla Stevens; *Has Winter Come?* by Wendy Watson; *The Little Red Lighthouse and the Great Gray Bridge* by Hildegarde Swift and Lynd Ward; *Over the River and Through the Wood* by Lydia Child, illustrated by Brinton Turkle; *Smokey* by Bill Peet; *The Snowman Who Went for a Walk* by Mira Lobe; *Winter's Coming* by Eve Bunting.

THE LEGEND OF THE BLUEBONNET
Retold by Tomie dePaola
Putnam (both), 1984
Pre S.–4
Here is the legend behind the bluebonnets that blanket the state of Texas— the story of the little Comanche Indian orphan who sacrificed her only doll in order to end the draught that was ravaging her village. Related Indian books: *Where the Buffaloes Begin* (p); *Annie and the Old One* by Miska Miles; *The Good Giants and the Bad Pukwudgies* by Jean Fritz; *Not Just Any Ring* by Danita Haller; *Small Wolf* by Nathaniel Benchley

Tomie dePaola is one of America's most beloved and prolific author/illustrators. His books often treat the theme of the human spirit and are marked with rambunctious humor and warmth. Among his works featuring old legends or retellings: *Big Anthony and the Magic Ring*; *The Clown of God*; *Finn M'Coul: The Giant of Knockmany Hill*; *Francis: the Poor Man of God*; *The Friendly Beasts*; *Georgio's Village*; *Helga's Dowry*; *The Lady of Guadalupe*; *The Legend of Befana*; *Noah and the Ark*; *The Prince of the Dolomites*; *Strega Nona*; *Strega Nona's Magic Lessons*.

His other books include: *The Comic Adventures of Old Mother Hubbard and her Dog; Flicks; The Hunter and the Animals* (wordless); *Michael Bird-Boy; Mother Goose; Oliver Button Is a Sissy; Pancakes for Breakfast* (wordless); *Watch Out for the Chicken Feet in Your Soup; When Everyone Was Fast Asleep.* Two of his books deal with the elderly: *Nana Upstairs & Nana Downstairs* and *Now One Foot, Now the Other.* In addition he has four excellent nonfiction books that blend fact and fun: *The Cloud Book; The Kids' Cat Book; The Popcorn Book; The Quicksand Book.*

LITTLE BEAR
by Else Holmelund Minarik • Illustrated by Maurice Sendak
Harper (both), 1957; 1978
Pre S.–1   54 pages
This series of books uses the simple but important elements of a child's life (clothes, birthdays, playing, and wishing) to weave poignant little stories about a child-bear and his family. The series has won numerous awards and is regarded as a classic in its genre. A former first-grade teacher, the author uses a limited vocabulary at no sacrifice to the flavor of the story. The series, which can be read in any order, includes: *Little Bear; A Kiss for Little Bear; Father Bear Comes Home; Little Bear's Friend; Little Bear's Visit.* Also by the author: *No Fighting, No Biting!* (p); Related books: *Frog and Toad Are Friends* (p); *The Empty Squirrel* by Carol Carrick; *Grandpa Bear* by Bonnie Pryor; *Uncle Elephant* by Arnold Lobel.

THE LITTLE ENGINE THAT COULD
by Watty Piper • Illustrated by George and Doris Hauman
Platt, 1961; Scholastic, 1979
Pre S.–2   36 pages
One of the most famous children's picture books of the twentieth century, this is the 1930 story of the little engine that smiled in the face of an insurmountable task and said, "I'm not very big but I'll do my best, and I think I can—I think I can—I think I can." A lesson in positive thinking, self-image, and persistence. This theme is one of the most recurrent in children's literature and can also be found in the following: *The Carrot Seed* (p); *The Contests at Cowlick* (p); *Katy and the Big Snow* (p); *The Little House* (p); *Little Toot* (p); *Smokey* by Bill Peet; *The Train* by David McPhail; *There's a Train Going by My Window* by Wendy Kesselman.

THE LITTLE HOUSE
by Virginia Lee Burton
Houghton Mifflin (both), 1942; 1978
Pre S.–3   40 pages
This Caldecott Medal winner uses a little turn-of-the-century country house to show the urbanization of America. With each page, the reader/listener becomes the little house and begins to experience the contentment, won-

der, concern, anxiety, and loneliness that the passing seasons and encroaching city bring. Many of today's children who daily experience the anxieties of city life will identify with the little house and her eventual triumph. Great use is made of the passing seasons as a means of describing the passage of time and the text is filled with the repetition of word patterns that provides a poetic tone to the story. Also by the author: *Katy and the Big Snow* (p); *Mike Mulligan and His Steam Shovel* (p). Related books: *The Best Little Town in the World* by Byrd Baylor; *Farewell to Shady Glade* and *Wump World* by Bill Peet; *Tattie's River Journey* by Shirley Murphy; *A Year at Maple Hill Farm* by Alice and Martin Provensen.

LITTLE TIM AND THE BRAVE SEA CAPTAIN
by Edward Ardizzone
Puffin, 1977 (paperback only)
Pre S.–3   48 pages

For more than forty years, Little Tim has enchanted and inspired children on both sides of the Atlantic. Each story provides children with the opportunity to achieve all the heroic tasks they dream about. All the books in the series follow Little Tim and one of his friends on a seafaring adventure filled with peril, during which the child overcomes great odds, and after which returns to the warmth and security of home. They are simple adventure stories—stories that are really impossible anywhere but in these books and in children's imaginations. The *Little Tim* series also includes *Lucy Brown and Mr. Grimes*; *Lucy in Danger*; *Ships's Cook Ginger*; *Tim All Alone*; *Tim and Charlotte**; *Tim and Ginger**; *Tim's Friend Towser**; *Tim in Danger*; *Tim's Last Voyage*; *Tim to the Lighthouse.** (* indicates editions available in hardcover from Oxford University Press).

Although some are now out of print, many of Ardizzone's other books are still available in libraries, including: *Johnny the Clockmaker*; *The Little Girl and the Tiny Doll*; *Nicholas and the Fast-Moving Diesel*; *Paul, the Hero of the Fire*; *Peter the Wanderer*; *Sarah and Simon and No Red Paint*; and *The Wrong Side of the Bed* (wordless).

LITTLE TOOT
by Hardie Gramatky
Putnam (both), 1939; 1978
Pre S.–1   100 (small) pages

There's no boat in American literary history so familiar to American children as this little tugboat and his growing pains as he waits in the watery shadow of a famous father and grandfather. The series can be read in any order after *Little Toot* and includes: *Little Toot on the Grand Canal*; *Little Toot on the Mississippi*; *Little Toot on the Thames*; *Little Toot Through the Golden Gate*. Related books: *The Little Engine That Could* (p); *The Little House* (p).

LIZA LOU AND THE YELLER BELLY SWAMP
by Mercer Mayer
Four Winds, 1976
Gr. 2–5 48 pages
In a style reminiscent of Brer Rabbit, this book tells of a young black girl's adventures in outwitting ghosts, witches, and monsters while crossing the Yeller Belly Swamp on her way to Gramma's house. Related books: *Household Stories of the Brothers Grimm* (Red Riding Hood) (p); *Madeline* (p); *Do Not Open* by Brinton Turkle; *The Gunniwolf* by Wilhelmina Harper.

MADELINE
by Ludwig Bemelmans
Viking, 1939; Puffin, 1977
Pre S.–2 54 pages
This series of five marvelous books is about a daring and irrepressible personality named Madeline and her eleven friends who all live together in a Parisian house. Because of the expressive illustrations and the originality of Madeline, the books are among the favorites of children around the world. The author's use of fast-moving verse, daring adventure, naughtiness, and glowing color keep it a favorite in early grades year after year. The other books in the series are: *Madeline and the Bad Hat; Madeline and the Gypsies; Madeline in London; Madeline's Rescue, Madeline's Christmas.* Related books: *How Tom Beat Captain Najork and His Hired Sportsmen* (p); *Henry the Explorer* (p); *Liza Lou and the Yeller Belly Swamp* (p); *Nice Little Girls* (p).

THE MAGGIE B.
by Irene Haas
Atheneum (both, 1975; 1984)
Pre S.–4 28 pages
One of the most beautiful books published in the 1970s, this is the story of a young girl's wish upon the North Star. Her wish is to sail on a boat of her own. When she wakes in the morning, she and her baby brother are safely aboard the most wonderful boat, filled to overflowing with food, flowers, coziness, and affection. To open the book's pages is to walk in a child's dream world. Related books: *The Sailor Dog* (p); *The Wreck of the Zephyr* (p); *Burt Dow Deep-Water Man* by Robert McCloskey.

MAKE WAY FOR DUCKLINGS
by Robert McCloskey
Viking, 1941; Puffin, 1976
Pre S.–2 62 pages
In this Caldecott Award-winning classic, we follow Mrs. Mallard and her eight ducklings as they make a traffic-stopping walk across Boston to meet

Mr. Mallard on their new island home in the Public Garden. Also by the author: *Blueberries for Sal* (p); *Burt Dow Deep-Water Man*; *Homer Price* (n); *Lentil*; *One Morning in Maine*. Related books: *Are You My Mother?* by P. D. Eastman; *The Story about Ping* by Marjorie Flack.

MAX'S FIRST WORD
by Rosemary Wells
Dial, 1979
Tod.   8 pages
This series of four books is intended to be used by the child as well as read to him or her. For this reason, the books are reinforced and all the pages are laminated to stand up to sticky fingers. Short and colorful, the books deal with those subjects close to all children's hearts: family, toys, clothes, and carriages. The series also includes: *Max's New Suit; Max's Ride; Max's Toys*. For related toddler books, see the listing at the end of *Family* (p) by Helen Oxenbury.

MIKE MULLIGAN AND HIS STEAM SHOVEL
by Virginia Lee Burton
Houghton Mifflin (both), 1939; 1977
K–4   42 pages
A modern classic, this is the heartwarming story of the demise of the steam shovel and how one shovel found a permanent home. Also by the author: *The Emperor's New Clothes*; *Katy and the Big Snow* (p); *The Little House* (p).

MILLIONS OF CATS
by Wanda Gag
Coward, McCann (both), 1928; 1977
Pre S.–2   30 pages
For more than fifty years this tale has enchanted children everywhere. An old man, in search of a cat to cure his loneliness, can't make up his mind which one he likes best and ends up taking a herd of cats home to his wife. Eventually the cats solve the problem themselves. Also by the author: *Gone Is Gone*; *The Sorcerer's Apprentice*. Related books: *The Boy Who Was Followed Home* by Margaret Mahy; *All the Cats in the World* by Sonia Levitin; *Cat and Canary* by Michael Foreman; *A Cat's Tale* by Rikki Cate; *Great Cat* by David McPhail; *The Kid's Cat Book* by Tomie dePaola.

MISS NELSON IS MISSING
by Harry Allard   •   Illustrated by James Marshall
Houghton Mifflin, 1977; Scholastic, 1978
Pre S.–4   32 pages
Poor, sweet Miss Nelson! Kind and beautiful as she is, she cannot control her classroom—the worst behaved children in the school. But when she is

suddenly absent, the children begin to realize what a wonderful teacher they had in Miss Nelson. Her substitute is the wicked-looking, strict Miss Viola Swamp, who works the class incessantly. Wherever has Miss Nelson gone and when will she return? A copy of this book should be in the hand of every elementary-level substitute teacher. Sequels: *Miss Nelson Is Back*; *Miss Nelson Has a Field Day*. Also by the author: *The Stupids Step Out* (p).

MISS RUMPHIUS
by Barbara Cooney
Viking, 1982; Puffin, 1985
Pre S. and up   30 pages
I cannot think of a book with art and prose that match more perfectly, nor a story more poignant than this tale of one woman's personal odyssey through life in search of fulfilling her grandfather's wish that she do something to make the world more beautiful. Her search begins in childhood, continues through world travels, and finally, in old age, she finds fulfillment in the seeds of flowers she spreads throughout her village by the sea. Be sure to have lupine flowers in a vase when you read this book; then try picking through a seed catalog for spring plantings. Also by the author: *Little Brother and Little Sister*; *The Little Juggler*. Related flower/garden stories: *The Legend of the Bluebonnet* (p); *The First Tulips in Holland* by Phyllis Krasilovsky; *The Great Blueness and Other Predicaments* by Arnold Lobel; *The Rainbow Goblins* by Ulde Rico; *The Rose in My Garden* by Anita Lobel; *The String Bean* by Edmond Sechan; *A Tree Is Nice* by Janice M. Udry.

MOONLIGHT
by Jan Ormerod
Lothrop, 1982; Puffin, 1983
Pre S.–K   26 pages
A series of wordless vignettes depicts a child's lingering last hours of the day, from dinner to bedtime, with special emphasis on the interaction between child and parents. A companion wordless book, *Sunshine*, depicts the child's first hours in the morning as the family rushes to get ready for work and school. Also by the author: *Dad's Back*; *Messy Baby*; *101 Things to Do with a Baby*; *Reading*; *Sleeping*. For related bedtime books, see *Goodnight Moon* (p); *The Napping House* (p); *The Tomorrow Book* (p); *A Story to Tell* by Dick Bruna.

MOTHER GOOSE, A TREASURY OF BEST LOVED RHYMES
by Watty Piper   •   Illustrated by Tim and Greg Hildebrandt
Platt, 1972
Tod.–2   66 pages
Of the two dozen nursery rhyme books available today, this volume—with easy-to-view, large-format illustrations that portray present- and olden-day

children in the 102 rhymes—is my favorite for extended use with children. Also recommended: *In a Pumpkin Shell* by Joan Walsh Anglund; *James Marshall's Mother Goose*; *Tiny Tim* by Jill Bennett; *Tomie dePaola's Mother Goose.*

Wallace Tripp's *Granfa' Grig Had a Pig and Other Rhymes Without Reason from Mother Goose* (Little Brown, ⟨both⟩, 1976) is a compilation of rhymes and is aimed at an older age group (K–5). Tripp takes 126 verses, many of which were previously incomprehensible to children, and makes obvious sense of them by sketching them as situation comedies played by Tripp's inimitable animal characters.

For related toddler books, see the listing of authors at the end of *Family* (p).

MY OLD GRANDAD
Oxford, 1984
by Wolf Harranth · Illustrated by C. Oppermann-Dimow
K–3   32 pages
An aging grandfather leaves his farm to come live with family and grandchildren in the city. The move (and old age) proves a challenge for all involved, and its positive and negative aspects are described with tenderness and understatement. Related books on aging: *Miss Rumphius* (p); *Old Mother Witch* (p); *Ella* by Bill Peet; *How Does It Feel to Be Old?* by Norma Farber; *I Know a Lady* by Charlotte Zolotow; *Miss Maggie* by Cynthia Rylant; *Mandy's Grandmother* by Liesel Skorpen; *Now One Foot, Now the Other* by Tomie dePaola; *A Special Trade* by Sally Whittman. For older children: *Grandma Didn't Wave Back* (s); *The Snailman* (n); *Weird Henry Berg* (n).

THE MYSTERIOUS TADPOLE
by Steven Kellogg
Dial (both), 1977; 1979
Pre S.–4   30 pages
When little Louis's uncle in Scotland sent him a tadpole for his birthday, neither of them had any idea how much havoc and fun the pet would cause in Louis's home, classroom, and school swimming pool. The tadpole turns out to be a direct descendant of the Loch Ness Monster (but what a cuddly monster this is!). Don't miss the tucked-away name of the junior high school. For other books by the author, see Index to Treasury. Related books: *The Great Green Turkey Creek Monster* (p); *The Boy Who Was Followed Home* by Margaret Mahy; *Great Cat* by David McPhail; *Patrick's Dinosaur's* by Carol Carrick; *Who Wants a Cheap Rhinoceros?* by Shel Silverstein.

NADIA THE WILLFUL
by Sue Alexander · Illustrated by Lloyd Bloom
Pantheon 1983
Gr. 2–6   48 pages

Unable to cope with his grief at his son's death, an Arab sheik bitterly decrees that none may utter his son's name again. It falls to his willful daughter to convince her father that memories are the only way we can keep the dead alive, a task she accomplishes with great poignancy. Also by the author: *Dear Phoebe; World Famous Muriel*. The following books all relate to the subject of grief and can be useful in helping young children to understand the loss of pets or loved ones: *The Accident* by Carol Carrick (pet); *The Big Red Barn* (p) (mother); *Do You Love Me?* (p) (pet); *Everett Anderson's Goodbye* by Lucille Clifton (father); *My Grandson Lew* by Charlotte Zolotow and *Nana Upstairs & Nana Downstairs* by Tomie dePaola (grandparents); *The Tenth Good Thing About Barney* (p) (pet). For older children, see the listing with *A Taste of Blackberries* (s).

THE NAPPING HOUSE
by Audrey Wood • Illustrated by Don Wood
Harcourt, 1984
Tod.–Pre S.   28 pages
This is one of the cleverest and most beautiful books for children. Its simple tale depicts a cozy bed on which are laid in cumulative rhymes a snoring granny, dreaming child, dozing dog and a host of other sleeping characters until the surprise ending at daybreak. The subtle lighting changes on the double-page illustrations show the gradual passage of time during the night and the clearing of a storm outside. (Cumulative rhymes are among the most powerful vocabulary builders for children.) Also by the author and illustrator: *Quick as a Cricket* (a child's book of similes); *The Big Hungry Bear*; *King Bidgood's in the Bathtub*. Related cumulative rhyme books: *Brown Bear, Brown Bear, What Do You See?* (p); *Ask Mr. Bear* by Marjorie Flack; *Drummer Hoff* by Barbara Emberley; *Mr. Magnolia* by Quentin Blake. Related bedtime books: see *Goodnight Moon* (p).

NICE LITTLE GIRLS
by Elizabeth Levy • Illustrated by Mordicai Gerstein
Delacorte (paperback only), 1978
Pre S.–2   44 pages
Jackie has a problem with her new school: her teacher insists upon stereotyping classroom assignments as "boy" or "girl" jobs. Told with humor and warmth, Jackie's liberated views help the teacher and class to realize that tool boxes and train sets are for *everyone*. The relationship between Jackie and her parents is especially warm and reassuring. Also by the author: *Something Queer at the Library* (series). Related books: *The Courage of Sarah Noble* (s); *Crow Boy* (p); *Free to be You and Me* (a); *Liza Lou and the Yeller Belly Swamp* (p); *Miss Rumphius* (p); *The Story of Ferdinand* (p); *William's Doll* (p); *The Girl Who Would Rather Climb Trees* by Miriam Schlein; *Like Jake and Me* by Mavis Jukes; *Max* by Rachel Isadora; *Need a House? Call Ms. Mouse!*

by George Mendoza; *Oliver Button Is a Sissy* by Tomie dePaola; *Once Upon a Test: Three Light Tales of Love* by Vivian Vande Velde; *Sleeping Ugly* by Jane Yolen; *Sloppy Kisses* by Elizabeth Winthrop; *Tammy and the Gigantic Fish* by Catherine and James Gray; *World Famous Muriel* by Sue Alexander.

NO BATH TONIGHT
by Jane Yolen • Illustrated by Nancy Winslow Parker
Crowell, 1978
Pre S.–2   30 pages
All week Jeremy uses a variety of scrapes and cuts as excuses for not taking a bath. But his cleverness is no match for his grandmother's ingenuity on Sunday. Also by the author: *Sleeping Ugly; The Girl Who Cried Flowers and Other Tales.* Related book: *Andrew's Bath* by David McPhail. Related grandparent books: *My Old Grandad* (p); *What's Under My Bed?* (p); *Coco Can't Wait* by Taro Gomi; *The Crack-of-Dawn Walkers* by Amy Hest; *Good as New* by Barbara Douglass; *Grandpa Bear* by Bonnie Pryor; *Grandma's House* by Elaine Moore; *Hurry Home, Grandma!* by Arielle Noth Olson; *The Littles' Surprise Party* by John Peterson; *Mandy's Grandmother* by Liesel Skorpen; *Now One Foot, Now the Other* by Tomie dePaola.

OLD MOTHER WITCH
by Carol and Donald Carrick
Clarion, 1975
Gr. 1–6   32 pages
A group of boys out trick-or-treating on Halloween decide to tease the cranky old woman who lives on their street—only to find a frightening surprise waiting for them. The old woman has suffered a heart attack and is lying unconscious on the porch. A young boy's brush with near tragedy and the sobering effect it has upon him will reach all children, inspiring a new sensitivity to the elderly in their neighborhoods. Also by the author: see *Sleep Out* (p). For related books on aging, see *My Old Grandad* (p).

PAT THE BUNNY
by Dorothy Kunhardt
Golden, 1962
Tod.   18 pages
This book is intended to actively involve the child's senses—patting a bunny picture that has a piece of furry material attached to it; smelling a scented flower picture; lifting a cloth flap on the page to play peek-a-boo with the boy beneath; turning the pages of the tiny book glued to one of the pages. This is a popular and important favorite of very young children. Sequel: *Pat the Cat* by Dorothy Kunhardt's daughter, Edith. Also by the author: *The Tiny Golden Library Animal Nonsense Stories*, a boxed set of twelve books, each measuring 3" by 2". Related toddler books, see listing at end of *Family* (p).

PETER SPIER'S RAIN
by Peter Spier
Doubleday, 1982
Tod.–1   36 pages

This magnificent wordless book traces the activities of brother and sister through a rainy day and night, inside and outside the house. Spier is a master observer of family and neighborhood life, and his 84 illustrations capture every feeling a child could possibly experience on a rainy day. His holiday book *Peter Spier's Christmas* uses the same successful formula.

Peter Spier's books have a universal appeal. In helping us find beauty in the commonplace or in simplifying the complex, Spier bridges all ages with a variety of perspectives. The 3-year-old looking at the garage scene in *Bored-Nothing to Do!*, where the boys are building a life-size airplane from house scraps, will enjoy the color and fun in the boys' task while a fifth-grade child will see the same page as a dream come true and appreciate the magnitude of the task.

Spier books for all ages: *Bored—Nothing to Do!; Noah's Ark; People; Peter Spier's Christmas; Peter Spier's Rain.*

For toddlers through kindergarten: *Crash! Bang! Boom!; Fast-Slow, High-Low; Gobble, Growl, Grunt.*

Gr. 1–5: *The Cow Who Fell in the Canal* (by Phyllis Krasilovsky); *Erie Canal; Fox Went Out on a Chilly Night; London Bridge Is Falling Down; Oh, Were They Ever Happy; The Star-Spangled Banner.* Because of the minute details of his illustrations, the Spier books are best read to small groups where the art can be appreciated close up.

THE POKY LITTLE PUPPY
by Janette S. Lowrey • Illustrated by Gustaf Tenggren
Golden, 1942
Tod.–K   24 pages

One of the all-time best sellers in the Golden Books mass-market line (forty-three-printings through 1979), here is the puppy-dog version of *Peter Rabbit*. The puppy keeps tripping over his curiosity and ends up late or left out of the dessert line at home. Sequels: *The Poky Little Puppy and the Patchwork Blanket; The Poky Little Puppy Follows His Nose Home; Poky Little Puppy's First Christmas.* Related books: *Sam's Cookie* (p); *Where's Spot?* (p); see Index to Treasury for list of Dick Bruna books.

THE RED BALLOON
by A. Lamorisse
Doubleday (both), 1956; 1978
Pre S.–3   48 pages

The fanciful story of the lonely little boy and the red balloon that follows him everywhere. The tale, told through photographs taken during the filming of the award-winning movie of the same name, is more successful in the large hardcover edition than in the smaller paperback. Related books: *Millions of Cats* (p); *The Boy Who Was Followed Home* by Margaret Mahy; *The Pirate Who Tried to Capture the Moon* by Dennis Haseley; *Stop That Ball* by Mike McClintock.

REGARDS TO THE MAN IN THE MOON
by Ezra Jack Keats
Four Winds, 1981
Tod.−3   32 pages

When the neighborhood children tease Louie about the junk in his back-yard, his father shows him how a little imagination can convert that rub-bish into a spaceship that will take him to the farthest galaxies. The next day, Louie and his friend Susie hurtle through space in their glorified wash-tub and discover that not even gravity can hold back a child's imagination. Related books: *The Aminal* (p); *How I Hunted the Little Fellows* (p); for older readers, *R, My Name is Rosie* (n); *And to Think That I Saw It on Mulberry Street* by Dr. Seuss; *Bored—Nothing to Do!* by Peter Spier; *The Pirate Who Tried to Capture the Moon* by Dennis Haseley.

Children experiencing the joys and discoveries of early childhood will find themselves cast as the central characters in Ezra Jack Keats's books. The settings for his stories are largely inner-city but the emotions are those of all children in all settings; the pride of learning how to whistle, the ex-citement of outwitting older children, the warmth that comes in helping a neighbor. As an author or illustrator, Keats has few peers. His works also include: *Apt. 3; Goggles; Hi, Cat; Jenny's Hat; John Henry; A Letter to Amy; Louie; Maggie and the Pirates; Peter's Chair; Pet Show; The Snowy Day; The Trip; Whistle for Willie.* Ezra Jack Keats fans will enjoy the books of Martha Alexander and Charlotte Zolotow; see Index to Treasury.

THE SAILOR DOG
by Margaret Wise Brown   •   Illustrated by Garth Williams
Golden, 1953
Pre S.−1   28 pages

This is a story about following your dreams and ambitions and realising them through determination. The dog Scupper is set on becoming a sailor and his odyssey leads him to sea, shipwreck, survival on a deserted island, and at last a cozy ship of his own. For other books by the author, see *Good-night Moon* (p). Related books: *Broderick* (p); *Little Tim and the Brave Sea Captain* (p); *Little Toot* (p); *Arnold of the Ducks* by Mordicai Gerstein; *Nicholas Bentley Stoningpot III* by Ann McGovern; *The Pirate Who Tried to Capture the Moon* by Dennis Haseley.

SAM'S COOKIE
by Barbro Lindgren • Illustrated by Eva Eriksson
Morrow, 1982
Tod.   24 pages
This highly successful series deals with childhood needs and the means of achieving them. Much of the success in the formula is due to the easily understood pictures, minimal text, everyday situations touched with the right amount of humor and gentle conflict, and the 6" × 6" format that is so comfortable with toddlers (I only wish the pages were laminated). In this case, Sam's dog wants Sam's cookie, and a tug or war ensues, happily settled by Sam's mother. Also in the series: *Sam's Ball*; *Sam's Bath*; *Sam's Car*; *Sam's Lamp*; *Sam's Teddy Bear*. Related books: *The Early Words Picture Book* and *The First Words Picture Book* both by Bill Gillham; "The Little Critter" series (Golden) by Mercer Mayer. For other related toddler books, see the listing of authors at the end of *Family* (p).

SARAH'S UNICORN
by Bruce and Katherine Coville
Lippincott, 1979
K–2   48 pages
Deep in the forest, Sarah lives happily with her Aunt Meg until the day a spell changes kind-hearted Aunt Meg into cruel-hearted Aunt Meg. Gathering spiders and toads for her aunt one day, Sarah meets a beautiful unicorn that brings sunshine into her life again. Also by Bruce Coville: *Sarah and the Dragon*; *The Monster's Ring* (s); *The Foolish Giant*. Related books: *The Book of Giant Stories* (p); *Liza Lou and the Yeller Belly Swamp* (p); *The Ordinary Princess* (n); *The Dragon of Og* by Rumer Godden.

THE SECRET BIRTHDAY MESSAGE
by Eric Carle
(Out of print, available only through libraries)
Pre S.–2   26 pages
On the night before his birthday, Tim finds a secret message under his pillow, advising him where to find his birthday present. The message leads Tim and the reader through caves, tunnels, and holes. The use of cutout pages to fit the shape of the holes, steps, doors, and caves makes it an exciting journey all the way. Also by the author: *The Very Hungry Caterpillar* (p).

THE SHRINKING OF TREEHORN
by Florence Parry Heide • Illustrated by Edward Gorey
Holiday House, 1971; Dell, 1980
Gr. 4–8   60 pages

When a young boy mentions to his social-climbing parents that he's begun to shrink, he's ignored. When he calls it to the attention of his teachers, his words fall on deaf ears. Day by day he grows smaller and day by day the adults continue to talk around him and his problem. Finally he must solve it himself. All children will recognize themselves here, but various age levels will bring different senses of humor and sympathy to the tale. Sequels: *Treehorn's Treasure*; *Treehorn's Wish*. (The *Shrinking* and *Treasure* books are included in one paperback volume under the Dell title *The Adventures of Treehorn*.) Also by the author: *Tales for the Perfect Child*. Related books: *The Indian in the Cupboard* (n).

THE SILVER PONY
by Lynd Ward
Houghton Mifflin, 1973
Pre S.–4   176 pages
The classic wordless book, this is the heartwarming story of a lonely farm boy and the flights of fancy he uses to escape his isolation. His imaginative trips take place on a winged pony and carry him to distant parts of the world to aid and comfort other lonely children. Also by the author: *The Biggest Bear* (p); *Nic of the Woods*. Illustrated by the author: *My Friend Mac*. Related books: *Henry the Explorer* (p); *The Maggie B.* (p); *Regards to the Man in the Moon* (p); *Up and Up* by Shirley Hughes.

SLEEP OUT
by Carol Carrick   ·   Illustrated by Donald Carrick
Clarion (both), 1973, 1982
K–5   30 pages
Christopher and his dog achieve that one great triumph that all children dream of accomplishing: they sleep out alone in the woods one night. This is the first in a series of six books about Christopher and his family. While the books can be enjoyed separately, they work best when read in sequence after *Sleep Out: Lost in the Storm*—Christopher searches for his lost dog after a long night's storm; *The Accident*—Christopher must come to terms with his grief after his dog is killed; *The Foundling*—Christopher adjusts to the idea of starting life anew after the dog's death; *The Washout*—Christopher and his new dog, Ben, rescue Christopher's stranded mother after a storm; *Ben and the Porcupine*—Christopher and his dog confront a neighborhood nuisance; *Dark and Full of Secrets*—Christopher timidly discovers the wonders of lake snorkeling.

Other Carrick books involving children include: *Old Mother Witch* (p); *The Climb*; *The Empty Squirrel*; *Harald and the Giant Knight*; *The Highest Balloon on the Common*; *Morgan and the Artist*; *Patrick's Dinosaur*; *Paul's Christmas Birthday*; *A Rabbit for Easter*; and two short novels: *Stay Away from Simon!* and *What a Wimp!*

The Carricks also have collaborated on a series of nature picture books for children: *Beach Bird; The Blue Lobster; The Brook; The Clearing in the Forest; The Crocodiles Still Wait; The Dirt Road; Octopus; The Pond; Sand Tiger Shark; The Tree; Two Coyotes.*

SNUFFY
by Dick Bruna
Dick Bruna Books, 1975
Tod.–Pre S.   24 (small) pages

After Mother Goose, one of Dick Bruna's books should be the next read-aloud for infants and toddlers, even preschoolers who are being introduced to books or read aloud to for the first time. These books also make excellent first readers for children just learning to read. *Snuffy* is typical of Bruna's style: a little dog canvasses the neighborhood until he finds a neighbor's lost little girl. Simple drawings, bright colors, easily discernible emotions in an uncomplicated story are the ingredients of Bruna's books, which have sold almost 48 million copies across the world. Among his more than 50 titles are: *Animal Book; The Apple; The Christmas Book; Circus; The Egg; The Fish; I Can Count; I Can Count More; I Can Dress Myself; I Can Read; I Can Read More; I Can Read Difficult Words; The King; I Know About Numbers; Lisa and Lynn; The Little Bird; Miffy; Miffy at the Beach; Miffy at the Playground; Miffy at the Zoo; Miffy Goes Flying; Miffy in the Hospital; Miffy in the Snow; Miffy's Birthday; Miffy's Dream; The Sailor; The School; Snuffy and the Fire; When I'm Big.*

A SPECIAL TRICK
by Mercer Mayer
Dial (both), 1970; 1976
Pre S.–5   32 pages

When the magician's houseboy discovers a dictionary of magic spells while he is dusting one day, he can't resist trying his hand at the art. Before he can say, "Sprittle sprattle, nattle tattle," the room is overrun with slithering tooth-gnashing monsters. Fortunately, little Elroy's spunk is up to the challenge. A story told with great color, imagination, and humor.

Mercer Mayer's books run from simple wordless books to daringly complicated fairy tales. His works are characterized by glowing watercolors and stories with a strong flavor of magic and fantasy.

His wordless books include: *Ah-Choo!; A Boy, a Frog and a Dog* (series); *Bubble, Bubble; Frog Goes to Dinner; Frog on His Own; Frog, Where Are You?; The Great Cat Chase; One Frog Too Many, Two Moral Tales; Two More Moral Tales.*

His picture books for preschoolers to early-elementary grades include: *I Am a Hunter; If I Had; There's a Nightmare in My Closet; Terrible Troll; What Do You Do With a Kangaroo?; You're the Scaredy Cat.*

His books for early-elementary to middle-school grades include: *East of the Sun, West of the Moon* (p); *Liza Lou and the Yeller Belly Swamp* (p); *Mrs. Beggs and the Wizard*; *The Sleeping Beauty*.

In addition, Mayer has been the illustrator for these books written by others: *Beauty and the Beast* (by Marianna Mayer); *Boy, Was I Mad* (by Kathryn Hitte); *The Crack in the Wall and Other Terrible Weird Tales* (by George Mendoza); *Everyone Knows What a Dragon Looks Like* (by Jay Williams); *Good-Bye Kitchen* (by Mildred Kantrowitz); *Outside My Window* (by Liesel M. Skorpen); *A Reward Worth Having* (by Jay Williams).

Many of Mayer's books are available in both hardcover and paperback.

THE STORY OF FERDINAND
by Munro Leaf   ·   Illustrated by Robert Lawson
Viking, 1936; Puffin, 1977
Pre S.–2   68 pages
This world-famous tale of a great Spanish bull who preferred sitting peacefully among the flowers to fighting gloriously in the bullring is one of early childhood's classics. It is illustrated by Robert Lawson in a simple black and white style that further enhances children's comprehension of the story about one of the world's most famous pacifists. Also by the author: *Wee Gillis*. Related books: *The Big Orange Splot* (p); *The Country Bunny and the Little Gold Shoes* (p); *Ira Sleeps Over* (p); *William's Doll* (p); *The Hare and the Tortoise* by Caroline Castle; *Oliver Button Is a Sissy* by Tomie dePaola.

THE STUPIDS STEP OUT
by Harry Allard   ·   Illustrated by James Marshall
Houghton Mifflin (both), 1974; 1977
Gr. 1–4   30 pages
The title alone is enough to intrigue children, and the pictures and text will more than live up to their expectations. The family of Stanley Q. Stupid is aptly named: when their behavior isn't stupid, it is at the very least silly—and children will love them. Because of the need to explore the pictures carefully in search of the humor, small groups are best suited for this read-aloud. Sequels: *The Stupids Die; The Stupids Have a Ball*. Also by the author: *It's So Nice to Have a Wolf Around the House; Miss Nelson Is Missing* (p). Related books: *Amelia Bedelia* (p); *Punnidles* by Bruce McMillan.

SUMMER BUSINESS
by Charles Martin
Greenwillow, 1984
K–3   30 pages
The island children go into business for themselves one summer and the result is the best summer they or their parents could imagine. This book and the others in the series, *Island Winter* and *Island Rescue*, provide an en-

chanting vision of life on an island. Other books that offer broadening views of community life: *The Best Town in the World* (turn-of-the-century life in the Texas hills) by Byrd Baylor; *Town and Country* (pictorial contrasts between city and country living) by Alice and Martin Provensen; *Lobo of the Tasaday* (the true story of a Stone Age boy in the modern world) by John Nance; *When I Was Young in the Mountains* (life in Appalachia coal country) by Cynthia Rylant.

SYLVESTER AND THE MAGIC PEBBLE
by William Steig
Simon & Schuster, 1969; Windmill, 1969
Pre S.–4   30 pages
In this contemporary fairy tale that won the Caldecott Medal, young Sylvester finds a magic pebble that will grant his every wish as long as he holds it in his hand. When a hungry lion approaches, Sylvester wishes himself into a stone. Since stones don't have hands with which to hold pebbles, the pebble drops to the ground and he cannot reach it to wish himself normal again. The subsequent loneliness of Sylvester and his parents is portrayed with deep sensitivity, making all the more real their joy a year later when they are happily reunited. Also by the author: *The Amazing Bone*; *Doctor De Soto* (p); *The Real Thief* (s). Related books: *The Chocolate Touch* (n); *The Maggie B.* (p); *The Whingdingdilly* (p); *Arnold of the Ducks* by Mordicai Gerstein; *The Golden Touch* by Paul Galdone.

THE TENTH GOOD THING ABOUT BARNEY
by Judith Viorst • Illustrated by Erik Blegvad
Atheneum (both), 1971; 1975
K–6   26 pages
One of the simplest and most sensitive treatments of death in modern children's literature. A child and his parents work to cope with the child's sense of loss with the death of his cat, Barney. The boy makes a list of good things about Barney, a list that takes his mind off his grief, a list that becomes a tribute to a devoted friend. This is an affectionate but down-to-earth approach. For a list of related books on the subject of grief, see *Nadia the Willful* (p).

THE THREE LITTLE PIGS
by Paul Galdone
Clarion (both), 1970; 1984
Tod.–1   36 pages
The classic tale of how the clever and industrious member of the pig family outwitted the wicked wolf. Many of the simpler folktales of Joseph Jacobs, the Brothers Grimm, and Hans Christian Andersen have been made into picture books by author-illustrator Paul Galdone. His versions are not meant

as replacements for the originals but merely as introductions to the fairy tale for very young children. Between first and second grades, the child's maturity and listening span should be developed enough to warrant longer, more complicated tales. (See Chapter 3 for a discussion of fairy tales.) Galdone's most popular books include: *Androcles and the Lion; The Bremen Town Musicians; Cinderella; The Frog Prince; The Gingerbread Boy; The Golden Touch; The Greedy Old Fat Man; Henny Penny; The House That Jack Built; The Hungry Fox and the Foxy Duck; Little Red Riding Hood; Old Mother Hubbard and Her Dog; Pandora's Box; The Princess and the Pea; Puss in Boots; Rumpelstiltskin; The Steadfast Tin Soldier; The Teeny-Tiny Woman; Three Aesop Fox Fables; The Three Bears; Three Billy Goats Gruff; The Turtle and the Monkey.* Related book: *The Fairy Tale Treasury* (a).

THY FRIEND, OBADIAH
by Brinton Turkle
Viking, 1969; Puffin, 1982
Pre S.−2   38 pages
This is one in a series of books about a 6-year-old boy and his colonial family on the island of Nantucket. The adventures deal with friendship, honesty, and courage while weaving a subtle history lesson. (Several of the titles may be out of print but can still be found in libraries.) Others in the series include: *The Adventures of Obadiah; Obadiah the Bold; Rachel and Obadiah.* Also by the author: *Deep in the Forest* (wordless); *Do Not Open; Fiddler on High Lonesome; It's Only Arnold;* and the following seasonal books: *Over the River and Through the Wood* (Thanksgiving); *The Elves and the Shoemaker* (Christmas).

TIKKI TIKKI TEMBO
by Arlene Mosel   ·   Illustrated by Blair Lent
Holt, 1968; Scholastic, 1972
Pre S.−3   40 pages
This little picture book tells the amusing legend of how the Chinese people changed from giving their first-born sons enormously long first names and began giving all children short names. Related books: *Crow Boy* (p); *The Emperor and the Kite* by Jane Yolen; *Liang and the Magic Brush* by Demi; *Shen of the Sea* by Arthur Bowie Chrisman (a collection of Chinese folk/fairy tales).

TINTIN IN TIBET
by Hergé
Little, Brown, (paperback only), 1975
Gr. 2−4   62 pages
When you've been in print for more than fifty years, been translated into twenty-two languages and praised in *The Times* of London and New York, you must be special. Tintin is just that. He's the boy-detective who hop-

scotches the globe in pursuit of thieves and smugglers. Loaded with humor, adventure, and marvelous artwork (700 pictures in each issue), Tintin's special appeal for parents who want to assist their child in reading is the fact that each Tintin contains more than 8,000 words. Having heard Tintin read aloud, children will want to obtain his other adventures and read them by themselves, oblivious to the fact that they are reading 8,000 words in the process. Because of the size of the pictures, Tintin is best read aloud to no more than two children at a time. There are more than twenty different adventures in the series, sold primarily in select bookstores. The Tintin series also includes: *The Black Island; The Broken Ear; The Calculus Affair; The Castafiore Emerald; Cigars of the Pharaohs; The Crab with the Golden Claws; Destination Moon; Explorers on the Moon; Flight 714; King Ottokar's Sceptre; Land of Black Gold; Prisoners of the Sun; Red Rackham's Treasure; The Red Sea Sharks; The Secret of the Unicorn; The Seven Crystal Balls; The Shooting Star; Tintin and the Picaros.*

THE TOMORROW BOOK
by Doris Schwerin • Illustrated by Karen Gundersheimer
Pantheon, 1984
Pre S.   32 pages

Few concepts are as difficult or as important for young children to understand as "tomorrow." Beginning simply by showing how tomorrows are born (by going to bed), this charming book describes all the promises that tomorrows bring—new games, new friends, and a new start. An excellent bedtime book—or one to pull out when the day has turned sour and it's time to think about a new beginning. Related books: *Moonlight* (p); *At This Very Minute* by Kathleen Rice Bowers; for older children, the passing of time through the seasons is described in: *Over and Over* and *Summer Is . . .* by Charlotte Zolotow; *The Year at Maple Hill Farm* by Alice and Martin Provensen. For a list of other bedtime books, see *Bedtime for Frances* (p).

TOO MANY BOOKS
by Caroline Feller Bauer • Illustrated by Diane Paterson
Warne, 1984
Pre S.–2   32 pages

A wonderful introduction to the birth of a book-lover, this fanciful story follows Maralou from her infant love of books through learning to read, discovering the library, receiving her first book as a gift and then developing an insatiable love of books that infects the entire town. Also by the author: *My Mom Travels a Lot*. Related books: *Broderick* (p); *Andy and the Lion* by James Dougherty; *Arthur's Prize Reader* by Lillian Hoban; *Fix-It* by David McPhail; *I Can Read* by Dick Bruna; *When Will I Read?* by Miriam Cohen; (for older children) *The Man Who Loved Books* by Jean Fritz.

THE VERY HUNGRY CATERPILLAR
by Eric Carle
Philomel/Putnam, 1969; Puffin, 1984
Tod.−1   38 pages

What an ingenious book! It is, at the same time, a simple, lovely way to teach a child the days of the week, how to count to five, and how a caterpillar becomes a butterfly. First, this is a book to look at—bright, bright pictures. Then it is something whose pages beg to be turned—pages that have little round holes in them made by the hungry little caterpillar. And as the number of holes grow, so does the caterpillar.

In a slightly more complicated book, *The Grouchy Ladybug,* Carle uses pages in odd sizes to show the passage of time and the growth in size of the ladybug's adversaries. In the middle of it all there's a nice little science lesson. Also by the author: *Do You Want to be My Friend?*; *The Mixed-Up Chameleon*; *The Secret Birthday Message.* For a list of related concept books, see *Brian Wildsmith's ABC* (p).

WHAT'S UNDER MY BED?
by James Stevenson
Greenwillow, 1983; Puffin, 1984
Pre S.−2   30 pages

In this ongoing series, Stevenson gives us a most endearing combination: two innocent but slightly worried grandchildren turn again and again for reassurance to their grandfather, who concocts imaginative tales about his childhood that make their worries pale by comparison. They've yet to invent the Superhero who can equal the hilarious heroics and hair-raising escapades of Grandpa as child. Also in the series: *Could Be Worse!*; *Grandpa's Great City Tour*; *The Great Big Especially Beautiful Easter Egg*; *That Dreadful Dog; That Terrible Halloween Night*; *We Can't Sleep*; *Worse Than Willy!* Also by the author: *The Night After Christmas*; *Wilfred the Rat*; *The Wish Card Ran Out*; *The Worst Person in the World.* For slightly longer fantastic tales, see Index to Treasury for James Flora books.

WHEN THE NEW BABY COMES I'M MOVING OUT
by Martha Alexander
Dial (both), 1979; 1981
Pre S.−1   28 pages

Jealousy surfaces for a little boy as he anticipates the arrival of a new baby in the house and that all the attention will be diverted from him. His anger is soothed when his mother tells him the special roles and privileges of big brothers. This is a companion book to *Nobody Asked Me If I Wanted a Baby Sister.*

With her gentle humor, Martha Alexander is especially adept at depicting preschoolers' concerns and their eventual resolution. Her books (most are in paperback) and themes include: *Bobo's Dream* (courage); *I'll Be the Horse If You'll Play With Me* (sibling rivalry); *I'll Protect You from the Jungle Beasts* (nightmares); *Marty McGee's Space Lab, No Girls Allowed* (sex roles); *Maybe a Monster* (anxiety); *Move Over, Twerp* (bullying); *No Ducks in Our Bathtub* (pets); *We Never Get to Do Anything* (stubbornness). In addition, Alexander has a set of four books that deal with a blackboard bear that comes to life in aid of a little boy squabbling with older playmates: *Blackboard Bear; And My Mean Old Mother Will Be Sorry, Blackboard Bear; I Sure Am Glad to See You, Blackboard Bear; We're in Big Trouble, Blackboard Bear.* Martha Alexander fans will enjoy books by Ezra Jack Keats and Charlotte Zolotow (see Index to Treasury).

WHERE THE BUFFALOES BEGIN
by Olaf Baker • Illustrated by Stephen Gammell
Warne (both), 1981; 1983
Gr. 2 and up   46 pages
After hearing the tribal legend of the sacred lake where the buffaloes begin their life, a young Great Plains Indian boy daringly sets off in search of the spot—only to end up in a fearful ride to save his own life and his tribe. For experienced listeners. For related Indian picture books, see *The Legend of the Bluebonnet* (p). Related Indian novels: *The Indian in the Cupboard* (n); *Sing Down the Moon* (n); *Stone Fox* (s); *Wait for Me, Watch for Me, Eula Bee* (n).

WHERE'S SPOT?
by Eric Hill
Putnam, 1980
Tod.−2   20 pages
In looking for her missing puppy, Spot's mother searches every corner and niche of the house. As she peeks into closets and pianos, under beds and rugs, the reader and listeners can imitate her search by lifting page flaps to find an assortment of animals in hiding. The flaps are reinforced and the pages durable enough to be handled by young children. The book is an entertaining introduction to household names, animals, and the concept of "No." Sequels (in order): *Spot's First Walk; Spot's First Christmas; Spot's Birthday Party; Spot Goes To The Beach; Spot Goes To School.* Related books: *Birthday Card, Where Are You?* and *Where's My Easter Egg?* both by Harriet Ziefert; *The Early Words Picture Book* and *The First Words Picture Book* both by Bill Gillham; *Pat the Bunny* (p). For other related toddler books, see the listing of authors at the end of *Family (p).*

WHERE THE WILD THINGS ARE
by Maurice Sendak
Harper (both), 1963; 1984
K−3   28 pages

This is the picture book that changed the course of modern children's literature. Sendak creates here a fantasy about a little boy and the monsters that haunt all children. The fact that youngsters are not the least bit frightened by the story, that they love it as they would an old friend, is a credit to Sendak's insight into children's minds and hearts. It was the 1964 winner of the Caldecott Medal. Actress Tammy Grimes does a magnificent reading of this book, along with selections from other Sendak works, on Caedmon recording No. CP1531, "Where the Wild Things Are and Other Stories." Also by the author: *Higglety Pigglety Pop!; In the Night Kitchen; Maurice Sendak's Really Rosie: Starring the Nutshell Kids;* the Nutshell Library, which includes *Alligators All Around; Chicken Soup with Rice; One Was Johnny; Pierre; Outside Over There; The Sign on Rosie's Door.* Related books: *Andrew's Bath* by David McPhail; *The Bear's Toothache* (p); *Harry and the Terrible Whatzit* (p); *The Beast in the Bed* by Barbara Dillon; *Do Not Open* by Brinton Turkle; *Nicholas Bentley Stoningpot III* by Ann McGovern; *Patrick's Dinosaurs* by Carol Carrick; *There's a Nightmare in My Closet* by Mercer Mayer.

WILFRED THE RAT
by James Stevenson
Greenwillow, 1977; Puffin, 1979
Pre S.–4   30 pages
Quite simply, this is a story about friendship—its joys and sorrows, the crying need in all of us for companionship and affection. Also by the author: *What's Under My Bed?* For other books by the author, see Index to Treasury. Related books: *Fair is Fair* (p); *Frog and Toad Are Friends* (p); *The Giving Tree* (p).

WILLIAM'S DOLL
by Charlotte Zolotow   •   Illustrated by William Pène du Bois
Harper, (both), 1972; 1985
Pre S.–4   32 pages
William's father wants him to play with his basketball or trains; William, to the astonishment of all, wishes he had a doll to play with. "Sissy," say his brother and friends. But William's grandmother says something else— something very important—to William, his father, and his brother. The message is one that all children and their parents should hear. For a list of related books, see *Nice Little Girls* (p); *When the New Baby Comes, I'm Moving Out* (p).

One of the most prolific (more than fifty books since 1944) and successful authors for children, Charlotte Zolotow is also one of the most beloved. She writes quiet little books with quiet simple sentences and her work is always illustrated by the best artists available. Few writers have their finger on the pulse of children's emotions as this author does. You'll have no trouble finding the many Zolotow books in your library—she has almost the entire "Z" shelf to herself. Your personal knowledge of your child's or class's emotional maturity should guide you in your Zolotow selections.

Here is a partial listing of her most popular read-alouds: *Big Sister and Little Sister* (siblings); *Do You Know What I'll Do?* (siblings); *A Father Like That* (fatherless boy); *The Hating Book* (anger, friendship); *Hold My Hand* (friendship); *I Know a Lady* (old age); *If It Weren't For You* (siblings); *If You Listen* (loneliness); *It's Not Fair* (envy); *Janey* (friend moves away); *May I Visit?* (family, future); *Mr. Rabbit and the Lovely Present* (sharing); *My Friend John* (friendship); *My Grandson Lew* (death); *Over and Over* and *Summer Is . . .* (seasons, time); *The Quarreling Book* (family friction); *The Sky Was Blue* (family genealogy); *Someone New* and *But Not Billy* (maturing); *Some Things Go To- gether* (rhymes); *The Storm Book* (electrical storms); *The Summer Night* (bed- time, family); *The Unfriendly Book* (jealousy); *Wake Up and Goodnight* (bed- time); *When the Wind Stops* (environmental questions); *The White Marble* (sharing, friendship).

THE WHINGDINGDILLY
by Bill Peet
Houghton Mifflin (both), 1970; 1982
Pre S.–5   60 pages
Discontented with his life as a dog, Scamp envies all the attention given to his beribboned neighbor—Palomar the wonder horse. But when a back- woods witch changes Scamp into an animal with the feet of an elephant, the neck of a giraffe, the tail of a zebra, and the nose of a rhinoceros, he gets more attention than he bargained for: he ends up a most unhappy cir- cus freak. Happily, all ends well, and tied into the ending is a subtle lesson for both Scamp and his readers: Be yourself! For a list of related books, see *Nice Little Girls* (p).

Bill Peet is one of the most popular of the contemporary author-illustra- tors and his picture books never fail to instruct, stimulate, and amuse chil- dren. Neither the text (often in rhyming verse) nor the art rests in the shadow of the other—they complement each other beautifully. Though never heavy- handed, many of his books have a fablelike quality. Two of his works— *Wump World* and *Farewell to Shady Glade*—were among the first children's books to call attention to the environmental crises during the 1960s. A sampling of his various themes includes: ambition *(Chester the Worldly Pig)*; arrogance *(Big Bad Bruce)*; aging *(Encore for Eleanor)*; conceit *(Ella)*; courage *(Cowardly Clyde)*; environment *(The Knats of Knotty Pine)*; hope *(The Caboose Who Got Loose)*; loyalty *(Jennifer and Josephine)*; mechanization *(Countdown to Christmas)*; peer pressure *(Fly Homer Fly)*; selfishness *(The Ant and the Ele- phant)*; timidity *(Merle the High-Flying Squirrel)*.

Other Bill Peet titles include: *Buford the Little Bighorn; Capyboppy* (short novel); *Cyrus the Unsinkable Sea Serpent; Eli; How Droofus the Dragon Lost His Head; Hubert's Hair-Raising Adventure; Huge Harold; Kermit the Hermit; The*

Kweeks of Kookatumdee; The Luckiest One of All; No Such Things; Pamela Camel; The Pinkish Purplish Bluish Egg; Randy's Dandy Lions; Smokey; The Spooky Tail of Prewitt Peacock.

Bill Peet fans will also enjoy the Dr. Seuss books; see Index to Treasury. Almost half of Peet's books are available in paperback.

WOLF! WOLF!
by Elizabeth and Gerald Rose
Faber, 1984 (paperback only)
Pre S.–2   30 pages
The classic tale of the naughty shepherd boy who cried "wolf!" as a practical joke and found that nobody believed him when he eventually told the truth. Related books: *The Hole in the Dike* (p); *Nobody Listens to Andrew* by Elizabeth Guilfoile; *Sam, Bangs, and Moonshine* by Evaline Ness.

THE WRECK OF THE ZEPHYR
by Chris Van Allsburg
Houghton Mifflin, 1983
K–5   30 pages
No one packs a greater sense of mystery into books than this author/illustrator. Long after you have finished reading his books, their imagery is still rolling around in the mind. In this tale, a boastful young sailor boy is carried by a storm to a land where boats can sail the skies and he is determined to bring the secret of such sailing home with him under the cover of darkness. The question for your listeners: Did he succeed or was he dreaming it all? Equally intriguing are the author's other books: *Ben's Dream* (wordless); *The Garden of Abdul Gusazi; Jumanji; The Mysteries of Harris Burdick* (nearly wordless book and excellent for creative writing classes); *The Polar Express.* Related books: *Dawn* (p); *How I Hunted the Little Fellows* (p); *Grasshopper and the Unwise Owl* (s); *The Maggie B.* (p); *The Red Balloon* (p); *Burt Dow Deep-Water Man* by Robert McCloskey; *Nicholas Bentley Stoningpot III* by Ann McGovern; *Up and Up* by Shirley Hughes.

Short Novels

AMONG THE DOLLS
by William Sleator
Dutton, 1975
Gr. 4–6   70 pages
A spooky psychological thriller about a girl who receives an old doll house for a birthday present, and finds herself drawn into the house and tormented by the very dolls she'd mistreated the day before. A spellbinder.

Also by the author: *Run*. Related books: *The Indian in the Cupboard* (n); *Prisoners at the Kitchen Table* (n); *The Dollhouse Murders* by Betty Wright.

BE A PERFECT PERSON IN JUST THREE DAYS!
by Stephen Manes
Clarion, 1982; Bantam, 1984
Gr. 3–6   76 pages
This is a laughing-aloud book. It is far from great literature but very close to the funny bone. A young boy, tired of bearing the brunt of everyone's taunts, begins a do-it-yourself course in becoming perfect—with hilarious and unpredictable results. Related book: *The Shrinking of Treehorn* (p).

THE BEARS' HOUSE
by Marilyn Sachs
Doubleday, 1971
Gr. 4–6   82 pages
A perfect vehicle for a discussion of values in the classroom, this novel deals with a 10-year-old girl whose mother is ill and can no longer care for the family after the father deserts. The girl decides to tend the family, all the while suffering the taunts of classmates because she sucks her thumb, wears dirty clothes, and smells. To escape, she retreats to the fantasy world she has created in an old doll house in her classroom. The need for greater understanding and patience among classmates is an inherent part of this read-aloud. Related books: *Burnish Me Bright* (s); *J.T.* (s); *R, My Name Is Rosie* (n).

THE BEST CHRISTMAS PAGEANT EVER
by Barbara Robinson
Harper, 1972; Avon, 1973
Gr. 2–6   80 pages
What happens when the worst-behaved family of kids in the town—the ones no mother would think of allowing her kids to play with—comes to Sunday school and muscles into all the parts for the Christmas pageant? The results are zany and heartwarming; a most unusual Christmas story. Related book: *Be a Perfect Person in Just Three Days!* (s).

BURNISH ME BRIGHT
by Julia Cunningham
Dell, 1980
Gr. 4–7   80 pages
A once-famous pantomimist, now retired and living on the edge of poverty, meets an orphaned mute boy who yearns to learn the art of mime. The subsequent sharing between man and boy cuts away the loneliness that enshrouded their lives. Filled with living definitions of love, friendship, and

courage it is also an excellent introduction to the art of pantomime. Sequels: *Far in the Day; The Silent Voice.* Related books: *The Cay* (n); *A Certain Small Shepherd* (s); *Child of the Silent Night* (n); *The Half-A-Moon Inn* (s).

CALL IT COURAGE
by Armstrong Sperry
Macmillan (both), 1940; 1971
Gr. 2–6   94 pages
Set in the South Seas before the traders or missionaries arrived, this story describes the struggle of a boy to overcome his fear of the sea. Finally the taunts of his peers drive him into open confrontation with his fears. A Newbery Award–winning study of fear and courage. Related books: *The Cay* (s); *A Lion to Guard Us* (s).

A CERTAIN SMALL SHEPHERD
by Rebecca Caudill   ·   Illustrated by William Pène du Bois
Holt (both), 1965; 1971
Gr. 2–6   48 pages
A mute child, assigned to the role of a shepherd in the school Christmas pageant, is heartbroken when a blizzard cancels the pageant. However, two visitors during the storm stir the depths of the child's soul and bring the story to a dramatic and touching end. Related books: *Burnish Me Bright* (s); *Child of the Silent Night* (n); *The Half-A-Moon Inn* (s); *My Friend Jacob* by Lucille Clifton; *The Story of Holly and Ivy* by Rumer Godden.

CHOCOLATE FEVER
by Robert K. Smith
Dell (paperback only), 1978
Gr. 1–5   94 pages
Henry Green is a boy who loves chocolate—he's insane over it. He even has chocolate sprinkles on his cereal and chocolate cake for breakfast. He thus becomes a prime candidate to come down with the world's first case of chocolate fever. Zany but with a subtle message on moderation in our eating habits. *Jelly Belly,* also by the author, uses humor and insight to describe the self-image problems of an overweight child. In *Jelly Belly,* as well as in *The War with Grandpa,* Smith paints a candid and powerful picture of the relationship between child and grandparent. Related book: *The Chocolate Touch* (n).

THE COURAGE OF SARAH NOBLE
by Alice Dalgliesh   ·   Illustrated by Leonard Weisgard
Scribner (both), 1954; 1974
K–3   54 pages

At the beginning of the eighteenth century, an 8-year-old girl journeyed many miles from home into the colonial wilderness with her father. With her family's instructions—"Keep up your courage!"—ringing in her ears, she faces the dangers of the dark forest while Father builds their new cabin. Just when she feels she has confronted all her fears, her father asks her to stay in the Indian village while he returns for the rest of the family. Based on a true incident, the story is an excellent introduction to the historical novel in a short form. A similar tale for older children can be found in *The Sign of the Beaver* (n). Also by the author: *Bears on Hemlock Mountain*. Related books on courage: *A Lion to Guard Us* (s); *The Lone Hunt* (n); *Stone Fox* (s); *Wagon Wheels* (s); *The Drinking Gourd* by E. F. Monjo.

DEXTER
by Clyde Robert Bulla
Crowell, 1973
Gr. 2–5   68 pages
One of the best of the author's more than fifty books, this is the story of a promise between two friends—friends who are eventually parted by neighbors and distance but never separated in their hearts. One boy promises to take care of the other's horse until he is able to return. Despite the threats of neighbors and the pains of winter storms, the boy clings to the promise—and to the hope his friend will someday return. For other books by the author, see *A Lion to Guard Us* (s). Related books: *Soup* (s); *Mrs. Fish, Ape, and Me, the Dump Queen* (n); *A Blue-Eyed Daisy* by Cynthia Rylant.

THE FALLEN SPACEMAN
by Lee Harding
Bantam (paperback only), 1982
Gr. 2–5   86 pages
An alien object drops to the earth's surface in view of two young brothers playing in the woods. The Army's efforts to deal with the aliens are complicated when one of the brothers wanders inside the object and encounters an alien child. A dramatic and touching science fiction tale, a rare treat for this age level. Related book: *Science Fiction Tales* (a).

FAMILY SECRETS:
FIVE VERY IMPORTANT STORIES
by Susan Shreve • Illustrated by Richard Cuffari
Knopf, 1979
Gr. 3–7   56 pages
Five stories about a boy and his family as they encounter the death of a pet, the suicide of a neighbor, an aging grandparent, a relative's divorce, and cheating in math class. Five fragile moments in a child's life, written with sensitivity, compassion, and hopefulness. Related books: *My Twin Sister Er-*

ika (s); *Mrs. Fish, Ape, and Me, the Dump Queen* (n); *Secrets of a Small Brother* (po); *A Blue-Eyed Daisy* by Cynthia Rylant.

FRECKLE JUICE
by Judy Blume
Four Winds, 1971; Dell, 1971
Gr. 2–5   32 pages
Andrew wishes he had freckles. Everyone else seems to have them. Thus, when his classmate Sharon sells him a recipe for freckles, he quickly swallows it—much to his stomach's dismay. Class rivalries, peer pressure, mixed with many laughs. Also by the author: *Tales of a Fourth Grade Nothing* (n). Related books: *Toad Food and Measle Soup* and *Lucky Charms and Birthday Wishes* both by Christine McDonnell.

GRANDMA DIDN'T WAVE BACK
by Rose Blue
Franklin Watts, 1972
Gr. 4–6   62 pages
Touching story of a 10-year-old girl who slowly realizes that her grandmother's memory is deteriorating and that she may have to go to a nursing home. The closeness between the child and the grandparent over the years is beautifully described, making the parting all the more touching. Related books: *Stone Fox* (s); *Now One Foot, Now the Other* by Tomie dePaola.

GRASSHOPPER AND THE UNWISE OWL
by Jim Slater
Holt, 1979
Gr. 1–5   88 pages
Here's a bundle of fascinating science lessons wrapped around the adventures of a young boy who is mistakenly reduced to the size of a mouse. Attempting to save his mother from an unscrupulous landlord, the shrunken child encounters a host of threatening animals and insects, each of whom he converts to his aid by capitalizing on their various natural characteristics. Exciting fantasy-adventure with just the right blend of humor. Related books: *The Chocolate Touch* (s); *Hans Andersen—His Classic Fairy Tales* (Thumbelina) (p); *The Indian in the Cupboard* (n); *The Littles* (s); *The Monster's Ring* (s); *The Shrinking of Treehorn* (p); *The Wish Giver* (n).

THE HALF-A-MOON INN
by Paul Fleischman
Harper, 1980; Scholastic, 1982
Gr. 2–6   88 pages
A chilling fantasy-adventure story about a mute boy separated from his mother by a blizzard and later kidnapped by the wicked proprietress of a village

inn. Fast-moving, white-knuckle reading. Also by the author: *The Animal Hedge; The Birthday Tree, Path of the Pale Horse* (n). Related books: *Among the Dolls* (s); *Burnish Me Bright* (s); *A Certain Small Shepherd* (p); *Child of the Silent Night* (n); *The Wish Giver* (n); *Lost in the Devil's Desert* by Gloria Skurzynski.

HELP! I'M A PRISONER IN THE LIBRARY
by Eth Clifford
Houghton Mifflin, 1979; Dell, 1981
Gr. 1–4   106 pages
When their father's car runs out of gas in a blizzard, Mary Rose and Jo-Beth are told to stay in the car while Dad goes for help. The two sisters, however, soon leave in search of a bathroom and end up mysteriously locked into an empty old stone library. Before long, the lights go out, the phone goes dead, and a threatening voice cries out "Off with their heads!" Dreadful moans emanate from the second floor. The dilemmas are all neatly solved when the girls find an old librarian who has fallen and hurt herself on the second floor. Sequels: *The Dastardly Murder of Dirty Pete; Just Tell Me When We're Dead!* Also by the author: *Harvey's Horrible Snake Disaster.* Related books: *Old Mother Witch* (p); *Hurricane* (s); *Day of the Blizzard* by Marietta Moskin.

"HEY, WHAT'S WRONG WITH THIS ONE?"
by Maia Wojciechowska
Harper, 1969
Gr. 3–6   96 pages
The wacky and hilarious adventures of three brothers who tire of their widowed father's reluctance to find a new wife. Taking matters into their own hands, they decide to find one for him. Amid the hilarity, some tender moments. Related books: *Us and Uncle Fraud* (n); *Be a Perfect Person in Just Three Days!* (s).

THE HUNDRED DRESSES
by Eleanor Estes
Harcourt (both), 1944; 1974
Gr. 3–6   78 pages
Wanda Petronski comes from the wrong side of the tracks and is the object of the class jokes until her classmates sadly realize their awful mistake and cruelty. But by then it's too late. Related books: *The Bear's House* (s); *Sara Crewe* (s); *Wild Violets* (n); *What If They Knew?* by Patricia Hermes.

HURRICANE
by Faith McNulty   •   Illustrated by Gail Owens
Harper, 1983
K–3   45 pages

‿ a hurricane approaches his community, a young boy wrestles with the questions that have confronted humankind throughout time: Why such a storm? How to control it? Where does it come from? Why does such violent strength both fascinate and intimidate? Instead of allowing this to become a bland piece of technical writing, the author wraps questions and answers around one family's struggle with Mother Nature and makes an exciting nature story. Divided into four short chapters. Also by the author: *How to Dig a Hole to the Other Side of the World*. Related books on storms: *Anna, Grandpa, and the Big Storm* by Carla Stevens; *Belinda's Hurricane* by Elizabeth Winthrop; *The Cay* by Theodore Taylor; *The Day of the Blizzard* by Marietta Moskin; *Flash, Crash, Rumble and Roll* by Franklin Branley; *A Horse Came Running* by Meindert DeJong.

INSIDE MY FEET: THE STORY OF A GIANT
by Richard Kennedy
Harper, 1979
Gr. 3–5   72 pages
In an age of *Star Wars* and revivals of *King Kong,* it is a rare story that can chill middle-graders, especially a story about a giant. But this tale of a frightened but determined child's battle to rescue his parents from an invisible giant will have children on the edge of their seats. This giant is no pushover—he's mean, conniving, and awesome—yet he carries a heavy heart, burdened with a bitter question: "What became of the child that I was?" Also by the author: *The Blue Stone; The Contests at Cowlick* (p). Related books: *Aladdin* (p); *Among the Dolls* (s); *Giant Kippernose and Other Stories* (a); *The Iron Giant* (s); *The Monster's Ring* (s); *Nightmares* (po); *The Selfish Giant* by Oscar Wilde.

THE IRON GIANT
by Ted Hughes
Harper (both), 1986
K–4   60 pages
The appeal and diversity of this story are such that it has been labeled science fiction, fantasy, a modern fairy tale—take your pick but don't miss it. With suspense dripping from every page, it describes an invincible iron giant—a robot without master—that stalks the land. Suddenly the earth faces a threat far greater than from the giant when an alien creature lands—forcing the iron man into a fight for his life. Related books on magic gone awry: *Aladdin* (p); *The Chocolate Touch* (n); *Cloudy With a Chance of Meatballs* (p); *The Monster's Ring* (s); *The Magic Finger* by Roald Dahl.

JACOB TWO-TWO MEETS THE HOODED FANG
by Mordecai Richler
Knopf, 1975; Bantam, 1977
Gr. 3–5   84 pages

For the crime of insulting a grownup, Jacob is sent to Children's Prison where he must confront the infamous Hooded Fang. A marvelous tongue-in-cheek adventure story, sure to delight all. Related books: *Giant Kippernose and Other Stories* (a); *Grasshopper and the Unwise Owl* (s); *The Monster's Ring* (s).

LAFCADIO, THE LION WHO SHOT BACK
by Shel Silverstein
Harper, 1963
Gr. 2–6   90 pages
Lafcadio decides he isn't satisfied being a lion—he must become a marksman and man-about-town and painter and world traveler and . . . Well, he tries just about everything and anything in hopes of finding happiness. If only he'd try being himself. A witty and thought-provoking book. Also by the author: see listing under *Where the Sidewalk Ends* (po). Related books: see list of picture books under *Nice Little Girls* (p).

A LION TO GUARD US
by Clyde Robert Bulla
Crowell, 1981; Scholastic, 1983
K–4   117 pages
In a simple prose style that is rich in character and drama, one of America's most noted writers for children gives us a poignant tale of the founding fathers of the Jamestown colony and the families they left behind in England. Here we see a plucky heroine named Amanda and her determination to hold fast to her brother and sister despite the grim agonies of her mother's death, poverty, and shipwreck—all while she clings to the dream that someday she will find the father who left them all behind. Few authors can write so intelligently and movingly for so young an audience as can Bulla. In another historical piece, *Charlie's House,* the author provides us with another New World face—this time a dreamy English boy turned out by his family and eventually indentured to Colonial farmers around 1750. Though sometimes told with grim realism, Charlie is a moving tribute to youthful determination and courage. Also by the author: *Dexter* (s); *Shoeshine Girl* (s); *The Wish at the Top; Daniel's Duck; John Billington, Friend of Squanto; Marco Moonlight; Squanto, Friend of the Pilgrims; Sword in the Tree.* Related books: *The Courage of Sarah Noble* (s); *The Lone Hunt* (n); *The Sign of the Beaver* (n); *Wagon Wheels* (p).

THE LITTLES
by John Peterson
Scholastic (paperback only), 1970
Gr. 1–4   80 pages
Children have always been fascinated with the idea of "little people"—from leprechauns to Lilliputians, from Thumbelina to hobbits. Unfortunately,

much of the famous fantasy literature is often too sophisticated for reading aloud to young children. The Littles series is the exception—short novels that provide fast-paced reading. While not great literature, they serve as excellent introductions to the notion of "chapters" in books, and are ideal springboards to more complicated literature.

The series centers on a colony of six-inch people who live inside the walls of the Bigg family's home. Their dramatic escapades with gigantic mice, cats, gliders, and telephones, while keeping their existence a secret, are a stimulant for reading appetites.

The Littles series also includes: *The Littles and the Big Storm; The Littles and Their Friends* (a guidebook to the series, complete with maps and anecdotes); *The Littles and the Trash Tinnies; The Littles Go to School; The Littles Have a Wedding; The Littles' Surprise Party; The Littles to the Rescue; Tom Little's Great Halloween Scare*. Related books: *Grasshopper and the Unwise Owl* (s); *The Indian in the Cupboard* (n); *Poor Stainless* by Mary Norton; *Tom Thumb* by Charles Perrault (illustrated by Linda Postma); *Thumbelina* by Hans Christian Andersen (illustrated by Susan Jeffers); *George Shrinks* by William Joyce.

THE LUCKY STONE
by Lucille Clifton • Illustrated by Dale Payson
Delacorte, 1979
Gr. 2–6   62 pages
A young black girl narrates the dramatic tale of how a tiny stone has brought luck to four generations of young black women, dating back to the time of slavery. Also by the author: *The Boy Who Didn't Believe in Spring; My Friend Jacob*. Related books: *Roll of Thunder, Hear My Cry* (n); *The Stories Julian Tells* (s); *Sylvester and the Magic Pebble* (p); *Wagon Wheels* (s).

THE MONSTER'S RING
by Bruce Coville
Pantheon, 1982
Gr. 2–4   87 pages
Just the thing for Halloween reading, this is a Dr. Jekyll/Mr. Hyde story of timid little Russell and the magic ring he buys that can turn him into a monster—not a make-believe monster but one with hairy hands, fangs and claws, one that roams the night, one that will make short order of Eddie the bully, and one that will bring out the worst in Russell. An exciting fantasy of magic gone awry. Also by the author: *Sarah's Unicorn* (p). Related books: *Among the Dolls* (s); *Grasshopper and the Unwise Owl* (s); *The Indian in the Cupboard* (n); *Black and Blue Magic* by Zilpha Keatley Snyder.

MY FATHER'S DRAGON
by Ruth S. Gannett
Random, 1948; Harper, 1985
K–2   78 pages
Here is a three-volume series bursting with fantasy, hair-raising escapes, and evil creatures. The tone is dramatic enough to be exciting for even mature preschoolers but not enough to frighten them. The narrator relates the tales as adventures that happened to his father when he was a boy. This is an excellent transition series for introducing children to longer stories with fewer pictures. The series, in order, also includes: *Elmer and the Dragon; The Dragons of Blueland.* Related books: *The Reluctant Dragon* (s); *The Knight and the Dragon* by Tomie dePaola.

MY TWIN SISTER ERIKA
by Ilse-Margaret Vogel
Harper, 1976
Gr. 1–4   54 pages
One in a series of books about a young German girl named Inge, this is a quiet little story (five chapters) about the relationship between two twin sisters as seen through the eyes of one, Inge. But like the others in the series, the quiet brevity belies its remarkable power. In this book, the sisters struggle to establish their separate identities through relationships, toys, and secrets. With those identities beginning to blossom, one of the two dies suddenly. The death is handled sensitively, with little or no melodrama, and the author allows plenty of room for us to watch as Inge works through her feelings of loss and anxiety, discovers a new role for herself in her mother's life, and continues her journey. In *My Summer Brother,* she encounters (at age 9) her first infatuation—the 20-year-old boy next door. *Tikhon,* which at 110 pages is the longest book, describes her mixed emotions when her parents secretly harbor a lonely Russian soldier in their basement. As a perfect introduction to all the Inge books, I would suggest *The Rainbow Dress and Other Tollush Tales,* four simple tales that center on a little girl and her widowed mother.

OWLS IN THE FAMILY
by Farley Mowat
Little, Brown, 1961; Bantam, 1981
Gr. 2–6   108 pages
No child should miss this experience of reliving with the author his rollicking boyhood on the Saskatchewan prairie, raising dogs, gophers, rats, snakes, pigeons, and—most dramatically of all—owls. It is an era we will never see again; the next best thing is to bask in it secondhand through this piece of nostalgia, filled with childhood's laughter and adventure. Also

by the author: *Lost in the Barrens*. Related books: *Gentle Ben* (n); *My Side of the Mountain* (n); *Storm Boy* (s); *Capyboppy* by Bill Peet.

THE REAL THIEF
by William Steig
Farrar (both), 1973; 1985
Gr. 3–5   58 pages
The author uses animals here (as he does in most of his books) to act out a story of theft, guilt, friendship, and pride. Standing up and admitting our mistakes is dealt with here in a touching manner. For experienced listeners. Also by the author: *Dr. De Soto* (p); *Sylvester and the Magic Pebble* (p). Related books: *The Adventures of Pinocchio* (n); *The Bad Times of Irma Baumlein* (n); *Mandy* (n); *Terpin* (s).

THE RELUCTANT DRAGON
by Kenneth Grahame   •   Illustrated by Ernest H. Shepard
Holiday House, 1953
Gr. 3–5   54 pages
The author of the classic *Wind in the Willows* offers us here a simple tale: simple in size (just an oversized short story); and simple in scope (a dragon, a boy, and a knight). But for all its simplicity, it is deep in charm. The dragon is not a devouring dragon but a reluctant dragon who wants nothing to do with violence. The boy is something of a local scholar, well versed in dragon lore and torn mightily between his desire to view a battle between the dragon and the knight and his desire to protect his friend the dragon. And the knight—he's no simple knight at all. He's the one and only St. George the Dragon Killer. This 1938 story is a charming introduction to a legendary time and place. For experienced listeners. Related books: *Saint George and the Dragon* by Margaret Hodges; *The Story of Ferdinand* (p); *Weird Henry Berg* (n); *The Dragon of Og* by Rumer Godden; *Everyone Knows What a Dragon Looks Like* by Jay Williams; *Sir Gawain and the Loathly lady* retold by Selina Hastings.

SARA CREWE
by Frances Hodgson Burnett
Putnam, 1981
Gr. 3–6   79 pages
This tale, as powerful today as it was nearly one hundred years ago when it was written, is the classic story of the star boarder at Miss Minchin's exclusive London boarding school who is suddenly orphaned and becomes a ward of the cruel headmistress. Now friendless, penniless, and banished to the attic as a servant, Sara holds fast to her courage and dreams—until at last she finds a friend and deliverance in a heart-warming surprise ending. For experienced listeners. *A Little Princess* is an expanded version of this

story. Also by the author: *The Secret Garden* (n); *Little Lord Fauntleroy*. Related books: *Mrs. Fish, Ape, and Me, the Dump Queen* (n); *Peppermints in the Parlor* (n); *Wild Violets* (s).

SHOESHINE GIRL
by Clyde Robert Bulla
Crowell, 1975; Scholastic, 1977
Gr. 2–4   84 pages
A spoiled and greedy little girl learns something about life, money, and friendship when she becomes a shoeshine girl. For other books by the author, see *A Lion to Guard Us* (s). Related books: *Mrs. Fish, Ape, and Me, the Dump Queen* (n); *Sara Crewe* (s).

SOUP
by Robert Newton Peck
Knopf, 1974; Dell, 1979
Gr. 4–6   96 pages
Two Vermont pals share a genius for getting themselves into trouble. The stories are set in the rural 1930s when life was simpler and the days were longer. But the need for a best friend was just as great then as now. Sequels: *Soup and Me; Soup for President; Soup on Wheels; Soup's Drum; Soup's Goat.* Also by the author: for older children, *A Day No Pigs Would Die* (n). Related books: *Dexter* (s); *Homer Price* (n); *Ida Early Comes Over the Mountain* (n); *Me and Caleb* (n); *Owls in the Family* (s); *Tramp Steamer and the Silver Bullet* by Jeffrey Kelly.

STONE FOX
by John R. Gardiner
Crowell, 1980; Harper, 1983
Gr. 1–7   96 pages
Here is a story that, like its 10-year-old hero, never stands still. It is filled to the brim with action and determination, the love of a child for his grandfather, and the loyalty of a great dog for his young master. Based on a Rocky Mountain legend, the story describes the valiant efforts of young Willy to save his ailing grandfather's farm by attempting to win the purse in a local bobsled race. The figure of Stone Fox, the towering favorite for the race, is an unusual departure from the Indian stereotype in children's literature. Pulsing with action, emotion, and originality. Also by the author: *Top Secret*. Related books: *Storm Boy* (s); *Where the Red Fern Grows* (n).

THE STORIES JULIAN TELLS
by Ann Cameron
Pantheon, 1981
Gr. K–3   72 pages

The author takes six short stories involving little Julian and his family and weaves them into a fabric that glows with the mischief, magic, and imagination of childhood. Though centered on commonplace subjects like desserts, gardens, loose teeth, and new neighbors, these stories of family life are written in an uncommon way that will both amuse and touch young listeners.

Don't miss the opportunity to incorporate related activities into these readings: everyone can enjoy pudding while listening to the dessert story, or make pudding afterwards; order seeds from a catalog or plant a garden after the garden story; measure everyone's height after the birthday fig tree story. Related books: *Free to Be You and Me* (a); *Liza Lou and the Yeller Belly Swamp* (p); *The Witch of Fourth Street* (s).

STORM BOY
by Colin Thiele • Illustrated by John Schoenherr
Harper, 1978
Gr. 3–6   64 pages
The story of an Australian hermit and his son who live an idyllic life in a shack by the sea. It is also the story of the loyal little pelican they adopt, train, and lose to thoughtless hunters. There is a haunting quality to the story that will have you licking your lips to taste the salt and wiping your eyes to clear the tears. Also by the author: *Fire in the Stone.* Related books: *Gentle Ben* (n); *My Side of the Mountain* (n); *Stone Fox* (s); *Capyboppy* by Bill Peet; *The Day of the Muskie* by Patricia Welch.

A TASTE OF BLACKBERRIES
by Doris B. Smith • Illustrated by Charles Robinson
Crowell, 1973; Scholastic, 1976
Gr. 4–7   52 pages
One of the first of contemporary authors to look at death from the child's point of view, Ms. Smith allows us to follow the narrator's emotions as he comes to terms with the death of his best friend, who died as a result of an allergic reaction to bee stings. The sensitivity with which the attendant sorrow and guilt are treated makes this an outstanding book. It blazed the way for many others which quickly followed, but few have approached the place of honor that this one holds. Eight short chapters. For a list of related picture books, see *Nadia the Willful* (p); for older children: *My Twin Sister Erika* (s); *Storm Boy* (s); *Tuck Everasting* (n); *Where the Red Fern Grows* (p); *Dead Birds Singing* by Mark Talbert; *The Magic Moth* by Virginia Lee.

TERPIN
by Tor Seidler
Farrar, Straus and Giroux, 1982
Gr. 5 and up   90 pages

Terpin, an easygoing, popular schoolboy, meets a disconsolate stranger and upon hearing the man's sad tale, the boy tells his own story, more tragic than the man's. Terpin's, however, is a lie, meant to make the stranger's story less tragic by comparison. Later the boy finds that his plan backfired and the man, so depressed by the story, has committed suicide. Resolved never to lie again—no matter how insignificantly—the boy soon finds himself ostracized at school and home because of his unflagging candor. The book covers his path from schoolboy to Supreme Court Justice and provides us with a disturbing figure that will raise many questions about values and goals. Reading a brief description of the life of Socrates will add an important dimension to this story. Related book: *Rain of Fire* (n).

TWENTY AND TEN
by Claire H. Bishop
Viking, 1952; Puffin, 1978
Gr. 3–6   76 pages
Set in occupied France during World War II, this book depicts the courage and ingenuity of twenty fifth-graders in hiding ten Jewish refugee children. The story is filled with high drama and history. Adult readers might give a brief explanation of the ration card system—both as a control system in peacetime (gas rationing) and wartime (food)—before reading the novel to children. Related books: *Lupita Manana* (n); *North to Freedom* (n); *Sing Down the Moon* (n); *The Drinking Gourd* by E. F. Monjo; *The Golem* by Isaac Bashevis Singer; *Snow Treasure* by Marie McSwigan.

THE VELVETEEN RABBIT
by Margery Williams • Illustrated by David Jorgensen
Knopf, 1985
Gr. 2–7   48 pages
The classic tale of how the long-loved nursery toy rabbit becomes real through the love of a little boy. Because of the sophisticated point of view and writing, older audiences (especially children who have bid good-bye to stuffed animals) tend to appreciate this tale more than younger ones. This edition comes with an excellent audio cassette with Meryl Streep narrating. For a related tale, see *The Story of Holly and Ivy* by Rumer Godden.

WAGON WHEELS
by Barbara Brenner • Illustrated by Don Bolognese
Harper (both), 1978; 1984
Pre S.–3   64 small pages
In this easy-reader three young black brothers follow a map to their father's homestead on the Western plains. Based on a real incident, the family braves storms, fires, and starvation to achieve their dream. Another black family's

travels are depicted in *The Drinking Gourd* by E. F. Monjo, a story of the underground railroad. Related pioneer books: *The Courage of Sarah Noble* (s); *A Lion to Guard Us* (s); *The Lone Hunt* (n); *The Lucky Stone* (s); *Charlie's House* by Clyde Robert Bulla.

WARTON AND MORTON
by Russell Erickson · Illustrated by Lawrence Di Fiori
Morrow, 1976; Dell, 1977
Gr. 1–4   60 pages
Combining adventure, brotherhood, and a sense of humor, here is a series of books that children will cherish. Two domesticated brother toads, Morton and Warton, display very different approaches to life and adventure. In all the stories there is the recurrent theme of adventure and facing adversity with a sense of courage, along with the warming bonds of brotherhood. The series also includes: *A Toad for Tuesday; Warton and the Castaways; Warton and the King of the Skies; Warton and the Traders; Warton's Christmas Eve Adventure.* Related books: *Charlotte's Web* (n); *Mrs. Frisby and the Rats of NIMH* (n); *Pearl's Promise* (n).

WILD VIOLETS
by Phyllis Green
Dell, 1980 (paperback only)
Gr. 3–6   104 pages
While the rags-to-riches, riches-to-rags theme may not be new to children's literature, it is hard to imagine it being done any better than this little story. Cornelia is the richest, prettiest, and most popular girl in her fourth-grade class. Ruthie is the homeliest, poorest, and least popular. Fate draws them together in friendship and then, through Cornelia's father's illness and Ruthie's father's good fortune, their roles are reversed. Also by the author: *Grandmother Orphan; Ice River.* Related books: *The Hundred Dresses* (s); *Mrs. Fish, Ape, and Me, the Dump Queen* (n); *The Secret Garden* (n); *Sara Crewe* (s); *What If They Knew* by Patricia Hermes.

THE WITCH OF FOURTH STREET
by Myron Levoy
Harper (paperback only), 1972
Gr. 2–5   110 pages
What a glorious collection of read-aloud short stories! Both its readability and subject matter make it must reading in every classroom and home. All the stories are set among the tenements of New York's Lower East Side during the early 1900s and deal with the daily crises, hopes, fears, laughter, and customs of a neighborhood melting pot of Russian, Polish, Irish, Italian, German, Protestant, Catholic, and Jewish families. Eight stories in all, approximately 13 pages each. Related books: *A Chair for My Mother* (p)

(series); *Ida Early Comes Over the Mountain* (n); *In the Year of the Boar and Jackie Robinson* (n); *Ike and Mama and the Once-in-a-Lifetime Movie* by Carol Snyder.

THE WONDERFUL STORY OF HENRY SUGAR & SIX MORE
by Roald Dahl
Knopf, 1977; Bantam, 1979
Gr. 4–7   226 pages
Here is a seven-story collection by Roald Dahl for experienced listeners. Two stories—"Lucky Break" and "A Piece of Cake"—are not good read-alouds. However, the other five pieces are excellent, especially the title story, one of the most imaginative tales I've ever read to myself or to a child. Other books by Roald Dahl, see *James and the Giant Peach* (n).

Novels

THE ADVENTURES OF PINOCCHIO
by Carlo Collodi
Macmillan, 1963; Scholastic, 1978
Gr. 1–5   252 pages
Unfortunately, whatever familiarity the modern child may have with this 1892 classic most often comes from having seen it emasculated in the movie version. Treat your children to the real version of the poor woodcarver's puppet who faces all the temptations of childhood, succumbs to most, learns from his follies, and gains his boyhood by selflessly giving of himself for his friends. The original is divided into 36 chapters, most as short as 2 pages. A well-condensed retelling has been done for younger children by Marianna Mayer in a Four Winds edition. Related books: *The Bad Times of Irma Baumlein* (n); *Mandy* (n); *The Real Thief* (s).

AND NOBODY KNEW THEY WERE THERE
by Otto Salassi
Greenwillow, 1984
Gr. 4–8   179 pages
As a publicity stunt, a demonstration squad of Marines disappears from a Houston fairground. With the news media and military officials debating their whereabouts, the nine men plan to walk 450 miles in twenty-six days and suddenly show up for a Fourth of July celebration in Mississippi. Their route is a nervy one—directly through Louisiana and Texas towns, farms, and woods, always under the cover of darkness. What they don't figure on is being discovered by two irrepressible 13-year-old boys, who quickly join the troop and prove themselves a hardy match for the Marines. Set up a

map of the area and plot the journey as you read this one. Related books: *Good Old Boy* (n); *Me and Caleb* (n); *Soup* (s).

THE BAD TIMES OF IRMA BAUMLEIN
by Carol Ryrie Brink
Macmillan (both), 1972; 1974
Gr. 3–6   134 pages
Irma, the new girl in school, tells a lie to impress her classmates, and before she knows it the lie steamrolls out of control. A witty and perceptive novel on truth, peer pressure, and friendship. Related books: *The Adventures of Pinocchio* (n); *Mandy* (n); *Rain of Fire* (n); *The Real Thief* (s); *Wild Violets* (s).

BAMBI
by Felix Salten
Grossett, 1969; Archway, 1982
Gr. 2–5   191 pages
Don't be misled by the Disney version. The forest life that sprang from the pen of Felix Salten is a far larger and deeper creation than the film. Against the backdrop of wonder, majesty, and mystery that is the forest, we focus on the birth of a roe deer, his subsequent maturity, and the eventual arrival of danger—in the form of man. One of the great animal stories of all time. Sequel: *Bambi's Children*. Related books: *Charlotte's Web* (n); *Pearl's Promise* (n); *Gentle Ben* (n); *The Midnight Fox* (n); *Mrs. Frisby and the Rats of NIMH* (n); *Storm Boy* (s); *The Faber Book of Animal Stories* by Johnny Morris.

THE BLACK STALLION
by Walter Farley
Random (both), 1944; 1977
Gr. 2–6   188 pages
When Walter Farley began writing this book as a Brooklyn high-school student, he could never have dreamed he was creating what *The New York Times* subsequently called "the most famous fictional horse of the century." He would go on to write more than fifteen sequels and see the stallion portrayed in a widely acclaimed motion picture. *The Black Stallion* is a novel with all the qualities of a thoroughbred—fast-paced, sleek in line, strong in character, dramatic in its turns. Among the sequels: *Black Stallion and Satan; Black Stallion Mystery; Black Stallion Returns*. Equally successful is Marguerite Henry's Newbery Award–winning *King of the Wind*, the true story of an Arabian stallion that rose from cart horse to siring the world's greatest thoroughbreds. Related books: *A Horse Came Running* by Meindert DeJong; *The Winged Colt of Casa Mia* by Betsy Byars.

BRIDGE TO TERABITHIA
by Katherine Paterson
Crowell, 1977; Avon, 1979
Gr. 4–7   128 pages
Few novels for children have dealt with so many emotions and issues so well: sports, school, peers, friendship, death, guilt, art, and family. A Newbery Award winner, this book deserves to be read or heard by everyone. Also by the author: *The Great Gilly Hopkins*. Related books: *A Day No Pigs Would Die* (n); *My Twin Sister Erika* (s); *R, My Name is Rosie* (n).

CADDIE WOODLAWN
by Carol Ryrie Brink
Macmillan (both), 1935, 1970; 1973
Gr. 4–6   286 pages
You take *The Little House on the Prairie;* I'll take *Caddie Woodlawn*. Ten times over, I'll take this tomboy of the 1860s with her pranks, her daring visits to Indian camps, her one-room schoolhouse fights and her wonderfully believable family. Try to pick up the 1973 revised edition with Trina Schart Hyman's sensitive illustrations. For experienced listeners. Sequel: *Magical Melons*. For an interesting comparative study, see *Introducing Shirley Braverman* (n). Related book: *Wait for Me, Watch for Me, Eula Bee* (n).

THE CALL OF THE WILD
by Jack London
Grosset, 1965; Bantam, 1969; Scholastic, 1970; Penguin, 1981
Gr. 6 and up   126 pages
This 1903 dog story, set amidst the rush for gold in the Klondike, depicts the savagery and tenderness between man and his environment in unforgettable terms. For experienced listeners. Read pages 10–32 in Irving Stone's biography *Jack London, Sailor on Horseback* for a portrait of London's deprived childhood and eventual awakening to books and writing. Also by the author: *White Fang*. Related books: *Best Tales of the Yukon* by Robert W. Service; *Lassie Come Home* (n); *Kavik the Wolf Dog* by Walt Morey; *Lost in the Barrens* by Farley Mowat.

CAPTAIN GREY
by Avi
Pantheon, 1977; Scholastic, 1982
Gr. 4–7   142 pages
A swashbuckling pirate story told in the classic adventure style, it deals with a young boy's determination to free himself from a band of pirates based on the New Jersey shoreline just after the Revolutionary War. For experienced listeners. One of today's most versatile authors, Avi's other books

include: *Emily Upham's Revenge; The History of Helpless Harry; The Fighting Ground; Shadrach's Crossing; Sometimes I Think I Hear My Name; A Place Called Ugly*. Related books, see listing with *Sarah Bishop* (n).

THE CASE OF THE BAKER STREET IRREGULAR
by Robert Newman
Atheneum (both), 1978; 1984
Gr. 4–8   216 pages
This finely crafted mystery novel is an excellent introduction for young readers to the world of Sherlock Holmes. A young orphan is suddenly pitted against the dark side of turn-of-the-century London when his tutor-guardian is kidnapped. Complete with screaming street urchins, sinister cab drivers, bombings, murder, back alleys, and a child's-eye view of the great sleuth himself—Sherlock Holmes. For experienced listeners. Sequels: *The Case of the Etruscan Treasure; The Case of the Frightened Friend; The Case of the Somerville Secret; The Case of the Threatened King; The Vanishing Corpse*. Related books: *Peppermints in the Parlor* (n); *The Curse of the Blue Figurine* by John Bellairs.

THE CAY
by Theodore Taylor
Doubleday, 1969; Avon, 1977
Gr. 2–6   144 pages
An exciting adventure about a blind white boy and an old black man shipwrecked on a tiny Caribbean island. The first chapters are slow but it builds with taut drama to a stunning ending. Related books: *Call It Courage* (s); *The Hurricane* (s); *Sign of the Beaver* (n); *Lost in the Devil's Desert* and *Swept in the Wave of Terror* both by Gloria Skurzynski.

CHARLOTTE'S WEB
by E. B. White   ·   Illustrated by Garth Williams
Harper (both), 1952
Gr. K–4   184 pages
One of the most universally acclaimed books in contemporary children's literature, it is loved as much by adults as by children. The tale centers on the barnyard life of a young pig who is slated to be butchered in the fall. The animals of the yard (particularly a haughty gray spider named Charlotte) conspire with the farmer's daughter to save the pig's life. While there is much humor in the novel, the author brings in wisdom and pathos in developing his theme of friendship within the cycle of life. Also by the author: *Stuart Little*. Related books: *Bambi* (n); *Cricket in Times Square* (n); *Pearl's Promise* (n); *Mrs. Frisby and the Rats of NIMH* (n); *Warton and Morton* (s); *Fantastic Mr. Fox* by Roald Dahl; *Pigs Might Fly* by Dick King-Smith.

CHILD OF THE SILENT NIGHT:
THE STORY OF LAURA BRIDGMAN
by Edith Fisher Hunter
Houghton Mifflin, 1963; Dell, 1984
Gr. 3–5   124 pages
When Charles Dickens visited the United States in 1842, the person he most wished to see was a 13-year-old girl in Boston named Laura Bridgman. And no wonder. This child's story is an inspiration to all who heard it then or hear it now. It was the triumphant efforts of this child and her teachers that eventually paved the way for another deaf, dumb, and blind child nearly forty years later—Helen Keller. Related books: *Burnish Me Bright* (s); *A Certain Small Shepherd* (s); *The Half-A-Moon Inn* (s); *Helen Keller: From Tragedy to Triumph* (n); *What If They Knew?* by Patricia Hermes.

THE CHOCOLATE TOUCH
by Patrick Skene Catling
Morrow, 1979; Bantam, 1981
Gr. 1–4   122 pages
Here is a new and delicious twist to the old King Midas story. Young John learns a dramatic lesson in self-control when everything he touches with his lips turns to chocolate—toothpaste, bacon and eggs, water, pencils, trumpet. What would happen, then, if he kissed his mother?

Either before or after reading this story, read or tell the original version, "The Golden Touch," which details King Midas's bout with greed and regret. For fifth grade and up, the tale is included as one of the stories in Hawthorne's *A Wonder Book* (a). Related books: *Chocolate Fever* (s); *The Search for Delicious* (n); *Jelly Belly* by Robert K. Smith.

CRICKET IN TIMES SQUARE
by George Selden • Illustrated by Garth Williams
Farrar, 1960; 1970
Gr. 3–6   156 pages
The fanciful story of a cat and mouse living in Times Square, where they discover the world's most talented cricket. Friendship and personal sacrifice are central issues. Related books: *Charlotte's Web* (n); *Pearl's Promise* (n); *Warton and Morton* (s); *Fantastic Mr. Fox* by Roald Dahl.

DANNY THE CHAMPION OF THE WORLD
by Roald Dahl
Knopf, 1978; Bantam, 1979
Gr. 3–6   196 pages
This is the exciting and tender story of a motherless boy and his father—"the most wonderful father who ever lived"—and their great adventure to-

gether. Teachers and parents should explain the custom and tradition of "poaching" in England before going too deeply into the story. Try comparing the experiences of Danny with those of Leigh Botts (a child of divorce) in *Dear Mr. Henshaw* (n). For other books by the author, see *James and the Giant Peach* (n).

A DAY NO PIGS WOULD DIE
by Robert Newton Peck
Knopf, 1972
Gr. 6 and up   150 pages
Set among Shaker farmers in Vermont during the 1920s, this poignant story deals with the author's coming of age at 13, his adventures, fears, and triumphs. As a novel of life and death, it should be read carefully by the teacher or parent before it is read aloud to children. A very moving story by the author of the Soup series (s). For experienced listeners. Related books: *Bridge to Terabithia* (n); *Where the Red Fern Grows* (n); *Words by Heart* (n); *Autumn Street* by Lois Lowry.

DEAR MR. HENSHAW
by Beverly Cleary
Morrow, 1983; Dell 1984
Gr. 3–6   134 pages
In this 1984 Newbery Medal winner, Beverly Cleary departs from her *Ramona* format to write a very different but every bit as successful book— perhaps the finest in her thirty-year career. Using only the letters and diary of a young boy (Leigh Botts), the author traces his personal growth from first grade to sixth. We watch the changes in his relationship with his divorced parents, his schools (where he always ends up the friendless "new kid"), an author with whom he corresponds over the years, and finally with himself. There is wonderful humor here but there is also much sensitivity to the heartaches that confront the growing number of Leigh Bottses in our homes and classrooms, and here too is a worthy role model in courage and perseverence. And, as icing on the cake, this book might do more for children's creative writing efforts than any textbook or classroom lesson you can offer. Also by the author: *Ramona the Pest* (series); *The Mouse and the Motorcycle* (series). Related books: *Danny the Champion of the World* (n); *J.T.* (n); *Mrs. Fish, Ape, and Me, the Dump Queen* (n); *Thank You, Jackie Robinson; The Amazing Memory of Harvey Bean* by Molly Cone.

DEATH RUN
by Jim Murphy
Clarion, 1982
Gr. 7 and up   174 pages

To all appearances, the death of the high school basketball player appeared to be an accident, the result of a seizure suffered alone in the park. But Brian knows otherwise. He was one of the four boys involved in the prank that ended in death. And like Raskolnikov in *Crime and Punishment,* his guilt and anxiety drive him into suspicious eccentricities that arouse the curiosity of a police detective. A suspenseful study of guilt, peer pressure, and a conscience struggling to be heard. Related books: *Killing Mr. Griffin* (n); *Terpin* (s); *Pursuit* by Michael French.

A DOG CALLED KITTY
by Bill Wallace
Holiday, 1980; Archway, 1984
Gr. 1–5   137 pages
In this first-person narrative, a young boy struggles to overcome the deep-seated fear of dogs caused by his traumatic experience with a vicious dog during early childhood. Don't be misled by the cutesy-sweet title of this book; it is a powerfully moving story of childhood and family, written by an Oklahoma elementary school principal. Also by the author: *Trapped in Death Cave; Shadow on the Snow.* Related books: *Hurry Home, Candy* (n); *Stone Fox* (s); *Where the Red Fern Grows* (n); *A Horse Came Running* by Meindert DeJong; *Kavic the Wolf Dog* by Walt Morey.

THE DOG DAYS OF ARTHUR CANE
by T. Ernesto Bethancourt
Holiday House, 1976; Bantam, 1980
Gr. 5–8   160 pages
When an affluent high-school boy is mysteriously transformed into a mongrel dog, he discovers exactly what is meant by the expression "a dog's life." Surviving on the streets of New York by his wits and the skin of his teeth, Arthur faces all the modern canine perils—dogcatchers, poisoned meat, speeding cars, even the gas chamber. Though the book has its humorous moments, much of its strength is in sheer drama. Readers may want to be alert to an occasional four-letter word. An equally effective story (for Gr. 4 and up) about a boy who becomes a cat is Paul Gallico's *The Abandoned,* now out of print but still found in the adult section of many libraries. Related book: *Lassie Come Home* (n).

THE 18th EMERGENCY
by Betsy Byars
Viking, 1973; Puffin, 1981
Gr. 4–6   126 pages
Benjie has made the mistake of angering the toughest boy in school. What to do when you fear the bully is waiting for you around every corner? Sooner

or later, one must face the consequences of one's actions, as Benjie does here. Also by the author: *The Midnight Fox* (n); *Trouble River* (n); *Summer of the Swans; The Winged Colt of Casa Mia.* Related books: *Call It Courage* (s); *Into the Painted Bear Lair* (n); *Introducing Shirley Braverman* (n).

EMILY UPHAM'S REVENGE
by Avi
Pantheon, 1978; Avon, 1979
Gr. 4–6   172 pages

Here's a book that is plain fun, an adventure story to help children realize that reading doesn't have to be connected with the tedium of workbooks. Written in a style that is reminiscent of an old-time silent movie and set in 1875, it is peopled with little lost Emily from a proper Boston family, an unscrupulous banker, crooks, frauds, and the fabulous 11-year-old Seth Marple. What a joy to read aloud!

Written in the same style is Avi's *The History of Helpless Harry,* forty fast-paced, spoofy, very short chapters. For other books by the author, see *Captain Grey* (n). Related book: *Humbug Mountain* (n).

THE ENORMOUS EGG
by Oliver Butterworth
Little, Brown, 1956; Dell, 1978
Gr. 3–6   188 pages

When a New Hampshire farm lad's diligence in caring for an oversized egg in the henhouse is rewarded with the birth of a prehistoric triceratops, his life takes a dramatic turn. Scientists, commercial entrepreneurs, reporters, and television cameramen descend on the little farm, all hoping to exploit the child and his famous "find." It is a book filled with humor—both warm and bittersweet. What was included in 1956 as some gentle satire on the media and Washington politics now in the 1980s reads more accurately than satirically. Sequel: *The Narrow Passage.* Related books: *The Flight of the Fox* (n); *The Iron Man* (s); *Mrs. Frisby and the Rats of NIMH* (n); *Weird Henry Berg* (n).

THE FLIGHT OF THE FOX
by Shirley Rousseau Murphy
(Out of print, available only through libraries)
Gr. 3–6   168 pages

The captivating story of an energetic young boy who joins ranks with a roguish kangaroo rat to rid a local airport of a dangerous flock of starlings. Combining fantasy with realism, the author confronts problems in modern technology, offers various plausible solutions, and stimulates the listener's imagination. The book provides many opportunities for class projects: rats, lemmings, starlings, airport problems, model airplanes. Also by the author: *Elmo Doolan and the Search for the Golden Mouse.* Related books: *Grasshopper and the Unwise Owl* (s); *Mrs. Frisby and the Rats of NIMH* (n); *Pearl's Promise* (n);

FROM THE MIXED-UP FILES OF MRS. BASIL E. FRANKWEILER
by E. L. Konigsburg
Atheneum (both), 1967; 1980
Gr. 4–7   162 pages
A bored and brainy 12-year-old girl talks her 9-year-old brother into running away with her. To throw everyone off their trail, Claudia chooses the Metropolitan Museum of Art in New York City as refuge, and amid centuries-old art they sleep, dine, bathe, and pray in regal secret splendor. An exciting story of hide-and-seek and a marvelous art lesson to boot. For experienced listeners. In related runaway books: a city boy hides in the wilderness—*My Side of the Mountain* (n); a city boy hides in the subway system—*Slake's Limbo* (n).

GENTLE BEN
by Walt Morey
Dutton, 1965; Avon, 1976
Gr. 3–6   192 pages
A young boy adopts a huge brown bear and brings to his family in Alaska all the joys and tears attendant to such a combination. Though the struggle to save animals from ignorant but well-intentioned human predators is one that has been written many times over, Morey's handling of characters, plot, and setting makes an original and exciting tale. He supports the pace of his story with many lessons in environmental science—from salmon runs to hibernation. Also by the author: *Kavik the Wolf Dog.* Related books: *Call of the Wild* (n); *The Midnight Fox* (n); *My Side of the Mountain* (n); *Storm Boy* (s); *The Grizzly* by Annabel and Edgar Johnson.

GOOD NIGHT, MR. TOM
by Michelle Magorian
Harper, 1981
Gr. 6 and up   318 pages
This is the longest novel in this list of recommended titles; it might also be the most powerful. Adults should preview it carefully before reading aloud. Simply put, this is the story of an 8-year-old boy evacuated during the London blitz to a small English village, where he is reluctantly taken in by a grumpy old man. The boy proves to be an abused child, terrified of everything around him. With painstaking care, the old man—Mr. Tom—begins the healing process, unveiling to the child a world he never knew existed—a world of kindness, friendships, laughter and hope. For experienced

listeners. Also by the author: *Back Home*. Related books: *North to Freedom* (n); *Slake's Limbo* (n); *A Blue-Eyed Daisy* by Cynthia Rylant.

GOOD OLD BOY
by Willie Morris
Yoknapatawpha Press (both), 1981
Gr. 5–8   128 pages
If Tom Sawyer had lived in the 1940s, this would have been the story Mark Twain would have written. In this funny and suspenseful boyhood memoir (based in part upon his award-winning *North Toward Home*), one of the South's finest writers tells us about growing up in the South. Originally published by Harper and Avon, it is now available only through Yoknapatawpha Press, P.O. Box 248, Oxford, MS 38655, where it is so beloved they boast of keeping it in print "forever." Related books: *Humbug Mountain* (n); *And Nobody Knew They Were There* (n); *Soup* (n). *The Great Brain* (series) by John D. Fitzgerald.

GREY CLOUD
by Charlotte Graeber
Four Winds, 1979
Gr. 4–8   124 pages
This is a book about being the new kid in school, about befriending the class oddball, about carrier pigeon racing, and about peer pressure. Its descriptions of pigeon racing alone make it fascinating reading, but combined with all its other facets, it is a book that is must reading for children at the age when their emotions are so fragile. Related books (on peer pressure): *Killing Mr. Griffin* (n); *Mrs. Fish, Ape, and Me, the Dump Queen* (n); *Rain of Fire* (n).

HANG TOUGH, PAUL MATHER
by Alfred Slote
Lippincott, 1973; Harper, 1985
Gr. 5–7   156 pages
A moving sports story about a boy with leukemia and his struggle to win— against both his disease and his baseball opponents. After reading this aloud, encourage your listeners to read on their own the many other Alfred Slote sports books. Related books: *It's a Mile From Here to Glory* (n); *Thank You, Jackie Robinson* (n); *Winning Kicker* (n); *Benny* by Barbara Cohen.

HELEN KELLER: FROM TRAGEDY TO TRIUMPH
by Katharine Wilkie
Bobbs Merrill (paperback only), 1969
Gr. 2–4   192 pages

This, the story of the famous blind and deaf woman and her tri
her handicap, is one of the "Childhood of Famous Americans S
also *Child of the Silent Night* (n). For decades this was a popular ......uover
series (many libraries still have them), and now many are available in softcover. The series, on small pages and in large print, also includes novelized
biographies of: Crispus Attucks; Clara Barton; Daniel Boone; Thomas Edi-
son; John F. Kennedy; Robert E. Lee; Abraham Lincoln; Babe Ruth; and
Martha Washington.

HOMER PRICE
by Robert McCloskey
Viking, 1943; Penguin, 1976
Gr. 2–5   160 pages
A modern classic, this is a hilarious collection of stories about a small-town
boy's neighborhood dilemmas. Whether it's the story of Homer's foiling
the bank robbers with his pet skunk or the tale of his uncle's out-of-control
doughnut maker, these six Homeric tales will long be remembered. Sequel:
Centerburg Tales. Related books: *Humbug Mountain* (n); *Me and Caleb* (n);
Peter Potts (s); *Pinch* (n); *Soup* (s).

HUMBUG MOUNTAIN
by Sid Fleischman
Little, Brown, 1978; Scholastic, 1980
Gr. 4–6   172 pages
Overflowing with humor, suspense, and originality, here are the captivating adventures of the Flint family as they battle outlaws, crooked riverboat
pilots, ghosts, and their creditors on the banks of the Missouri River in the
late 1800s. Very reminiscent of Mark Twain. Also by the author: *By the
Great Horn Spoon; Chancy and the Grand Rascal; The Ghost in the Noonday
Sun; The Ghost on Saturday Night; Longbeard the Wizard; Me and the Man on
the Moon-eyed Horse; Mr. Mysterious and Company.* Related books: *Homer Price*
(n); *Pinch* (n); *Soup* (s); *The Wish Giver* (n).

HURRY HOME, CANDY
by Meindert DeJong
Harper (both), 1953
Gr. 2–6   244 pages
With a childlike sense of wonder and pity, this book describes the first year
in the life of a dog—from the moment she is lifted from her mother's side,
through the children, adults, punishments, losses, fears, friendships, love,
and trust that flesh out this moving story. Also by the author: *A Horse Came
Running.* Related books: *A Dog Called Kitty* (n); *Lassie Come Home* (n); *Stone
Fox* (s); *Kavik the Wolf Dog* by Walt Morey.

IDA EARLY COMES OVER THE MOUNTAIN
by Robert Burch
Viking, 1980; Avon, 1982
Gr. 2–6   145 pages
During the Depression, an ungainly young woman shows up to take over the household chores for Mr. Sutton and his four motherless children. The love that grows between the children and the unconventional Ida is, like Ida's tall tales, a joyous experience. She has been rightly described as a Mary Poppins in the Blue Ridge Mountains. Sequel: *Christmas With Ida Early*. Also by the author: *Queeny Peavy*. Related books: *Mrs. Fish, Ape, and Me, the Dump Queen* (n); *Introducing Shirley Braverman* (n); *Us and Uncle Fraud* (n); *Sarah, Plain and Tall* by Patricia MacLachlan.

INCIDENT AT HAWK'S HILL
by Allan W. Eckert
Little, Brown, 1971; Dell, 1972
Gr. 6 and up   174 pages
An extremely timid 6-year-old who wandered away from his family's farm in 1870 is adopted by a ferocious female badger, à la Mowgli in the Jungle Books. The boy is fed, protected, and instructed by the badger through the summer until the family manages to recapture the now-wild child. Definitely for experienced listeners. Reading this aloud, I would paraphrase a large portion of the slow-moving prologue. Related books: *The Dog Days of Arthur Cane* (n); *My Side of the Mountain* (n); *The Pond* (n); *Tales from the Jungle Book* retold by Robin McKinley.

THE INDIAN IN THE CUPBOARD
by Lynne Reid Banks
Doubleday, 1981; Avon, 1983
Gr. 2–6   182 pages
A witty, exciting, and poignant fantasy tale of a 9-year-old English boy who accidentally brings to life his three-inch plastic Indian Boy. Once the shock of the trick wears off, the boy begins to realize the immense responsibility involved in feeding, protecting, and hiding a three-inch human being from another time (1870s) and culture. An excellent values clarification model. Readers-aloud should note beforehand that the miniature cowboy in the story occasionally uses the word "damn" in his exclamations. Related books: *The Flight of the Fox* (n); *Grasshopper and the Unwise Owl* (s); *Into the Painted Bear Lair* (n); *The Littles* (s); *Poor Stainless* by Mary Norton.

IN THE YEAR OF THE BOAR AND JACKIE ROBINSON
by Bette Bao Lord • Illustrated by Marc Simont
Harper, 1984
Gr. 1–5   169 pages

Over the course of the year 1947, we watch a little Chinese girl as she and her family begin a new life in Brooklyn. Told with great warmth and humor and based on the author's own childhood, Shirley Temple Wong's cultural assimilation will ring true with any child who has had to begin again—culturally or socially. To know this little girl is to fall in love with her—and her neighbors and classmates. Two comparative studies can be done with this book: one with Frances Hodgson Burnett's classic *Little Lord Fauntleroy,* in which a poor American boy is confronted with the cultural adjustment of moving into his grandfather's English estate; the other with *Homesick,* an autobiographical novel by Jean Fritz about her childhood in China. Related books: *Introducing Shirley Braverman* (n); *Sara Crewe* (s); *Thank You, Jackie Robinson* (n); for Gr. 4 and older, *The Voyage of the Lucky Dragon* by Jack Bennett.

INTO THE PAINTED BEAR LAIR
by Pamela Stearns • Illustrated by Ann Strugnell
Houghton Mifflin, 1976
Gr. 3–6 154 pages
This outrageously witty, touching, and unconventional fantasy-fairy tale concerns a young boy who can't find his way back to the toy store from whence he entered this strange land, a female knight named Sir Rosemary who is involved in a dangerously chilling mission, and a ferocious bear named Bear who would like nothing more than to devour the boy and the knight. And yet, for all its seeming foolishness, this is a novel of beautiful prose and dramatic dialogue showing that life is a succession of choices, and that the amount of happiness in our lives depends on how we handle those choices. Not the least of those choices, the author demonstrates, is friendship and the value we place on it. The fantasy will bring the reader and listener to new heights of imagination. Related books: *The Lion, the Witch and the Wardrobe* (n); *The Ordinary Princess* (n); *Search for Delicious* (n).

INTRODUCING SHIRLEY BRAVERMAN
by Hilma Wolitzer
Farrar, 1975; Dell, 1981
Gr. 3–5 154 pages
This novel covers slightly less than a year in the life of a Brooklyn, N.Y., girl during World War II. In 22 short, fast-paced chapters, we glimpse family life as it is affected by the war (air-raid practices, letters from soldier neighbors, telegrams from the War Department, the triumphant return of peace) and family life as it is usually lived: spelling bee competitions, visiting grandpa in the nursing home, curing your little brother of his timidity, facing down the neighborhood bully, and dress-up games on rainy days. This book makes a sensitive and enlightening comparative study with *Caddie Woodlawn.* Many similar family and community situations appear in the

two novels and the nearly 100-year difference in their settings offers a unique social and cultural study. Related books: *Me and Caleb* (n); *Ramona the Pest* (n); *Us and Uncle Fraud* (n); *In the Year of the Boar and Jackie Robinson* (n).

IT'S A MILE FROM HERE TO GLORY
by Robert C. Lee
Little, Brown, 1972
Gr. 4–7   150 pages
An inspiring sports story about an antagonistic farm boy who gains a new sense of self-worth and insight into those around him while competing on his school track team. Guaranteed to spur an interest in running. Related books: *Hang Tough, Paul Mather* (n); *Terpin* (s); *Winning Kicker* (n).

JAMES AND THE GIANT PEACH
by Roald Dahl   •   Illustrated by Nancy Ekholm Burkert
Knopf, 1961; Bantam, 1978
Gr. 1–6   120 pages
Young James, orphaned, is sent to live with his mean aunts and appears resigned to spending the rest of his life as their humble servant. It is just about then that a giant peach begins growing in the backyard. Waiting inside that peach is a collection of characters that will captivate your audience as well they did James. Few books hold up over six grade levels as well as this one does. It's my all-time favorite. The book also has been adapted as a dramatization: *James and the Giant Peach: A Play* by Richard George (Puffin). Also by the author: *Danny the Champion of the World* (n); *The Wonderful Story of Henry Sugar* (s); *The BFG; Charlie and the Chocolate Factory; The Enormous Crocodile; Fantastic Mr. Fox.*

J.T.
by Jane Wagner   •   Photographs by Gordon Parks
Dell (paperback only), 1971
Gr. 3–5   124 pages
J.T. is an inner-city black child, harassed by neighbors and teenagers and the despair of his mother. He is, in fact, tottering on the brink of delinquency when an old, one-eyed alley cat brings out his sensitivity and responsibility. Excellent book about inner-city life, individual responsibility, life and death. Related books: *Dear Mr. Henshaw* (n); *Roll of Thunder, Hear My Cry* (n); *The Stories Julian Tells* (s); *One More Flight* by Eve Bunting.

JUMP SHIP TO FREEDOM
By James L. Collier and Christopher Collier
Delacorte, 1982
Gr. 5–9   200 pages

This is the first book in an award-winning historical trilogy that describes the troubles and triumphs in the black experience during the post-Revolutionary War period. It deals with Daniel Arabus, a courageous young slave, attempting to recover money earned by his father during the Revolution, money that will buy freedom for himself and his mother. The second book, *War Comes to Willy Freeman,* portrays the struggles of a young free black girl (disguised as a boy) as she searches for her mother who has been captured by the British. *Who Is Carrie?,* the third book, covers the further adventures of Dan Arabus and Carrie, a kitchen slave in the household of President Washington. All three novels are fast-paced and present a vivid picture of the slavery issues confronting the new nation. Readers aloud are advised to first read the authors' note at the end of each book and their remarks regarding the use of the word "nigger." Another Revolutionary War book by the same authors: *My Brother Sam Is Dead.* Related books: *Captain Grey* (n); *Listen Children* (a); *North to Freedom* (n); *Roll of Thunder, Hear My Cry* (n); *Sarah Bishop* (n); *Wagon Wheels* (s); *Words by Heart* (n).

KILLING MR. GRIFFIN
by Lois Duncan
Little, Brown, 1978; Dell, 1980
Gr. 7 and up   224 pages
This young-adult story offers a chilling dissection of peer pressure and group guilt. Because of the subject matter and occasional four-letter words, care should be used in its presentation. The story deals with five high-school students who attempt to scare their unpopular English teacher by kidnapping him. When their carefully laid plans slowly begin to unravel towards a tragic catastrophe, they find themselves unable to handle the situation. For a discussion of this book's use in the classroom, see Chapter 3. For experienced listeners. Also by the author: *Ransom; The Third Eye.* Related books: *Death Run* (n); *Good Night, Mr. Tom* (n); *Terpin* (s).

LASSIE COME HOME
by Eric Knight
Holt, 1940, 1971 (revised); Dell, 1972
Gr. 4 and up   200 pages
This is one of the greatest dog stories you could ever hope to read. It reads so easily, the words ring with such feeling, that you'll find yourself coming back to it year after year. As is the case with most dog stories, there are the usual sentiments of loss, grief, courage, and struggle. But here these feelings are presented in such a way that most other dog stories pale by comparison. Set between the Scottish Highlands and Yorkshire, England, in the early 1900s, the novel describes the triumphant struggle of a collie dog to return the 100 miles to her young master. Unfortunately, Holly-

wood and television have badly damaged the image of this story with their tinny, affected characterization. This is the original Lassie story. Related books: *The Call of the Wild* (n); *The Dog Days of Arthur Cane* (n); *Hurry Home, Candy* (n); *Stone Fox* (s); *Where the Red Fern Grows* (n); *Kavik the Wolf Dog* by Walt Morey.

THE LION, THE WITCH AND THE WARDROBE
by C. S. Lewis
Macmillan (both), 1950; 1970
Gr. 3–6   186 pages
Four children discover that the stuffy wardrobe closet in an empty room leads to the magic kingdom of Narnia—a kingdom filled with heroes, witches, princes, and intrigue. The first of seven enchanting books called the Narnia Chronicles. The sequels, in order are: *Prince Caspian; The Voyage of the "Dawn Treader"; The Silver Chair; The Horse and His Boy; The Magician's Nephew;* and *The Last Battle.* Related books written in the fantasy/fairy tale genre: *Into the Painted Bear Lair* (n); *The Ordinary Princess* (n); *R, My Name Is Rosie* (n); *The Search for Delicious* (n); *A Walk Out of the World* (n); *The Wonderful Wizard of Oz* (n).

THE LONE HUNT
by Willian O. Steele
Harcourt (paperback only), 1976
Gr. 1–4   176 pages
Flavored with the language of the Tennessee frontier, this is the story of 12-year-old Yancy's rebellion against apron strings and chores. In the thick of a snowstorm, he sets off with his dog to hunt the last buffalo in the Cumberland Mountains. Amid the adventure story we also witness the boy's awakening to manhood and responsibility. Other wilderness stories by the author: *The Buffalo Knife; The Perilous Road; Trail Through Danger; Winter Danger.* Related books: *The Courage of Sarah Noble* (s); *A Lion to Guard Us* (s); *The Sign of the Beaver* (n); *Trouble River* (n); *Wagon Wheels* (s).

THE LONG JOURNEY
by Barbara Corcoran
Atheneum (paperback only), 1970
Gr. 3–6   188 pages
In a desperate effort to aid her stricken grandfather, 13-year-old Laurie sets off on horseback in search of her uncle at the other end of Montana. Skirting cities and towns for fear of trouble, this gritty heroine encounters both unexpected danger and friendship in a fast-paced contemporary story. Related books: *Lupita Mañana* (n); *North to Freedom* (n); *Trouble River* (n); *The Voyage of the Lucky Dragon* by Jack Bennett.

LUPITA MAÑANA
by Patricia Beatty
Morrow, 1981
Gr. 4–8 192 pages
Here is a moving and closeup view of the illegal immigrant problem in America, bringing to life the heartache of people driven out or hunted like animals. With the death of her beloved father, 13-year-old Lupita emigrates illegally into the United States. In slum alleyways, under the cover of night, in dark freight cars, across the desert, plucky Lupita—posing as a boy—learns the meaning of fear as immigration police haunt her thoughts night and day. The hope and heartbreak of poor families—wherever they be—are described in moving detail in this tribute to courageous determination. Related books by the author: In *Turn Homeward, Hannalee*, a determined young Southern girl journeys home after being one of two thousand textile workers captured by Union forces and shipped to work in Northern mills; *Wait for Me, Watch for Me, Eula Bee* (n). Other related books: *North to Freedom* (n); *Our John Willie* (n); *The Voyage of the Lucky Dragon* by Jack Bennett.

MANDY
by Julie Andrews Edwards
Harper, 1971; Bantam, 1973
Gr. 3–6 196 pages
Ten-year-old Mandy climbs the orphanage wall one day to explore the woods—and finds a deserted cottage. A book dealing with the pitfalls of "little white lies," as well as love and friendship. For experienced listeners. Related books: *The Bad Times of Irma Baumlein* (n); *Mrs. Fish, Ape, and Me, the Dump Queen* (n); *Peppermints in the Parlor* (n); *Sara Crewe* (s).

ME AND CALEB
by Franklyn Mayer
Scholastic (paperback only), 1982
Gr. 4–6 160 pages
Don't miss this collection of adventures. The escapades of two brothers make entertaining as well as tender reading. The book's chapters are divided by months; thus the subjects match the seasons. Sequel: *Me and Caleb Again*. Related books: *Homer Price* (n); *Ida Early Comes Over the Mountain* (n); *The Great Brain* (series) by John D. Fitzgerald.

THE MIDNIGHT FOX
by Betsy Byars
Viking, 1968; Penguin, 1981
Gr. 4–6 160 pages

From the very beginning, young Tommy is determined he'll hate his aunt and uncle's farm where he must spend the summer. His determination suffers a setback when he discovers a renegade black fox. His desire to keep the fox running free collides with his uncle's wish to kill it, and the novel builds to a stunning moment of confrontation and courage. An excellent book about values and superb character development. Also by the author: *The 18th Emergency* (n); *The Pinballs* (n); *Trouble River* (n); *Summer of the Swans.* Related books: *Gentle Ben* (n); *Stone Fox* (s); *Storm Boy* (s); *Weird Henry Berg* (n); *A Horse Came Running* by Meindert DeJong.

MR. POPPER'S PENGUINS
by Richard and Florence Atwater • Illustrated by Robert Lawson
Little, Brown, 1938; Dell, 1978
Gr. 2–4   140 pages
When you add twelve penguins to the family of Mr. Popper the house painter, you've got immense food bills, impossible situations, and a freezer full of laughs. Extra-short chapters that will keep your audience hungry for more. Related books: *Grasshopper and the Unwise Owl* (s); *Owls in the Family* (s); *Ramona the Pest* (n); *Fantastic Mr. Fox* by Roald Dahl.

MRS. FISH, APE, AND ME, THE DUMP QUEEN
by Norma Fox Mazer
Dutton, 1980; Avon, 1982
Gr. 3–6   138 pages
Living with her homely but loving uncle (the manager of the town dump), Joyce is taunted unmercifully by her classmates. The walls she has built to resist such derision are beginning to weaken when help comes from a most unlikely source—Mrs. Fish, the "crazy" school custodian. For all its candidness in describing the cruelty of the peer group, the book also portrays the powerful effects of love as an anchor in the lives of three different people. Related books: *Dexter* (s); *Grey Cloud* (n); *The Hundred Dresses* (s); *Sara Crewe* (s); *Wild Violets* (s); *A Blue-Eyed Daisy* by Cynthia Rylant.

MRS. FRISBY AND THE RATS OF NIMH
by Robert C. O'Brien
Atheneum (both), 1971
Gr. 4–6   232 pages
A fantasy-science fiction tale that can only be described as "unforgettable." A group of rats have become super-intelligent through a series of laboratory injections. Though it opens with an almost fairy-tale softness, it grows into a taut and frighteningly realistic tale. Also by the author: *The Silver Crown,* a lesser known but equally exciting sci-fi tale. Related books: *The Enormous Egg* (n); *The Twenty-One Balloons* (n).

MY BROTHER SAM IS DEAD
by James Lincoln Collier and Christopher Collier
Four Winds, 1974; Scholastic, 1977
Gr. 5 and up   251 pages
In this award-winning historical novel, the inhumanity of war is examined at close hand through the experiences of one sharply divided Connecticut family during the Revolutionary War. Told in the words of a younger brother, the heartache and passions described here hold true for all wars in all times, and the authors' balanced accounts of British and American tactics allow plenty of latitude for readers to come to their own conclusions. This book makes a good comparative study with *Rain of Fire* (n), in which a young brother is startled by the effect WW II had upon his brother. Regarded as leading figures in American historical fiction for children, the authors also have written an exciting trilogy that deals with the black experience during the same period—see *Jump Ship to Freedom* (n). Related books: *Captain Grey* (n); *Otto of the Silver Hand* (n); *Sarah Bishop* (n); *The Fighting Ground* by Avi.

MY SIDE OF THE MOUNTAIN
by Jean George
Dutton (both), 1959; 1975
Gr. 3–8   178 pages
A modern-day Robinson Crusoe in adolescence, city-bred Sam Gribley describes his year surviving as a runaway in a remote area of the Catskill Mountains. His diary of living off the land is marked by moving accounts of the animals, insects, plants, people, and books that helped him survive. See *Sarah Bishop* for comparative study. For experienced listeners. Also by the author: *Julie of the Wolves*. Related books: *The Cay* (n); *From the Mixed Up Files of Mrs. Basil E. Frankweiler* (n); *Gentle Ben* (n); *Incident at Hawk's Hill* (n); *The Pond* (n); *Slake's Limbo* (n); and three excellent wilderness survival stories by Gloria Skurzynski: *Caught in the Moving Mountains, Lost in the Devil's Desert,* and *Trapped in Sliprock Canyon.*

NORTH TO FREEDOM
by Anne Holm
Harcourt (paperback only), 1974
Gr. 4 and up   190 pages
This is a magnificent and unforgettable book. Picture a 12-year-old boy, raised in an East European prison camp, who remembers no other life. Suddenly the opportunity to escape presents itself, and he begins not only a terrifying odyssey across Italy, Switzerland, France, and into Denmark but also a journey into human experience. David must now deal with the normal experiences and knowledge that had been denied him in prison. Here are wondrous but confusing moments when he meets for the first time: a

baby, flowers, fruit, a church, children playing, a toothbrush. Meanwhile, he learns how to smile, the meaning of conscience, the need to trust. For experienced listeners. Related books: *Captain Grey* (n); *The Long Journey* (n); *Lupita Mañana* (n); *Wait for Me, Watch for Me, Eula Bee* (n).

THE ORDINARY PRINCESS
by M. M. Kaye
Doubleday, 1984
Gr. 2–5   112 pages
In a most unconventional but liberated fairy tale, we see a young princess who is marked by her fairy godmother with the gift of "ordinariness"— that is, straight hair, grayish-brown eyes, a freckled nose, awkwardness, and even an ordinary name: Amy. The princes are as uninterested in her as she is in them, to the point where she runs away and gets her first job in the kitchen of a neighboring kingdom. While the warm spoof lays to rest some old stereotypes, it also gives us a captivating princess. Related books: *Into the Painted Bear Lair* (n); *The Maid of the North* (a); *The Dragon of Og* by Rumer Godden; *Once Upon a Test: Three Light Tales of Love* by Vivian Vande Velde; and two books by Barbara Cohen: *R, My Name is Rosie* and *Seven Daughters and Seven Sons* (with Bahija Lovejoy).

OTTO OF THE SILVER HAND
by Howard Pyle
(Out of print, available only through libraries)
Gr. 5–8   132 pages
First published in 1888 and written by one of the leading figures of American children's literature, this book is an ideal introduction to the classics. Set in the Middle Ages, the narrative spins the tale of a young boy's joy and suffering as he rises above the cruelty of the world. Though the language may be somewhat foreign to the listener at the start, it soon adds to the flavor of the narrative. The story literally rings with the clash of armored knights and the solemn knell of monastery bells. For experienced listeners. *Knights* by Julek Heller and Deirdre Headon (Schocken) is a comprehensive illustrated book on the traditions, heroes, and equipment associated with medieval times. Other related books: *Robin Hood* (n); *The Search for Delicious* (n); *Looking into the Middle Ages* by Huck Scarry.

OUR JOHN WILLIE
by Catherine Cookson
Bobbs-Merrill, 1974; New American Library, 1975
Gr. 4–8   192 pages
A gothic novel set in the mine country of northern England, this book portrays the unselfish love between two orphaned brothers (one is a deaf-mute). Add to this the forbidding figure of Miss Peamarsh, the village mystery

woman, and you have a gripping historical novel set in the 1850s. Teachers and parents should note pages 152–53, which mention a child born out of marriage. For experienced listeners. This book usually is shelved among adult fiction in libraries and bookstores. Related books: *Burnish Me Bright* (s); *Child of the Silent Night* (n); *Peppermints in the Parlor* (n); *The Secret Garden* (n).

PATH OF THE PALE HORSE
by Paul Fleischman
Harper, 1983
Gr. 6 and up   144 pages
More than one hundred years before Walter Reed discovered the cause of yellow fever, one-tenth of Philadelphia's population died of the fever. In this story, a 14-year-old boy is apprenticed to a doctor working in the heat of the epidemic, and we are given a fascinating view of how entangled were the worlds of myth and science in 1793. For experienced listeners. Also by the author: *The Half-A-Moon Inn* (s).

PEARL'S PROMISE
by Frank Asch
Delacorte, 1984; Dell 1984
K–4   152 pages
Adventure, danger, heartache, tenderness, romance, and courage—all are woven tightly into this fast-moving novel about a pet store mouse who promises her young brother that she will save him somehow from the snake that is about to make a breakfast of him. Fans of *Charlotte's Web* and *Stuart Little* will love the spunky Pearl, who gives us a study in courage and determination while at the same time allowing us a mouse's eye-view of the world. Related novels: *Warton and Morton* (s); *The Mouse and the Motorcycle* by Beverly Cleary; *Mrs. Frisby and the Rats of NIMH* (n); *Feldman Fieldmouse: A Fable* by Nathaniel Benchley; *Stuart Little* by E. B. White. For a listing of picture books on mice, see *Broderick* (p).

PEPPERMINTS IN THE PARLOR
by Barbara Brooks Wallace
Atheneum, 1980
Gr. 3–7   198 pages
When the newly orphaned Emily arrives in San Francisco, she expects to be adopted by her wealthy aunt and uncle. What she finds instead is a poverty-stricken aunt held captive as a servant in a shadowy, decaying home for the aged. Filled with Dickensian flavor, there are secret passageways, tyrannical matrons, eerie whispers in the night, and a pair of fearful but plucky kids. Also by the author: *Hawkins*. Related books: *Our John Willie* (n); *Sara Crewe* (s); *The Secret Garden* (n); *The Wolves of Willoughby Chase* (n).

THE PINBALLS
by Betsy Byars
Harper, 1977; Scholastic, 1979
Gr. 5–7   136 pages

Brought together under the same roof, three foster children prove to each other and the world that they are *not* pinballs to be knocked around from one place to the next; they have a choice in life—to try or not to try. The author has taken what could have been a maudlin story and turned it into a hopeful, loving, and very witty book. Very short chapters with easy-to-read dialogue. No wonder 58,000 school children in Georgia voted it their favorite in 1979. For other books by the author, see *The Midnight Fox* (n); Related books: *Ida Early Comes Over the Mountain* (n); *Mandy* (n); *Mrs. Fish, Ape, and Me, the Dump Queen* (n); *Sara Crewe* (s); *A Blue-Eyed Daisy* by Cynthia Rylant.

PINCH
by Larry Callen
Little, Brown, 1976
Gr. 4–6   180 pages

Pinch, a boy growing up in the country, becomes involved with a pig he trains to hunt and a mean, crafty neighbor who teaches Pinch the art of trickery. The story deals with family and community relationships and personal honesty with a sense of drama and humor. Sequels: *The Deadly Mandrake; The Muskrat War.* Callen continues in the same homespun manner with a new set of characters in *Who Kidnapped the Sheriff?* Related books: *Good Old Boy* (n); *Homer Price* (n); *Me and Caleb* (n); *And Nobody Knew They Were There* (n).

THE POND
by Robert Murphy
(Out of print, available only through libraries)
Gr. 6 and up   254 pages

In my opinion, this is one of the finest juvenile novels ever written. I've yet to meet someone who has read it and not been deeply moved. It's about history: urban and suburban life in America in 1917. It's about nature: the mutual effects and affections between mankind and a patch of Virginia backwoods with its giant bass, wild turkeys, minks, and squirrels. It's about human nature: a young boy's coming of age as he realizes his own capacity for good and evil—whether through the gun he carries into the woods or through the kindness he carries into others' lives. The winner of numerous awards, *The Pond* has often been compared to *The Yearling* and *Rascal;* as a read-aloud, it wins any such comparison hands down. For experienced listeners. Related books: *A Day No Pigs Would Die* (n); *Incident at Hawk's Hill* (n); *My Side of the Mountain* (n).

PRISONERS AT THE KITCHEN TABLE
by Barbara Holland
Clarion, 1979
Gr. 3–6   122 pages
Two neighborhood friends (a timid boy and boisterous girl) are pitted against a bickering husband-and-wife kidnapping team, a creepy, secluded farmhouse, and a week of waiting—waiting for food, waiting for ransom, waiting for a chance to escape. Along with a nice blend of humor and suspense, the author provides us with an excellent study of character development. Your listeners will think twice before accepting a ride with stangers after hearing this story. Also by the author: *The Pony Problem; Creepy-Mouse Coming To Get You.* Related books on kidnapping: *Captain Grey* (n); *The Half-A-Moon Inn* (s); *Peppermints in the Parlor* (n); *Wait for Me, Watch for Me, Eula Bee* (n).

RAIN OF FIRE
by Marion Dane Bauer
Clarion, 1983
Gr. 3–6   153 pages
Matthew's experiences in Japan during World War II have left him a different person, and no one is more affected than his kid brother, Steve. Matthew's talk of the shame and inhumanity in war confuses his 12-year-old brother, who is looking for a war hero. When Steve's peers accuse Matthew of being a coward, Steve concocts heroic war stories in his defense—with near-tragic results. This is a powerful story, suggesting the seeds of warfare between nations often are sown first in backlots and alleyways among children. Matthew's recollections of Hiroshima will be etched in children's minds long after the book is read. Also by the author: *Shelter from the Wind.* Related books: *The Bicycle Man* (p); *My Brother Sam Is Dead* (n); *Otto of the Silver Hand* (n); *The Butter Battle Book* by Dr. Seuss; *Hiroshima No Pika* by Toshi Maruki; *Sadako and the Thousand Paper Cranes* by Eleanor Coerr.

RAMONA THE PEST
by Beverly Cleary
Morrow, 1968; Dell, 1982
Gr. K–4   144 pages
Not all of Beverly Cleary's books make good read-alouds. A prolific writer for the early reader, her books sometimes move too slowly to hold read-aloud interest. But that's not so with *Ramona the Pest,* which follows the outspoken young lady through her early months in kindergarten. All children will smile in recognition at Ramona's encounters with the first day of school, show and tell, seat work, a substitute teacher, Halloween, young love—and dropping out of kindergarten. Long chapters can easily be divided. Early grades should have some experience with short novels before

trying *Ramona*. The sequels follow Ramona as she and her family grow older and experience the challenges of modern life (like unemployment, Mom going back to work, after-school babysitters): *Ramona the Pest; Ramona and Her Father; Ramona and Her Mother; Ramona Quimby, Age 8; Ramona Forever*. Also by the author: *Dear Mr. Henshaw* (n); *The Mouse and the Motorcycle*. Related books: *Ida Early Comes Over the Mountain* (n); *Us and Uncle Fraud* (n).

R, MY NAME IS ROSIE
by Barbara Cohen
Lothrop, 1978; Scholastic, 1980
Gr. 4–6   188 pages

In this book, the author offers us two complete stories, neatly intertwined. The first is that of Rosie—11 years old, fat, and forgotten. Her widowed mother manages the inn where Rosie and her brother and sister live, and in Rosie's eyes, she also manages to overlook Rosie's potential. The second story (90 pages long) runs intermittently through the book, in the form of a serialized fairy tale created by Rosie and her friend the bartender during their daily meetings. Young listeners will recognize both Rosie's insecurities and her need for a fantasy world to which she can retreat. Try reading some of the original Andersen and Grimm fairy tales after this book. In a similar vein for older children (Gr. 5–9), the author has written *Seven Daughters and Seven Sons* (with Bahija Lovejoy), an Arabic tale of a "liberated" daughter in a poor Bagdad family who achieves great financial success while disguised as a male merchant—only to have her plans disturbed when she falls in love. Also by the author: *Thank You, Jackie Robinson; King of the Seventh Grade; Benny*. Related books: *Bridge to Terabithia* (n); *Into the Painted Bear Lair* (n); *The Ordinary Princess* (n).

ROBIN HOOD—PRINCE OF OUTLAWS
by Bernard Miles   •   **Illustrated by Victor Ambrus**
Rand McNally, 1979
Gr. 3–6   124 pages

Of the more than 700 books written on the famous outlaw of Sherwood Forest, this is one of the most ambitious and most successful of contemporary efforts. Relying as much as possible on fact and personal observation of the historic English locale, the author has humanized Robin while retaining his medieval flavor. His updating of the language to nearer present-day usage brings the story within the listening bounds of children as young as third grade. The books's format is large and allows for brilliant full-color illustrations on every page. For experienced listeners. Also by the author and illustrator: *Favorite Tales From Shakespeare*. A perfect companion to this book is *Knights* by Julek Heller and Deirdre Headon (Schocken), a comprehensive illustrated book on the traditions, heroes, and equipment associated with medieval times. Other related books: *Otto of the Silver Hand* (n); *The*

Search for Delicious (n); *The Dragon Kite* by Nancy Luenn; *Sir Gawain and the Loathly Lady* retold by Selina Hastings.

ROLL OF THUNDER, HEAR MY CRY
by Mildred Taylor
Dial, 1976; Bantam, 1978
Gr. 5 and up   276 pages
Filled with the lifeblood of a black Mississippi family during the Depression, this novel throbs with the passion and pride of a family that refuses to give in to threats and harassments by white neighbors. The story is told through daughter Cassie, age 9, who experiences her first taste of social injustice and refuses to swallow it. She, her family, her classmates and neighbors will stir listeners' hearts and awaken many children to the problems of minorities in our society. Winner of the Newbery Award. For experienced listeners. Sequel: *Let the Circle Be Unbroken*. Related books: *Jump Ship to Freedom* (n); *Listen Children* (a); *The Lucky Stone* (s); *Lupita Mañana* (n); *Words by Heart* (n); *Philip Hall Likes Me, I Reckon Maybe* by Bette Greene.

SARAH BISHOP
by Scott O'Dell
Houghton Mifflin, 1980; Scholastic, 1982
Gr. 5 and up   184 pages
Based on an actual historical incident, this is the story of a courageous and determined young girl who flees war-torn Long Island after her father and brother are killed at the outbreak of the Revolutionary War. In the Connecticut wilderness, she takes refuge in a cave where she begins her new life. It is a story of constant courage, as well as a historical account of a time that shaped our nation's destiny. *Sarah Bishop* makes an interesting comparative study with two other read-aloud novels dealing with children running away: *Slake's Limbo* (n) and *My Side of the Mountain* (n). Each approaches the subject from a different point in time but each poses the same question: Is any man or woman really an island unto themselves? For experienced listeners. Also by the author: *Sing Down the Moon* (n); *The King's Fifth*. Related books: *Captain Grey* (n); *Jump Ship to Freedom* (n); *My Brother Sam Is Dead* (n); *Rain of Fire* (n); *The Sign of the Beaver* (n).

THE SEARCH FOR DELICIOUS
by Natalie Babbitt
Farrar, 1969; Avon, 1974
Gr. 3–7   160 pages
Here is a small masterpiece: fantasy and the English language as they were meant to be written. After a nasty argument among the King, Queen, and their court over the correct meaning of the word "delicious," the Prime Minister's adopted son is dispatched to poll the kingdom and determine the

choice of the people. The foolishness of man, his pettiness and quarrelsome nature are suddenly aroused by the poll: Everyone has a different personal definition of "delicious" and civil war looms. An excellent book about values that is guaranteed to challenge every child's sense of the word "delicious." Also by the author: *Tuck Everlasting* (n). Related books: *Chocolate Fever* (s); *The Chocolate Touch* (n); *The Ordinary Princess* (n); *Robin Hood* (n).

THE SECRET GARDEN
by Frances Hodgson Burnett • Illustrated by Tasha Tudor
Lippincott, 1962; Dell, 1971
Gr. 2–5   256 pages
Few books spin such a web of magic about its readers (and listeners) as does this children's classic (first published in 1911) about the contrary little orphan who comes to live with her cold, unfeeling uncle on the windswept English moors. Wandering the grounds of his immense manor house one day, she discovers a secret garden, locked and abandoned. This leads her to discover her uncle's invalid child hidden within the mansion, her first friendship, and her own true self. For experienced listeners. Also by the author: *Sara Crewe* (s); *Little Lord Fauntleroy; A Little Princess; The Lost Prince.* Related books: *Bridge to Terabithia* (n); *Mandy* (n); *Peppermints in the Parlor* (n).

THE SIGN OF THE BEAVER
by Elizabeth George Speare
Houghton Mifflin, 1983; Dell, 1984
Gr. 3 and up   135 pages
This is the story of two boys—one white, the other Indian—and their coming of age in the Maine wilderness prior to the Revolutionary War. It is also an insightful study of the awkward relationship that develops when the starving boy is forced into teaching the reluctant Indian to read. A similar pioneer survival story for younger readers is *The Courage of Sarah Noble* (s). Also by the author: *Calico Captive; The Witch of Blackbird Pond.* Related books: *The Cay* (n); *The Lone Hunt* (n); *Sarah Bishop* (n); *Stone Fox* (s); *Wait for Me, Watch for Me, Eula Bee* (n).

SING DOWN THE MOON
by Scott O'Dell
Houghton Mifflin, 1970; Dell, 1973
Gr. 3–6   138 pages
Through the first-person narrative of a 14-year-old Navaho girl, we follow the plight of the American Indian in 1864 when the U.S. government ordered the Navahos out of their Arizona homeland and marched them 300 miles to Fort Sumner, New Mexico, where they were imprisoned for four years. Known as "The Long Walk," it is a journey that has since become

a part of every Navaho child's heritage. The injustices and the subsequent courage displayed by the Indians should be known by all Americans. The novel also provides a detailed account of daily Indian life during the period. Short chapters are told with the vocabulary and in the style appropriate to a young Indian child. After reading *Sing Down the Moon* you might follow up with an article, "The Navajos," from the December 1972 *National Geographic,* for an updated view of the Navajo nation. Also by the author: *Sarah Bishop* (n). Related books: *Lupita Mañana* (n); *North to Freedom* (n); *Sign of the Beaver* (n); *Wait for Me, Watch for Me, Eula Bee; Where the Buffaloes Begin* (p); *Annie and the Old One* by Miska Miles.

SLAKE'S LIMBO
by Felice Holman
Scribner, 1984
Gr. 5–8   117 pages
A 15-year-old takes his fears and misfortunes into the New York City subway one day, finds a hidden construction mistake in the shape of a cave near the tracks, and doesn't come out of the system for 121 days. The story deals simply but powerfully with the question: Can anyone be an island unto himself? It is as much a story of survival as it is a tale of personal discovery. This book makes an interesting comparative study with two other books which discuss running away, hiding, and personal discovery: *My Side of the Mountain* (n) and *Sarah Bishop* (n). For experienced listeners. Other related books: *Good Night, Mr. Tom* (n); *Lupita Mañana* (n); *North to Freedom* (n).

THE SNAILMAN
by Brenda Sivers
Little, Brown, 1978
Gr. 3–6   118 pages
When a lonely young boy adopts the village's homely eccentric as his friend, he must stand against intense family and peer pressure to do otherwise. A novel that deals with overcoming loneliness. Related books: *Mrs. Fish, Ape, and Me, the Dump Queen* (n); *Weird Henry Berg* (n); *The Day of Muskie* by Patricia Welch.

SNOW-BOUND
by Harry Mazer
Delacorte, 1973; Dell, 1975
Gr. 5–8   146 pages
Two teenagers, a boy and a girl, marooned by a car wreck during a severe snowstorm, fight off starvation, frostbite, wild dogs, broken limbs, and personal bickering in order to survive. An excellent example of people's lives being changed for the better in overcoming adversity. Adults should be ad-

vised of occasional four-letter words in the dialogue. Related books: *The Cay* (n); *My Side of the Mountain* (n); *Fire Storm* by Robb White.

A STRANGER CAME ASHORE
by Mollie Hunter
Harper (both), 1975; 1977
Gr. 4–7   163 pages
The handsome stranger who claims to be the sole survivor of a shipwreck off the Scottish coast is really the Great Selkie, come to lure the Henderson family's beautiful daughter to her death at the bottom of the sea. Here is a novel brimming with legend and suspense. Related books: *A Walk Out of the World* (n); *The Wish Giver* (n); *The Leopard's Tooth* by William Kotzwinkle.

TALES OF A FOURTH GRADE NOTHING
by Judy Blume
Dutton, 1972; Dell, 1976
Gr. 3–5   120 pages
A perennial favorite among schoolchildren, this story deals with the irksome problem of a kid brother and his hilarious antics with his fourth-grade brother, Peter. Sequel: *Superfudge* (Readers-aloud should be cautioned that this book deals with the question: Is there or is there not a Santa Claus?). Also by the author: *Freckle Juice* (s). Related books: *Ida Early Comes Over the Mountain* (n); *Ramona the Pest* (n); *Toad Food and Measle Soup* and *Lucky Charms and Birthday Wishes* by Christine McDonnell.

THANK YOU, JACKIE ROBINSON
by Barbara Cohen
Lothrop, 1974
Gr. 5–7   126 pages
Set in the late 1940s, this is the story of young Sam Green, one of that rare breed known as the True Baseball Fanatic and a Brooklyn Dodger fan. His widowed mother runs an inn and when she hires a 60-year-old black cook, Sam's life takes a dramatic turn for the better. They form a fast friendship and begin to explore the joys of baseball in a way that the fatherless boy has never known. A tender book that touches on friendship, race, sports, personal sacrifice, and death. *Benny* is another Cohen book with an underlying sports theme; for other books by the author, see *R, My Name is Rosie* (n). Related books: *The Cay* (n); *In the Year of the Boar and Jackie Robinson* (n); *The Snailman* (n); *Trouble River* (n).

TROUBLE RIVER
by Betsy Byars
Viking, 1969; Scholastic, 1972
Gr. 3–6   158 pages

A pioneer lad takes his cantankerous grandmother downriver on his make-shift raft to avoid an Indian attack. Forty miles later, they have learned much about each other's resolve and courage. For other books by the author, see *The Midnight Fox* (n). Related books: *The Lone Hunt* (n); *The Long Journey* (n); *Stone Fox* (s).

TUCK EVERLASTING
by Natalie Babbitt
Farrar, 1975, 1985; Bantam, 1976
Gr. 4–7   124 pages
A young girl stumbles upon a family that has found the "Fountain of Youth," and in the aftermath there is a kidnapping, a murder, and a jailbreak. This touching story suggests a sobering answer to the question: What would it be like to live forever? For experienced listeners. Also by the author: *Search for Delicious* (n). Related books: Ray Bradbury's short story "Hail and Farewell" contained in *Young Mutants* edited by Isaac Asimov; *A Day No Pigs Would Die* (n); *My Twin Sister Erika* (s); *A Taste of Blackberries* (s).

THE TWENTY-ONE BALLOONS
by William Pène du Bois
Viking, 1947; Dell, 1969
Gr. 4–6   180 pages
Here is a literary smorgasbord; there are so many different and delicious parts one hardly knows which to mention first. The story deals with a retired teacher's attempts to sail by balloon across the Pacific in 1883, his crash landing and pseudo-imprisonment on the island of Krakatoa and, finally, his escape. The book is crammed with nuggets of science, history, humor, invention, superior language, and marvelous artwork. Winner of the Newbery Medal. For experienced listeners. You might follow up this book by reading "Mount St. Helens," an in-depth study of volcanoes in the January 1981 issue of *National Geographic*. Related books: *Mrs. Frisby and the Rats of NIMH* (n); *A Walk Out of the World* (n); *Weird Henry Berg* (n); *Volcanoes* by Franklyn Branley.

US AND UNCLE FRAUD
by Lois Lowry
Houghton, 1984
Gr. 2–6   160 pages
Was Uncle Claude, Mom's vagabond blacksheep brother, really a world traveler? Had he really hidden Russian jewels in the house for his niece and nephew? Or was he, as Dad suggested, a fraud? Did he rob the Leboff estate? This is one family's timeless story that brims with laughter, drama, and boundless affection. Also by the author: *Autumn Street*. Related books: *Humbug Mountain* (n); *Ida Early Comes Over the Mountain* (n); *Me and Caleb* (n); *Pinch* (n).

WAIT FOR ME, WATCH FOR ME, EULA BEE
by Patricia Beatty
Morrow, 1978
Gr. 4 and up   221 pages
In this spellbinding, realistic portrayal of a Texas teenager's year-long struggle
to free his 4-year-old sister from her Comanche captors, we find a violent
yet often tender picture of Western life in the 1860s. With historical pre-
cision, the author presents the Indian wars from both the red and white
perspectives, and manages to include a remarkable amount of fascinating
data about Indian and frontier life. As an enriching background study, take
a day's break from the text and read aloud the story *Where the Buffaloes Begin* (p). Also by the author: *Turn Homeward; Hannalee; Lupita Mañana* (n).
Related books: *Caddie Woodlawn* (n); *North to Freedom* (n); *The Sign of the
Beaver* (n); *Down the Long Hills* by Louis L'Amour.

A WALK OUT OF THE WORLD
by Ruth Nichols
Harcourt, 1969
Gr. 3–8   192 pages
Reminiscent of *The Lion, the Witch, and the Wardrobe* and *The Hobbit,* this
fantasy novel follows a brother and sister into the woods one day and ob-
serves as they enter an ancient kingdom of Water Folk, Stone People, and
Forest People and are quickly involved in ancient magic and a fast-paced
tribal war. For experienced listeners. Related book: *The Hobbit* by J. R.
Tolkien.

WEIRD HENRY BERG
by Sarah Sargent
Crown, 1980; Dell, 1981
Gr. 4–6   114 pages
Twelve-year-old Henry is content to play the role of class weirdo and family
recluse until the family heirloom he inherited from his grandfather hatches
into a dragon. That's when Henry begins to change. That is also the moment when the dragon's relatives in Wales send an emissary to Henry's
hometown in search of the newborn member of the clan. Henry's subsequent adventures with Millie, the town's elderly eccentric, in pursuit of the
dragon are filled with a happy blend of mystery, humor, and fantasy. Related books: *A Walk Out of the World* (n); *The Reluctant Dragon* (s).

WHERE THE RED FERN GROWS
by Wilson Rawls
Doubleday, 1961; Bantam, 1974
Gr. 3–7   212 pages
A 10-year-old boy growing up in the Ozark mountains, praying and saving
for a pair of hounds, finally achieves his wish. He then begins the task of

turning the hounds into first-class hunting dogs. It would be difficult to find a book that speaks more definitively about perseverance, courage, family, sacrifice, work, life and death. Long chapters are easily divided. Related books: *Bridge to Terabithia* (n); *A Day No Pigs Would Die* (n); *The Dog Days of Arthur Cane* (n); *Lassie Come Home* (n); *Stone Fox* (s).

WINNING KICKER
by Thomas J. Dygard
Morrow, 1978
Gr. 6–8   190 pages
A hard-nosed football coach at the end of a long and successful career is jolted in his final season when a girl makes his high-school team as a place-kicker, potentially turning the season into a three-ring circus. In a companion novel, *Rebound Caper,* a high school boy, benched by his basketball coach, retaliates by joining the girls' team. The author offers a liberated and sensitive view of the family, school, and community pressures that result. Sure to stir the interest of both sexes and make for lively discussion. Also by the author: *Outside Shooter; Point Spread; Quarterback Walk-On; Running Scared; Soccer Duel; Wilderness Peril.*

THE WISH GIVER
by Bill Brittain
Harper, 1983
Gr. 4–8   181 pages
Into the town of Coven Tree comes a mysterious stranger who sets up a tent at the church social, promising wishes-come-true for 50 cents. Three young people in this tiny New England town find out the hard way that sometimes we'd be better off if our wishes didn't come true. There is lots of homespun merriment and fast-moving suspense here. Before reading the tale aloud, have your listeners write down a secret wish and hide it. After completing the book, have them rethink their wish. Also by the author: *The Devil's Donkey; Who Knew There'd Be Ghosts.* Related books: *Among the Dolls* (s); *The Dog Days of Arthur Cane* (n); *Humbug Mountain* (n); *Weird Henry Berg* (n); *The Wonderful Story of Henry Sugar* (title story) (s); *Black and Blue Magic* by Zilpha Keatley Snyder.

THE WITCH OF BLACKBIRD POND
by Elizabeth George Speare
Houghton Mifflin, 1958; Dell, 1972
Gr. 6 and up   250 pages
This Newbery Award-winning novel portrays an impetuous 16-year-old girl's struggles and growth in a Puritan community of Connecticut Colony. After being raised in a free-thinking tropical home, Kit balks at the narrow-minded ways of her aunt and uncle with whom she goes to live after the death of her grandfather. Seeking a port in her emotional storm, she wanders into

friendship with a lonely old woman who is suspected by villagers of being a witch—a suspicion that is eventually pinned on the rebellious Kit as well. Particularly well drawn is the community's peer pressure and ostracism of the old woman because of her independent and unconventional ways. An excellent novel about values for experienced listeners. Also by the author: *The Sign of the Beaver* (n); *Calico Captive*. Related books: *My Brother Sam Is Dead* (n); *Sarah Bishop* (n); *The Snailman* (n).

THE WOLVES OF WILLOUGHBY CHASE
by Joan Aiken
Doubleday, 1962; Dell, 1981
Gr. 3–6   168 pages
Here is Victorian melodrama in high gear: a great English estate surrounded by hungry wolves, two young girls mistakenly left in the care of a wicked, scheming governess, secret passageways and tortured flights through the snow in the dark of night. For experienced listeners. Sequels: *Black Hearts in Battersea; The Cuckoo Tree; Nightbirds on Nantucket; The Stolen Lake.* Related books: *Peppermints in the Parlor* (n); *The Secret Garden* (n); *Sara Crewe* (s).

THE (WONDERFUL) WIZARD OF OZ
by L. Frank Baum
Holt, 1983; Dover, 1960; Puffin, 1983
Gr. 1–5   260 pages
Before your children are exposed to the movie version, treat them to the magic of this 1900 book many regard as the first American fairy tale, as well as early American science fiction. (Incidentally, the book is far less terrifying for children than the film version.) The magical story of Dorothy and her friends' harrowing journey to the Emerald City is but the first of 14 books on the Land of Oz by the author. If your audience already has seen the movie, introduce them to one of the sequels: *Dorothy and the Wizard of Oz; The Emerald City of Oz; Glinda of Oz; The Lost Princess of Oz; The Magic of Oz; The Marvelous Land of Oz; Ozma of Oz; The Patchwork Girl of Oz; Rinkitink of Oz; The Road to Oz; The Scarecrow of Oz; Tik-tok of Oz; The Tin Woodman of Oz.*

WORDS BY HEART
by Ouida Sebestyen
Little, Brown, 1979; Bantam, 1981
Gr. 5 and up   162 pages
A young girl and her family must summon all their courage and spirit in order to survive as the only black family in this 1910 Texas community. The child's spunk, her father's tireless patience, and the great faith in God he leaves with her make this an unforgettable book. For experienced listeners. The slow-moving first chapter can be edited with prereading. Se-

quel: *On Fire.* Related books: *Jump Ship to Freedom* (n); *Lupita Mañana* (n); *Roll of Thunder, Hear My Cry* (n).

Poetry

THE BEST LOVED POEMS OF THE AMERCIAN PEOPLE
Edited by Hazel Felleman
Doubleday, 1936
Gr. 3 and up   648 pages
As editor of the Queries and Answers page of *The New York Times Book Review,* Hazel Felleman was fully aware of the nation's tastes in poetry. By keeping track of the *Times*'s readers' poetry correspondence, she was able to compile the most often requested poems. Parents and teachers could not have been better served, especially when she arranged her anthology under various themes, thereby easing the burden of those who go in search of a poem to fit a particular child or occasion. Here are poems that tell a story (the best loved by children), poems of friendship, inspiration, home and motherhood, childhood, patriotism, humor, and animals. Usually filed in the poetry section of your library, most of these 575 poems are for experienced listeners.

CASEY AT THE BAT
by Ernest Thayer • Illustrated by Wallace Tripp
Coward, 1978; Peppercorn, 1982
Gr. 2 and up   28 pages
This should be part of every child's poetic heritage. It describes a small-town baseball game and local hero. The color has neither changed nor faded from the game and its fans in the one hundred years since this poem was first written. The illustrations imbue the poem with a fablelike quality by casting it with animal characters wearing the fashions of 1888. When children have been treated to *Casey at the Bat,* they'll enjoy follow-up readings of lesser-known sequels: *Casey's Revenge* by James Wilson and *Casey: 20 Years Later* by S. P. McDonald, both included in *The Best Loved Poems of the American People* (po).

THE COVERED BRIDGE HOUSE
by Kaye Starbird • Illustrated by Jim Arnosky
Four Winds, 1979
Gr. 1–6   53 pages

A collection of 35 narrative poems about such whimsical children as the girl who hops on her horse one day and rides from New York to Vermont without leaving word with a soul; the leg-in-a-cast girl who becomes the world's highest jumper; sly little Beverly who becomes the scourge of Camp Blue Sky; and Artie Dole who can't control his imagination. Related book: *Jelly Belly* by Dennis Lee.

ELLA
by Bill Peet
See listing under *The Whingdingdilly* (p.)

HAILSTONES AND HALIBUT BONES
by Mary O'Neill • Illustrated by Leonard Weisgard
Doubleday (both), 1961; 1973
Pre S.–6   60 pages
Twelve poems which explore the spectrum of colors in the world around us and the feelings aroused by those colors. Mary O'Neill takes the commonplace object and shows us the glowing colors we've been taking for granted or missing. Related book: *Surprises* by Lee Bennett Hopkins.

HONEY, I LOVE
by Eloise Greenfield • Illustrated by Diane and Leo Dillon
Crowell, 1978
Pre S.–3   42 pages
Here are 16 short poems about the things and people children love: friends, cousins, older brothers, keepsakes, mother's clothes, music, and jump ropes. Set against an urban background, the poems elicit both joyous and bitter-sweet feelings.

A HOUSE IS A HOUSE FOR ME
by Mary Ann Hoberman • Illustrated by Betty Fraser
Viking, 1978; Puffin, 1982
Pre S.–6   44 pages
On the surface this book is a rhyming picture book about the variety of dwelling places people, animals, and insects call home. Below the surface it is an ingeniously entertaining study of metaphor: "cartons are houses for crackers," "a rose is a house for a smell," "a throat is a house for a hum." Such imagination-expanding thoughts can be easily developed after the book is finished. Encourage the class or child to compile their own list of houses. Also by the author: *Bugs; The Cozy Book; I Like Old Clothes; Nuts to You and Nuts to Me; The Raucous Auk; Yellow Butter Purple Jelly Red Jam Black Bread.*

IF I RAN THE ZOO
by Dr. Seuss
See page 142.

IF I WERE IN CHARGE OF THE WORLD
AND OTHER WORRIES
by Judith Viorst
Atheneum (both), 1981; 1984
Gr. 3 and up   56 pages
If the meter or rhyme in these 41 poems is occasionally imperfect, it is easily overlooked in light of their perfect pulse and timing. In prescribing these short verses "for children and their parents," this contemporary American humorist offers a two-point perspective: Children reading these poems will giggle, then recognize themselves, their friends and enemies, and think "That's really the way it is!" Parents will recognize in the poems the child they used to be. Witty, introspective, sometimes bittersweet poems on children's hopes, fears, and feelings. Also by the author: *Alexander and the Terrible, Horrible, No Good, Very Bad Day* (p); *I'll Fix Anthony; The Tenth Good Thing About Barney* (p); *Alexander Who Used to Be Rich Last Sunday; My Mama Says There Aren't Any Zombies, Ghosts, Vampires, Creatures, Demons, Monsters, Fiends, Goblins or Things; Rosie and Michael*.

MOTHER GOOSE,
A TREASURY OF BEST LOVED RHYMES
See page 149.

THE NIGHT BEFORE CHRISTMAS
by Clement Moore   •   Illustrated by Tomie dePaola
Holiday House (both), 1980
Pre S.–6   30 pages
One of the most beloved American poems, it is still attracting the efforts of new artists 150 years after its creation. Using his own hundred-year-old farmhouse in a small New Hampshire village as a model and bordering each of the large-format pages with brightly colored New England quilt patterns, dePaola has created one of the most memorable editions of the classic. For other books by Tomie dePaola, see Index to Treasury. For a list of other Christmas books, see *Babushka* (p).

NIGHTMARES: POEMS TO TROUBLE YOUR SLEEP
by Jack Prelutsky   •   Illustrated by Arnold Lobel
Greenwillow, 1976
Gr. 4 and up   40 pages
Here are a dozen poems to make your children squirm but never lose interest. The poet's haunting imagery brings out the worst of bogeymen, vampires, dragons of death, trolls, and ogres. Beneath the cobwebs and gloom, young listeners will find a crackling sense of humor. Sequel: *The Headless Horseman Rides Tonight*. Also by the author: for younger children, *The Baby Uggs are Hatching; Circus; It's Halloween; The Mean Old Hyena; The*

New Kid on the Block; The Pack Rat's Day and Other Poems; The Queen of Eene; The Snope on the Sidewalk; The Wild Baby (po); *Zoo Doings.* Related books: *Scary Stories to Tell in the Dark* (a); *The Terrible Tales of Happy Days School,* cautionary tales by Lois Duncan.

NOW WE ARE SIX
by A. A. Milne • Illustrated by Ernest H. Shepard
Dutton, 1927; Dell, 1975
K and up   104 pages
This best-selling classic celebrates the dreams and nonsense of childhood in 31 narrative poems: stories of good children and naughty children, foolish kings, and imaginary friends. For experienced listeners. Also by the author: *The House at Pooh Corner; When We Were Very Young* (poetry); *Winnie-the-Pooh.* Related book: *Once Upon a Rhyme* by Corrin.

OUT IN THE DARK AND DAYLIGHT
by Aileen Fisher • Illustrated by Gail Owens
Harper, 1980
Pre S.−5   152 pages
This award-winning poet's specialty is polishing the drab, taken-for-granted things in a child's life in such a way that we see colors and dimensions we've never observed before. Only Aileen Fisher would ask if rabbit ears hear better than horses' ears, or if basset ears hear better than robins'. Only she would ask what kind of debt a caterpillar owes for all of his nibbles, or if parks grow lonely in the winter. In asking such questions, she stirs a child's sense of wonder. These 140 short poems are arranged chronologically by seasons and holidays for easy reference. Other poetry by the author: *Anybody Home?; Cricket in a Thicket; Do Bears Have Mothers, Too?; Easter; Going Barefoot; In One Door and Out the Other; I Stood Upon a Mountain.* Related book: *Surprises* by Lee Bennett Hopkins.

THE RANDOM HOUSE BOOK OF POETRY FOR CHILDREN
selected by Jack Prelutsky • Ilustrated by Arnold Lobel
Random House, 1983
K–5   248 pages
One cannot find enough superlatives to describe this anthology of 572 poems and 400 illustrations. It is by far the best of its kind. Poet Jack Prelutsky recognizes that the common language of childhood is laughter and wonder. The poems he has selected are short—but they are long on laughter, imagery, and rhyme. While there are excellent contributions from traditional poets like Frost, Milne and even Shakespeare, the bulk is from contemporary poets grouped around fourteen categories that include food, goblins, nonsense, home, children, animals, and seasons. For collections of Prelutsky's own poetry, see *Nightmares: Poems to Trouble Your Sleep* (po). Related book: *Jelly Belly* by Dennis Lee.

SECRETS OF A SMALL BROTHER
by Rickard J. Margolis • Illustrated by Donald Carrick
Macmillan, 1984
K–4   34 pages
In these 22 short poems, we look at the relationship of two brothers through
the eyes of the younger: the teasing, questioning, sharing, wondering and
watching that takes place between siblings. Much of it is written in un-
rhymed verse and each poem is illustrated with some of Donald Carrick's
most sensitive illustrations. Related books: *Alexander and the Terrible, Horrible, No Good, Very Bad Day* and *I'll Fix Anthony* both by Judith Viorst;
My Twin Sister Erika (s); *Sisters* by David McPhail.

SEE MY LOVELY POISON IVY
by Lilian Moore • Illustrated by Diane Dawson
Atheneum, 1975
Pre S.–4   48 pages
If a witch's child asked her mother to tell her a story these 35 poems would
be just what she wanted. Filled with tongue-in-cheek drama and eeriness,
they touch upon shadows, cats, trolls, ghouls and ghosts, monsters, haunted
houses, ogres, and witches. Typical of Moore's light touch is the poem about
a child who has misplaced his head and is worried because everything he
needs is in it.

WHEN THE DARK COMES DANCING: A BEDTIME
POETRY BOOK
Selected by Nancy Larrick • Illustrated by John Wallner
Philomel, 1983
Tod.–K   78 pages
A collection of 45 poems, lullabies and lyrics, that quietly celebrate the
close of day. Accompanied by magnificently colorful illustrations that sweep
from page to page, there are old favorites and contemporaries in this cozy
volume by one of America's most respected anthologists. Also by the author: *On City Streets, Piping Down the Valleys Wild, Room for Me and a Mountain Lion;* for adults: *A Parent's Guide to Children's Reading.* Related bedtime
books: see listing below *Bedtime for Frances* (p), *Goodnight Moon* (p).

WHERE THE SIDEWALK ENDS
by Shel Silverstein
Harper, 1974
K–8   166 pages
This is, without question, the best-loved collection of poetry for children.
(It sold 1 million copies during its first eight years in print.) When it comes
to knowing children's appetites Silverstein is pure genius. The titles alone
are enough to bring children to rapt attention: "Bandaids"; "Boa Constric-

tor"; "Crocodile's Toothache"; "The Dirtiest Man in the World"; "If I Had a Brontosaurus"; "Recipe for a Hippopotamus Sandwich." Here are 130 poems that will either touch children's hearts or tickle their funny bones. Silverstein's second collection of poems, *A Light in the Attic,* was the first children's book (of any kind) to make *The New York Times* bestseller list, where it remained for more than one hundred and twenty weeks. The multitalented Silverstein also has thirty-eight selections from *Sidewalk* on an exciting forty-minute cassette (Harper). Also by the author/illustrator: *The Giving Tree* (p); *Lafcadio, the Lion Who Shot Back* (s); *Who Wants a Cheap Rhinoceros?* Related book: *Jelly Belly* by Dennis Lee.

THE WILD BABY
by **Barbro Lindgren** • Illustrated by **Eva Eriksson**
Greenwillow, 1981
Pre S.–5 22 pages
Adapted from the Swedish by American poet Jack Prelutsky, this rhyming narrative follows a mischievous child whose naughty exploits never dampen his mother's love for him Sequel: *The Wild Baby Goes to Sea.* Also by the author: *Sam's Cookie* (p). Related books: *The Complete Adventures of Peter Rabbit* (p); *Deep in the Forest* (p).

Anthologies

AMERICAN BEAT
by **Bob Greene**
Atheneum, 1983; Penguin, 1984
Gr. 7 and up 301 pages
Here are eighty-eight stories (averaging five pages apiece) from one of today's most respected journalists, all having appeared originally either as newspaper or magazine columns. I consider them to be the best of their kind. These are true stories but not news stories. They are stories about people, and each is presented matter-of-factly by Greene the observer, leaving you to draw your own conclusions. Greene is a master at finding stories that highlight the human condition. He writes about people who inspire courage and respect—as well as those you will detest, people at home, in school, in business, in life and in death. The story entitled "Rush Week," one that should be heard in every junior and senior high, will give you an exact pulse on the book. Readers aloud should preview each story before reading—a few deal with subject matter that may not be appropriate for your child or class. Also by the author: *Cheeseburgers.*

ANIMALS CAN BE ALMOST HUMAN
Compiled by Reader's Digest
Reader's Digest, 1979
Gr. 3 and up   416 pages
This collection of 82 true-to-life animal stories offers something for everyone and every moment: from rib-ticklers to heart-stoppers, from parakeets to porcupines, from the jungles to Jersey, from the long to the short. Beautifully illustrated throughout. Related book: *The Faber Book of Animal Stories* by Johnny Morris.

BEST-LOVED FOLKTALES OF THE WORLD
Selected by Joanna Cole
Doubleday (both), 1981; 1983
Gr. 3 and up   792 pages
Here is today's most comprehensive collection of world folklore, 200 tales told (but not bowdlerized) in a most accessible way. From ten areas of the world, we have the witty and the clever, princes and paupers, heroes and heroines, magic and cunning—all woven into centuries-old stories and legends from oral and written traditions. For experienced listeners. Also by the author: *A New Treasury of Children's Poetry: Old Favorites and New Discoveries.* Related book: *The Faber Book of Modern Fairy Tales* by Sara and Stephen Corrin.

CLASSICS TO READ ALOUD TO YOUR CHILDREN
by William Russell
Crown, 1984
K and up   400 pages
Recognizing that not all great literature can be comfortably read aloud and that those classics that are suitable are spread out in separate volumes that require hours of searching out, Russell has compiled in one book thirty-eight selections of the very best from poetry, fairy tales, myths, short stories and novels. The works are divided into three listening levels: age 5–7; 8–10; 11–13, the last being works from Crane, London and Twain that can be enjoyed by 60-year-olds as well. Each selection is prefaced with a brief paragraph about the story, an estimate of the reading time, and notes on any unusual vocabulary in text. Most entries are complete in themselves; some excerpts are used from novels. Related books: *A Wonder Book* (a); *The World Treasury of Children's Literature* (a); *The Faber Book of Modern Fairy Tales* by Sara and Stephen Corrin; *Fables from Aesop* retold by James Reeves; *The St. Nicholas Anthology* edited by Henry Steele Commager.

THE FAIRY TALE TREASURY
Collected by Virginia Haviland   •   Illustrated by Raymond Briggs
Coward, 1972; Dell, 1980
Pre S.–4   191 pages

While head of the children's book section of the Library of Congress, Virginia Haviland selected 32 of the most popular fairy tales of all time, including favorites from Andersen, Grimm, Jacobs, and Perrault. Her choices range from the short and simple "Henny Penny" to the more complex "Snow White." Presented in large format with full-color illustrations in both hardcover and paper.

FREE TO BE YOU AND ME
Edited by Carole Hart, Letty C. Pogrebin, Mary Rodgers,
and Marlo Thomas
McGraw-Hill (paperback only), 1974
Pre S.–3   116 pages
This is a liberated collection of stories, songs, poems, drawings, and photos aimed at encouraging children to the highest goals regardless of sex or race. With humor and sensitivity, many contemporary stereotypes are challenged and subdued here by a variety of authors for children, including: Judy Blume, Lucille Clifton, Carol Hall, Betty Miles, Carl Reiner, Mary Rodgers, Shel Silverstein, Judith Viorst, and Arnold Lobel. A record of the book's songs is also available through libraries and record stores. For related books, see listing at the end of *Nice Little Girls* (p).

GIANT KIPPERNOSE AND OTHER STORIES
by John Cunliffe
Deutsch, 1972
Gr. 1–4   112 pages
This collection of the author's short stories for primary-grade youngsters (an area that is largely ignored in the short-story field) has everything this age group demands in its books: originality, suspense, humor, ferocious villains, and happy endings. Typical is the giant in the title story: When Kippernose comes to town, people flee the streets, bolt the doors, and lock their windows—despite his tearful pleadings that he only wants to be their friend. Unbeknownst to Kippernose, it is not his size they fear—it is his smell. He hasn't taken a bath, changed his socks, or brushed his teeth in a hundred years. But who has the nerve (or the nose) to instruct a giant on personal hygiene? Related books: *The Book of Giant Stories* (p); *Inside My Feet* (s); *The Iron Giant* (s).

THE GOLDEN TREASURY OF CHILDREN'S LITERATURE
Edited by Louis Untermeyer
Golden, 1985
Pre S.–5   544 pages
For many years the only book of its kind, this has now been reissued by Golden Press. Built along the same lines as the four volumes of *The Treasury of World Literature* (a), this mass market single volume may prove to

be the most economical. Drawing from a wide variety of sources—*The Jungle Book, Mary Poppins, Winnie-the-Pooh, Uncle Remus, Pinocchio, Bambi,* and *The Arabian Nights,* to name a few, the 70 selections are colorfully illustrated and include fairy tales, myths, fantasy, humor, and selections from novels. Related books: *The Fairy Tale Treasury* (a); *The World Treasury of Children's Literature.*

LISTEN CHILDREN
edited by Dorothy S. Strickland
Bantam, 1982 (paperback only)
K–5   122 pages
This short collection of black literature is a true anthology—managing to squeeze into its few pages little gems from poetry, myth and folklore, plays, speeches, and, surprisingly, biography. One seldom sees biography included in most literature collections, and the book is all the better for including moments from the lives of Rosa Parks, Wilma Rudolph, and Stevie Wonder. All the entries underline the black experience, but they also speak of course to the human condition. The selection from Maya Angelou's biography happens to be one of my lifetime favorites, and it is something that will touch every child. Related titles on the black experience: *Honey, I Love* (po); *Roll of Thunder, Hear My Cry* (n); *The Stories Julian Tells* (s); *Wagon Wheels* (p); *The People Could Fly* by Virginia Hamilton.

THE MAID OF THE NORTH
by Ethel Johnston Phelps
Holt (both), 1981; 1983
Gr. 2 and up   174 pages
In an effort to balance a field that is top-heavy with heroes, this collection of fast-moving folk and fairy tales offers us twenty-one heroines from seventeen different ethnic cultures. Like their counterparts of the opposite sex, they are resourceful, clever, confident, with a clear sense of self-worth, sometimes physically attractive but always morally attractive. These tales have the perfect balance of compassion, humor, and conflict. They will appeal to boys as well as girls, and each can be read in a single sitting. Also by the author: *Tatterhood and Other Tales* (feminist fairy tales). Related books: *Into the Painted Bear Lair* (n); *Nice Little Girls* (p); *The Ordinary Princess* (n); *R, My Name Is Rosie* (n); *The Emperor and the Kite* and *Sleeping Ugly* both by Jane Yolen.

PAUL HARVEY'S THE REST OF THE STORY
by Paul Aurandt
Doubleday, 1977; Bantam, 1978
Gr. 6 and up   234 pages
These collections of broadcaster Paul Harvey's five-minute radio show, *The Rest of the Story,* are perfect for teachers and parents trying to win older

students to the art of listening. Nearly all of these pieces deal with famous people past and present. The person's name is saved for the last few lines of the tale and serves as an O. Henry punch. The 81 stories average 2 pages in length. Other books in the series: *Destiny; More of Paul Harvey's The Rest of the Story*. Related book: *American Beat* (a).

SCIENCE FICTION TALES:
INVADERS, CREATURES, AND ALIEN WORLDS
Edited by Roger Elwood
Rand McNally (both), 1973
Gr. 3–6   124 pages
These 7 tales are an excellent science fiction sampler for middle-grade young people, an age level that is largely overlooked in sci-fi publishing. Sequel: *More Science Fiction Tales*. Related books: *The Fallen Spaceman* (s); *Baleful Beasts and Eerrie Creatures* edited by Roger Elwood.

SCARY STORIES TO TELL IN THE DARK
Collected by Alvin Schwartz   ·   Illustrated by Stephen Gammell
Lippincott, 1981; Harper, 1983
Gr. 5 and up   112 pages
Dipping into the folk vaults of the past and present, the author presents 29 American "horror" stories and songs guaranteed to make your listeners cringe. The text includes suggestions for the reader-aloud on when to pause, when to scream, even when to turn off the lights. The selections run the gamut from giggles to gore and average 2 pages in length. In addition, a source section briefly traces each tale's origin in the U.S. (Discretion is advised because of the subject matter.) Sequel: *More Scary Stories to Tell in the Dark*. Related book: *Nightmares* (po).

A TASTE FOR QUIET AND OTHER DISQUIETING TALES
by Judith Gorog
Philomel, 1982
Gr. 5 and up   128 pages
A dozen modern fantasy and fairy tales, always rooted in the familiar but giving rise to the bizarre and unexpected. Ranging from the short to the long, from eerie to tender, from human to supernatural, they are always thought-provoking. The short story "Those Three Wishes" will give you a good gauge of the book's contents. For experienced listeners. Related book: *Young Mutants* edited by Azimov, Greenberg, and Waugh.

A WONDER BOOK
by Nathaniel Hawthorne
Airmont, 1966; Grosset, 1967
Gr. 4–8   160 pages

Fearing that the classical tone of the ancient myths would frighten future generations of children away from these great stories, Nathaniel Hawthorne produced this collection in 1851. Translating the classical language into modern romantic, he used a keen ear that was carefully tuned to children. Sadly, the book is not well known by today's parents and educators.

The book is divided into six chapters, each treating a different myth. The stories are supposedly told by a college student to his cousins, and his conversations with them serve as transitions between the various tales. These conversations are the least successful and the least necessary parts of the book, and I recommend that you skip them entirely.

Many everyday expressions and symbols have their roots in these myths, and children will gain a new appreciation for such expressions after hearing them. The myths include: "The Gorgon's Head," a marvelous monster story; "Paradise of Children," the story of Pandora's box; "The Golden Touch," the story of King Midas; "The Three Golden Apples," the story of Hercules; "The Miraculous Pitcher," the rewards of a charitable heart; "The Chimaera," the story of Pegasus, the winged horse. Of the six tales I find "The Three Golden Apples" to be the least successful for reading aloud. For experienced listeners. Related books: *Classics to Read Aloud to Your Children* (a); *The World Treasury of Children's Literature* (a).

THE WORLD TREASURY OF CHILDREN'S LITERATURE
by Clifton Fadiman
Little, Brown, 1984; 1985
Pre S.–6   Four volumes in two slipcases (200 pages in each book)
Before even thinking about purchasing a set of encylopedias for my children I would first make sure my family owned these four volumes. One of the most respected names in publishing, Fadiman has assembled the rhymes, poems, myths, fairy tales, and novels that are the essence of children's literature. For want of a better description, this is the Hall of Fame for children's books. Finally under one roof—including much of their original artwork—are *Madeline* and *Curious George, The Little House* and *Little Bear, Peter Rabbit* and *Alexander* (both of whom know about terrible, horrible, no-good very bad days). From the Brothers Grimm and Aesop to Dr. Seuss and Beverly Cleary—these volumes speak to the heart and soul of childhood. The first two volumes are geared to younger children (Pre S.–3).

ZLATEH THE GOAT AND OTHER STORIES
by Isaac B. Singer   •   Illustrated by Maurice Sendak
Harper, 1966
Gr. 3–6   90 pages
The magic of one of the world's great storytellers and winner of the Nobel Prize for literature is seen in these seven folk tales. Derived from the East-

ern European Jewish oral tradition, the captivating blend of humor, fantasy, and devilry in these stories has become a Singer trademark. For experienced listeners. Also by the author: *The Golem; The Power of Light: Eight Stories of Hanukkah; Stories for Children; Why Noah Chose the Dove.*

Notes

CHAPTER 1

1. Courtney B. Cazden, *Child Language and Education* (New York: Holt, Rinehart and Winston, 1972).
2. Stanley N. Wellborn, "Ahead: A Nation of Illiterates?" *U.S. News and World Report,* May 17, 1982, pp. 53–57. B. Dalton Bookseller (Community Relations Department, One Corporate Center, 7505 Metro Blvd., Minneapolis, MN 55435) also offers an excellent packet entitled "National Literacy Initiative."
3. Television Bureau of Advertising (477 Madison Avenue, New York, NY 10022), January 1984 report.
4. Harry F. Waters, "What TV Does to Kids," *Newsweek,* February 21, 1977, p. 63.
5. Lynn Minton, *Movie Guide for Puzzled Parents* (New York: Delacorte, 1984) p. 6.
6. John Steinbeck, *The Acts of King Arthur and His Noble Knights* (New York: Farrar, Straus and Giroux, 1976), p. 3.
7. Izaak Wirszup, "Education and National Survival," *Educational Leadership,* December/January 1984, p. 6.
8. *The New York Times,* August 11, 1981, p. C6.
9. *The New York Times,* April 26, 1983, p. C8.
10. *Educational Leadership,* September, 1983, p. 16.

11. Fred M. Hechinger, "Report Faults Army's Teaching of Basic Skills," *The New York Times,* July 12, 1983, p. 6. This article is based on the General Accounting Office report, June 20, 1983, "Poor Design and Management Hamper Army's Basic Skills Education Program."

12. Jason DeParle, "High-Tech Trend-Speak," *The New Republic,* October 25, 1982, p. 12.

13. *The New York Times Book Review,* "The Paperback Evolution," January 10, 1982, p. 7. Statement by Ronald Busch, former president of Pocket Books.

14. Remarks by Jonathan Kozol, director of National Literacy Coalition in Boston, reported in *Marketing News* May 13, 1983, p. 18.

15. Book Industry Study Group, Inc., "The 1983 Consumer Research Study on Reading and Book Purchasing," a summary report presented at the Library of Congress April 11, 1984.

16. Terry Ley, *Media and Methods,* March 1979, p. 244.

17. Barbara Bush, wife of Vice President George Bush and an honorary member of Literacy Volunteers of America, in remarks to literacy volunteers in Wyoming County, NY, in 1982.

18. Remarks by Jonathan Kozol, director of National Literacy Coalition in Boston, reported in *Marketing News* May 13, 1983, p. 18.

19. Chow Loy Tom, "What Teachers Read to Pupils in the Middle Grades," (Dissertation, Ohio State University, 1969), p. 174. See also: Chow Loy Tom, "Paul Revere Rides Ahead: Poems Teachers Read to Pupils in the Middle Grades," *Library Journal,* Vol. 43 (January 1973), pp. 27–38.

20. California State Department of Education, "Student Achievement in California Schools, 1979–80 Annual Report" (Sacramento, CA, 1980).

21. Richard Allington, "If They Don't Read Much How They Gonna Get Good?" *Journal of Reading,* October 1977, pp. 57–61. See also: Richard Allington, "Sustained Approaches to Reading and Writing," *Language Arts,* September 1975, pp. 813–15.

22. Bruno Bettelheim, *The Uses of Enchantment: The Meaning and Importance of Fairy Tales* (New York: Knopf, 1976), pp. 3–6.

23. Robert Penn Warren, "Why Do We Read Fiction," *The Saturday Evening Post,* October 20, 1962, pp. 82–84.

24. Edward B. Fiske, "Eight Year Study of Public Schools Finds Chronic Problems in System," *The New York Times,* July 19, 1983, p. 1.

25. "Hers is a room full of success," *Boston Globe,* June 21, 1982, p. 6.

26. Dorothy Cohen, "The Effect of Literature on Vocabulary and Reading Achievement," *Elementary English,* Vol. 45 (February 1968), pp. 209–213, 217. See also: Bernice Cullinan, Angela Jaggar, and

Dorothy Strickland, "Language Expansion for Black Children in the Primary Grades: A Research Report," *Young Children*, Vol. 29 (January 1974), pp. 98–112.

CHAPTER 2

1. These remarks were made during a half-hour interview (September 3, 1979) with Dr. Brazelton conducted by John Merrow for *Options in Education*, a co-production of National Public Radio and the Institute for Educational Leadership of the George Washington University. See note 7 below.
2. Sharon Begley and John Carey, "The Wisdom of Babies," *Newsweek*, January 12, 1981, pp. 71–72.
3. Dorothy Butler, *Cushla and Her Books* (Boston: The Horn Book, 1980).
4. Anthony Brandt, "Literacy in America," *The New York Times*, August 25, 1980, p. 25.
5. Benjamin Bloom, *Stability and the Change in Human Characteristics* (New York: Wiley, 1964), p. 72.
6. J. McV. Hunt, *Intelligence and Experience* (New York: Ronald Press, 1961).
7. Martin Deutsch, "The Disadvantaged Child and the Learning Process," in *Education in Depressed Areas*, ed. A. Harry Passow (New York: Teachers College, 1963), pp. 168–78.
8. Jerome Kagan, "The Child: His Struggle for Identity," *Saturday Review*, December 1968, p. 82. See also: Steven R. Tulkin and Jerome Kagan, "Mother-Child Interaction in the First Year of Life," *Child Development*, March 1972, pp. 31–41.
9. A complete transcript of this interview is available by writing: *Options in Education*, 2025 M Street, N.W., Washington, D.C., 20036.
10. Further examples of "concept-attention span" can be found in Jerome Kagan, "The Child: His Struggle for Identity," p. 82.
11. Dolores Durkin, *Children Who Read Early* (New York: Teachers College, 1966). See also: Anne D. Forester, "What Teachers Can Learn from 'Natural Readers,' " *Reading Teacher*, November 1977, pp. 160–66; Margaret M. Clark, *Young Fluent Readers* (London: Heinemann, 1976).
12. *The New York Times*, March 22, 1959, Section IV, p. 9.
13. John Holt treats this concept at length in his essay, "How Teachers Make Children Hate Reading," *Redbook*, November 1967.
14. Paula Fox's comments are reported by Augusta Baker in a biographical note on Fox for *Newbery and Caldecott Medal Books 1966–1975* (Boston: The Horn Book, 1975), pp. 124–25.

CHAPTER 3

1. Grace B. Martin and Russell D. Clark III, "Distress Crying in Neonates: Species and Peer Specificity," *Developmental Psychology*, 1982, Vol. 18, No. 1, pp. 3–9.
2. Otto Friedrich, "What Do Babies Know?" *Time*, August 15, 1983, pp. 52–59.
3. Nancy Rubin, "Learning How Children Learn from the First Moments of Life," *The New York Times Winter Survey of Education*, January 10, 1982, Section 13, pp. 36–37.
4. Otto Friedrich, "What Do Babies Know?" *Time*, August 15, 1983, pp. 52–59.
5. Nancy Rubin, "Learning How Children Learn from the First Moments of Life," *The New York Times Winter Survey of Education*, January 10, 1982, Section 13, pp. 36–37.
6. Sharon Begley and John Carey, "The Wisdom of Babies," *Newsweek*, January 12, 1981, pp. 71–72.
7. Otto Friedrich, "What Do Babies Know?" *Time*, August 15, 1983, pp. 52–59.
8. Sharon Begley and John Carey, "The Wisdom of Babies," *Newsweek*, January 12, 1981, pp. 71–72.
9. Clifton Fadiman, *Empty Pages: A Search for Writing Competence in Schools and Society* (Belmont, CA: Fearon Pitman, 1979), p. 157.
10. Barbara Cass-Beggs, *Your Baby Needs Music* (New York: St. Martin's, 1980). A poignant example of this phenomenon is described by Barry Farrell in *Pat and Roald* (New York: Random, 1969), p. 22. When actress Patricia Neal (then married to author Roald Dahl) was struck by a series of near-fatal strokes, she suffered a total loss of language memory. While her loss of language was complete and required more than a year's recovery, she never lost the language or memory of the songs she learned as a child. Her first words after twenty-two days of total silence were the words of a childhood song.
11. Dorothy White, *Books Before Five* (Portsmouth, NH: Heinemann Educational Books, 1984), p. 2.
12. Bruno Bettelheim, *The Uses of Enchantment: The Meaning and Importance of Fairy Tales* (New York: Knopf, 1976), pp. 17–18.
13. Kornei Chukovsky, *From Two to Five*, trans. Miriam Morton (Berkeley, CA: University of California, 1963), pp. 7, 9.
14. Eli M. Bower, "The Magic Symbols," *Today's Education*, Vol. 57 (January 1968), pp. 28–31. See also: Vincent R. Rogers, "Laughing With Children," *Educational Leadership*, April 1984, pp. 46–50.
15. Donald Barr, *Who Pushed Humpty Dumpty? Dilemmas in American Education Today* (New York: Atheneum, 1971), p. 69.

16. Richard Abrahamson, "An Analysis of Children's Favorite Picture Storybooks," *Reading Teacher,* November 1980, pp. 167–70. *Children's Choices* is an annual publication of the International Reading Association in conjunction with the Children's Book Council. Its purpose is to publicize the favorite books of U.S. schoolchildren, and a copy can be obtained by sending an SASE, (first-class postage for two ounces) to Children's Book Council, 67 Irving Place, New York, NY 10003.

17. William F. Coughlin, Jr. and Brendan Desilets, "Frederick the Field Mouse Meets Advanced Reading Skills as Children's Literature Goes to High School," *Reading Journal,* December 1980, pp. 207–11.

18. Robert C. O'Brien, "Newbery Award Acceptance," *Newbery and Caldecott Medal Books 1966–1975* (Boston: The Horn Book, 1975), pp. 83–89.

19. Daniel N. Fader and James Duggins, Tom Finn, and Elton B. McNeil, *The New Hooked on Books* (New York: Berkley, 1976), pp. 95–96.

20. Katherine Paterson, "National Book Award Acceptance," *The Horn Book,* August 1979, pp. 402–3.

21. Bernice E. Cullinan, with Mary K. Karrer, and Arlene M. Pillar, *Literature and the Child* (New York: Harcourt Brace Jovanovich, 1981), p. 250.

22. Donald Barr, *Who Pushed Humpty Dumpty?,* pp. 313–14.

23. Arthur Schlesinger, Jr., "Advice From a Reader-Aloud-to-Children," *The New York Times Book Review,* November 25, 1979.

24. Emma Halstead Swain, "Using Comic Books in Teaching Reading and Language Arts," *Journal of Reading,* December 1978, pp. 253–58. See also: Larry Dorrell and Ed Carroll, "Spider-Man at the Library," *School Library Journal,* August 1981, pp. 17–19.

CHAPTER 5

1. Michael H. Kean, Anita H. Summers, Mark Raivetz, and Irvin J. Farber, "What Works in Reading? Summary and Results of a Joint School District/ Federal Reserve Bank Empirical Study in Philadelphia," The School District of Philadelphia: ERIC Report ED176216, May 1979.

2. "An Expert Urges Multiple Reforms," *The New York Times,* July 7, 1983, p. C1, 7.

3. Elliot A. Medrich, Judith A. Roizen, Victor Rubin, and Stuart Buckley of Children's Time Study, *The Serious Business of Growing Up* (Berkeley, CA: University of California, 1982).

4. Julius Lester, "The Beechwood Staff," *The Horn Book,* April 1984, p. 161.

5. David Elkind, *The Hurried Child* (Reading, MA: Addison-Wesley, 1981), p. 19.

6. Daniel Goleman, "Rethinking I.Q. Tests and Their Value," *The New York Times,* July 22, 1984, p. E22. See also: R. C. Lewontin, Peter Rose, and Leon Kamin, *Not in Our Genes* (New York: Pantheon, 1984); and Daniel Goleman, "Successful Executives Rely on Own Kind of Intelligence," *The New York Times,* July 31, 1984, p. C1.

7. Desmond Morris, *The Naked Ape* (New York: McGraw-Hill, 1967), p. 29.

8. Mortimer J. Adler, *The Paideia Proposal: An Educational Manifesto* (New York: Macmillan, 1982), p. 9.

CHAPTER 7

1. Television Bureau of Advertising (477 Madison Avenue, New York, NY 10022), January, 1984 report.

2. "National Report on College-Bound Seniors, 1984," The College Board, 888 Seventh Avenue, New York, NY 10106.

3. Paul Copperman, *The Literacy Hoax: The Decline of Reading, Writing, and Learning in the Public Schools and What We Can Do About It* (New York: Morrow, 1980), p. 166.

4. California Department of Education, "Student Achievement in California Schools, 1979–80 Annual Report," P.O. Box 271, Sacramento, CA 96802.

5. M. Morgan and L. Gross, "Television and Educational Achievement and Aspiration," in D. Pearl, L. Bonlithilet, and J. Lazar, *Television and Behavior: Ten Years of Scientific Progress and Implications for the Eighties,* Rockville, MD: NIMH, 1982.

6. Donald Hayes and Dana Birnbaum, *Developmental Psychology* Vol. 16, No. 5 and Vol. 17, No. 2. See also: *Psychology Today,* June 1982, pp. 78–79.

7. Meg Schwartz, "Broadcasting Books to Young Audiences," *RE:ACT,* Spring/Summer 1980, p. 19. Mr. Rushnell's remarks were made at a symposium cosponsored by Action for Children's Television (ACT) and the Library of Congress Center for the Book. *RE:ACT* is a nonprofit journal published by ACT.

8. Neil Postman, *Teaching as a Conserving Activity* (New York: Delacorte, 1980), pp. 77–78.

9. Jackie S. Busch, "TV's Effects on Reading: A Case Study," *Phi Delta Kappan,* June 1978, pp. 668–71.

10. Wilbur Schramm, Jack Lyle, and Edwin B. Parker, *Television in the Lives of Our Children* (Stanford, CA: Stanford, 1961).

11. Frank Mankiewicz and Joel Swerdlow, *Remote Control: Television and*

the Manipulation of American Life (New York: Times Books, 1978), pp. 6, 15–72.

12. Neil Postman, *Teaching as a Conserving Activity,* p. 208.
13. Frank Mankiewicz and Joel Swerdlow, *Remote Control,* p. 6.
14. Linda S. Lichter and S. Robert Lichter, *Crooks, Conmen and Clowns* (Washington, DC: Media Institute, 1981); "Television and Behavior," The National Institute of Mental Health, 1982; Earle Barcus, *Images of Life on Children's Television: Sex Roles, Minorities, and Families* (New York: Praeger, 1983).
15. Bob Keeshan's remarks were made during an interview September 24, 1979, with John Merrow for *Options in Education,* a co-production of National Public Radio and the Institute for Educational Leadership of the George Washington University.
16. John Leo, "How the Hostages Came Through," *Time,* February 9, 1981, p. 52; Gregg W. Downey, "Keough Ponders the Lessons of Captivity," *Executive Educator,* May 1981, pp. 24–29.
17. Further evidence can be found in Alexander Dolgun's autobiographical account of his role as a "storyteller" for 129 Soviet prisoners in a labor cell measuring 16' wide by 40' long. See Alexander Dolgun, with Patrick Wilson, *Alexander Dolgun's Story: An American in the Gulag* (New York: Knopf, 1975), pp. 138–49.
18. Kornei Chukovsky, "The Battle of the Fairy Tale: Three Stages," *From Two to Five* (Berkeley, CA: University of California, 1963), pp. 122–130.
19. Sylvia Ashton-Warner, *Spearpoint: "Teacher" in America* (New York: Vintage, 1974), pp. 85–88.
20. Jane Mayer, "Some Cried a Lot, But Youths Survived Week Without TV," *The Wall Street Journal,* January 6, 1982, p. 1, 19.
21. Rhoderick J. Elen, "Listening: Neglected and Forgotten in the Classroom," *Elementary English,* February 1972, pp. 230–32.
22. Paul Kresh, "Short Stories Can Make Lively Disks," *The New York Times,* December 13, 1981, pp. 28–29. The author offers an extensive listing of spoken-word records and cassettes in this article. See also: "To the Dickens and Other Authors by Way of Cassette," *The New York Times,* June 13, 1982, p. 4H.
23. Marie Carbo, "Teaching Reading With Talking Books," *Reading Teacher,* December 1978, pp. 267–73.

CHAPTER 8

1. John I. Goodlad, *A Place Called School* (New York: McGraw-Hill, 1984), p. 107.
2. Robert A. McCracken, "Instituting Sustained Silent Reading," *Journal of Reading,* May 1971, pp. 521–24, 582–83.

3. Mark Sadoski, "An Attitude Survey for Sustained Silent Reading Programs," *Journal of Reading,* May 1980, pp. 721–26.

4. Richard Allington, "If They Don't Read Much, How They Gonna Get Good," *Journal of Reading,* October 1977, pp. 57–61.

5. Michael H. Kean, Anita H. Summers, Mark Raivetz, and Irvin J. Farber, "What Works in Reading? Summary and Results of a Joint School District/ Federal Reserve Bank Empirical Study in Philadelphia," The School District of Philadelphia: ERIC Report ED176216, May 1979, p. 8 of Document Resume.

6. Martha Efta, "Reading in Silence," *Teaching Exceptional Children,* Fall 1978, pp. 12–24.

7. Robert A. McCracken and Marlene J. McCracken, "Modeling Is the Key to Sustained Silent Reading," *Reading Teacher,* January 1978, pp. 406–8. See also: Linda B. Gambrell, "Getting Started with Sustained Silent Reading and Keeping It Going," *Reading Teacher,* December 1978, pp. 328–31.

CHAPTER 9

1. Jacques Barzun, *Teacher in America* (Garden City, NY: Doubleday, 1954), pp. 60–62, 136.

Bibliography

Adler, Mortimer. *Paideia Problems and Possibilities*. New York: Macmillan, 1983.

———. *The Paideia Proposal: An Educational Manifesto*. New York: Macmillan, 1982.

Ashton-Warner, Sylvia. *Spearpoint: "Teacher" in America*. New York: Vintage, 1974.

Barr, Donald. *Who Pushed Humpty Dumpty? Dilemmas in American Education Today*. New York: Atheneum, 1971.

Barzun, Jacques. *Teacher in America*. Garden City, New York: Doubelday, 1954.

Bernard, Harold W. *Child Development and Learning*. Boston: Allyn and Bacon, 1973.

Bettelheim, Bruno. *The Uses of Enchantment: The Meaning and Importance of Fairy Tales*. New York: Knopf, 1976.

Bettleheim, Bruno and Zelan, Karen. *On Learning to Read*. New York: Knopf, 1982.

Bloom, Benjamin. *Stability and the Change in Human Characteristics*. New York: Wiley, 1964.

Butler, Dorothy. *Babies Need Books*. New York: Atheneum, 1980.

———. *Cushla and Her Books*. Boston: The Horn Book, 1980.

Cass-Beggs, Barbara. *Your Baby Needs Music*. New York: St. Martin's, 1980.

Cazden, Courtney B. *Child Language and Education*. New York: Holt, Rinehart and Winston, 1972.

Chukovsky, Kornei. *From Two to Five*. Translated by Miriam Morton. Berkeley, Calif.: University of California Press, 1963.

Clark, Margaret M. *Young Fluent Readers*. London: Heinemann, 1976.

Copperman, Paul. *The Literacy Hoax: The Decline of Reading, Writing, and Learning in the Public Schools and What We Can Do About It*. New York: Morrow, 1980.

Cousins, Norman. *Human Options*. New York: Norton, 1981.

Cullum, Albert. *Aesop in the Afternoon*. New York: Citation Press, 1972.

Cullinan, Bernice E., with Karrer, Mary K., and Pillar, Arlene M. *Literature and the Child*. New York: Harcourt Brace Jovanovich, 1981.

Davies, Robertson. *One Half of Robertson Davies*. New York: Viking, 1977.

Del Rey, Lester. *Early Del Rey*. New York: Doubleday, 1975.

Dodson, Fitzhugh. *How to Father*. Los Angeles: Nash, 1974.

———. *How to Parent*. Los Angeles: Nash, 1970.

Dolgun, Alexander, with Watson, Patrick. *Alexander Dolgun's Story: An American in the Gulag*. New York: Knopf, 1975.

Durkin, Dolores. *Children Who Read Early*. New York: Teachers College, 1966.

Egoff, Sheila; Stubbs, G. T.; and Ashley, L. F., eds. *Only Connect: Readings on Children's Literature*. Toronto: Oxford, 1969.

Elkind, David. *The Hurried Child: Growing Up Too Soon Too Fast*. Reading, MA: Addison Wesley, 1981.

Fader, Daniel N., and McNeil, Elton B. *Hooked on Books: Program and Proof*. New York: Berkley, 1968.

Fadiman, Clifton, and Howard, James. *Empty Pages: A Search for Writing Competence in School and Society*. Belmont, Calif.: Fearon Pitman and the Council for Basic Education, 1979.

Fadiman, Clifton. *The Lifetime Reading Plan*. New York: World, 1960.

———. *Reading I've Liked*. New York: Simon and Schuster, 1941.

———. *The Selected Writings of Clifton Fadiman,* New York: World, 1955.

Fisher, Margery. *Who's Who in Children's Literature*. New York: Holt, Rinehart and Winston, 1975.

Gibson, Janice T., and Blumberg, Phyllis. *Growing Up: Readings on the Study of Children*. Reading, Mass.: Addison-Wesley, 1978.

Glazer, Susan Mandel. *Getting Ready to Read*. Englewood Cliffs, NJ: Prentice-Hall, 1980.

Goodlad, John I. *A Place Called School: Prospects for the Future*. New York: McGraw-Hill, 1984.

Greene, Graham. *The Lost Childhood and Other Essays*. New York: Viking, 1951.

Haviland, Virginia. *Children and Literature: Views and Reviews*. New York: Lothrop, Lee & Shepard, 1973.

Hayden, Torey L. *One Child*. New York: Putnam's, 1980.

Hearne, Betsy. *Choosing Books for Children: A Commonsense Guide*. New York: Delacorte, 1981.

Herndon, James. *How to Survive in Your Native Land*. New York: Simon & Schuster, 1971.

Highet, Gilbert. *Man's Unconquerable Mind*. New York: Columbia University Press, 1954.

Hopkins, Lee Bennett. *Books Are by People*. New York: Citation, 1969.

————. *Let Them Be Themselves*. 2nd ed. New York: Citation, 1974.

————. *More Books by More People*. New York: Citation, 1974.

Huck, Charlotte S. *Children's Literature in the Elementary School*. 3rd ed. New York: Holt, Rinehart and Winston, 1976.

Kimmel, Margaret Mary and Segel, Elizabeth. *For Reading Out Loud!* New York: Delacorte, 1983.

Kingman, Lee, ed. *Newbery and Caldecott Medal Books 1966–1975*. Boston: The Horn Book, 1975.

Larrick, Nancy. *A Parents Guide to Children's Reading*. 4th ed. New York: Bantam, 1975.

Lee, Barbara and Rudman, Masha Kabakow. *Leading to Reading*. New York: Berkeley, 1983.

Maeroff, Gene I. *Don't Blame the Kids*. New York: McGraw-Hill, 1982.

Mankiewicz, Frank, and Swerdlow, Joel. *Remote Control: Television and the Manipulation of American Life*. New York: Times Books, 1978.

Martin, Everett Dean *The Meaning of a Liberal Education*. Garden City, NY: Garden City, 1926.

Mussen, Paul Henry; Conger, John Janeway; and Kagan, Jerome. *Child Development and Personality*. 4th ed. New York: Harper and Row, 1974.

Passow, Harry A., ed. *Education in Depressed Areas*. New York: Teachers College, 1963.

Paulin, Mary Ann. *Creative Uses of Children's Literature*. Hamden, CT: Library Professional Publications, 1982.

Pines, Maya. *Revolution in Learning*. New York: Harper and Row, 1967.

Postman, Neil. *The Disappearance of Childhood*. New York: Harper and Row, 1982.

————. *Teaching as a Conserving Activity*. New York: Delacorte, 1980.

Prescott, Orville. *A Father Reads to His Children: An Anthology of Prose and Poetry*. New York: Dutton, 1965.

Reasoner, Charles. *Bringing Children and Books Together: A Teacher's Guide to Early Childhood Literature*. New York: Dell, 1979.

————. *Releasing Children to Literature*. New York: Dell, 1976.

————. *When Children Read*. New York: Dell, 1975.

————. *Where the Readers Are*. New York: Dell, 1972.

Rudman, Masha. *Children's Literature: An Issues Approach*. Lexington, Mass.: Heath, 1976.

Rutstein, Nat. *"Go Watch TV!"* New York: Sheed and Ward, 1974.

Sabine, Gordon and Sabine, Patricia. *Books That Made a Difference.* Hamden, CT.: Library Professional Publications, 1983.

Schramm, Wilbur; Lyle, Jack; and Parker, Edwin B. *Television in the Lives of Our Children.* Stanford, Calif.: Stanford, 1961.

Simon, Sidney B.; Howe, Leland W.; and Kerschenbaum, Howard. *Values Clarification: A Handbook of Practical Strategies for Teachers and Students,* rev. ed. New York: A & W, 1978.

Smith, Frank. *Understanding Reading.* 3rd ed. New York: Holt, Rinehart and Winston, 1982.

Steinbeck, John. *The Acts of King Arthur and His Noble Knights.* New York: Farrar, Straus and Giroux, 1976.

Sutherland, Zena, and Arbuthnot, May Hill. *Children and Books.* 5th ed. Glenview, Ill.: Scott, Foresman, 1977.

White, Dorothy. *Books Before Five.* Portsmouth, NH: Heinemann Educational Books, 1984.

Winn, Marie. *The Plug-in Drug.* New York: Viking, 1977.

Wintle, Justin, and Fisher, Emma. *The Pied Pipers: Interviews With the Influential Creators of Children's Literature.* New York: Paddington, 1974.

Yolen, Jane. *Touch Magic.* New York: Philomel, 1981.

Author-Illustrator Index to Treasury

Italics are for illustrator only; * after page number gives location of a group of books by an author or illustrator.